Climate Change & The Humanities
2017

Also by Emil Morhardt

Climate Change & The Humanities
2017

J. Emil Morhardt, Editor

CloudRipper Press

Cutting Edge Books

CloudRipper Press
    Santa Barbara, California
    www.CloudRipperPress.com
    Copyright © 2017 J. Emil Morhardt
    All rights reserved. No part of this
book may be reproduced in any form
without written permission from the author.
    Morhardt, J. Emil
        Climate Change & The
    Humanities 2017
        J. Emil Morhardt, Editor.
    ISBN 978-0-9963536-7-0 (paper)

TABLE OF CONTENTS

Food and Water Supplies and Climate Change.............237

FORWARD

by Emil Morhardt

Climate change, the result of global warming, which is in turn the result of our massive burning of fossil fuels, is the province of the natural sciences; the vast majority of the information we have about these topics is clearly the result of scientific research. On the other hand, climate change is caused by human behavior, driven by economic considerations and the universal human desire for a better life, and ultimately affects all aspects of human endeavor including the "imaginative practices from the arts and humanities [that] play a critical role in thinking through our representations of environmental change" (Yusoff and Gabrys, 2011).

Mike Hulme, writing in *Nature Climate Change*, one of the premier scientific journals dealing with climate change, in a 2011 opinion piece titled *Meet the Humanities*, asserted that "Although climate is inarguably changing society, social practices are also impacting on the climate. Nature and culture are deeply entangled, and researchers must examine how each is shaping the other. But they are largely failing to do so" (Hulme, 2011). This was likely the first time that many climate scientists thought much about the humanities as relevant to what they were studying.

That was true in my case, and stimulated me to propose a course at Claremont McKenna College entitled "The Human Response to Climate Change". My working definition of suitable material was any serious writing or research about climate change produced by non-scientists, and by that I meant people who were not some version of physicists, chemists, biologists, geologists, or engineers. In other words, I include the humanities and social sciences, but none of the natural sciences.

The idea was to have students scour the academic literature for relevant papers in these areas and write a weekly summary of a paper they found interesting with the instructions that the writing style would be journalistic; jargon-free, informative, and easy to assimilate. Along the way the selection criteria were relaxed a little to include a variety nonacademic writing, including that in newspapers, and various presentations in the arts, but the main focus remained academic output. The result has been three books—this is the third annual version—comprising summaries of work published in the previous year (in this case 2016 and 2017) which provide an interesting readible overview of the sorts of things non-scientists are writing about climate change.

The authors, as authors often are—or at least appear to be to editors—were somewhat intractable, with two of them sometimes writing about the same publication, or wandering over the humanities line I drew in the sand and reporting on scientific papers instead. I included all of these pieces under the general operating principal that more is better, as long as it is well-enough written.

To add a modicum of organization, I have grouped the summaries into sections; within each section the summaries are arranged alphabetically by author, making it easy for the reader to read everything by a specific author, but causing similar topics within a section to be separated, which is particularly disorienting when two authors have written about the same paper. *C'est la vie.* In addition, many of the papers could equally well have been inserted into a different section instead. For example, a paper about the behavior of religiously-motivated people written by psychologists could have been equally accurately placed into the religion or psychology section, so a reader interested only in religion will need to look in the psychology section as well (and *vice versa*) for complete coverage.

How well does the involvement of the humanities clarify the problem of climate change and what to do about it? The novelest Jonathan Franzen, writing in The New Yorker a while back (Franzen, 2015) identified the problem more clearly than most scientists would: "We're taking carbon that used to be sequestered and putting it into the atmosphere, and unless we stop we're fucked." Most scientists believe this; maybe people in the humanities like Franzen can get through to politicians better.

Two other takes on the value of the humanities in addressing climate change follow.

Franzen, J., 2015. Carbon Capture: Has climate change made it harder for people to care about conservation? The New Yorker, 56-65.
Hulme, M., 2011. Meet the humanities. Nature Climate Change 1, 177-179.
Yusoff, K., Gabrys, J., 2011. Climate change and the imagination. Wiley Interdisciplinary Reviews: Climate Change 2, 516-534.

The Need for Social Sciences in Climate Policy

by Becky Strong (from Climate Change & The Humanities [2016])

In 2015, David G. Victor, a professor of international relations at the University of California, San Diego wrote about the importance of looking into the social sciences when seeking to implement policies about climate change. Victor believes that the Intergovernmental Panel on Climate Change (IPCC) has become irrelevant to climate policy due to its focus on only the most well-known facts about climate change and avoidance of controversy. He believes that in order to find insights that truly matter regarding climate change, one must look beyond the natural sciences. Looking into fields in the social sciences such as political science and sociology is the best way to understand how people react to climate change, and therefore how to implement the best policy. Victor claims that so far, the only field outside of the natural science represented in the IPCC deliberations is economics. He feels that many other disciplines have knowledge of many policy relevant questions. The problem with using only scientists in climate change research is that they are under the intense scrutiny of governments, leading them to steer clear of the controversial topics which could be pivotal in good decision making. The social sciences, he writes, can help provide answers to questions such as how voters will react to changes in climate policy and which countries will be most affected by climate change. Victor believes that it is important for the IPCC to incorporate social scientists in climate policy development because they can provide approaches different from those suggested by natural scientists, some of which would be more effective and relevant. Victor thinks that the IPCC displays major bias in the way it only focuses on "known knowns and known unknowns" instead of on deeper uncertainties that might stir the pot. The social sciences may not have much literature on climate change, but the IPCC needs to be able to ask social scientists the right questions in order to find relevant answers that would prove to be very helpful in climate policy.

Victor, G. D., 2015. Embed the social sciences in climate policy. Nature 520, 27-29. http://www.des.ucdavis.edu/faculty/handy/ESP178/Embed_social_sciences_in_climate_policy.pdf

Why Environmental Science Needs the Humanities

by Emily Segal (from Climate Change & The Humanities [2015])

In the past, those working to combat environmental problems were generally thought of as natural scientists utilizing technology, economics, and policy to come up with solutions for reducing and preventing climate change. The truth is that humanist thinkers were an integral part of the first phase of the environmental revolution. They were early journalists, philosophers and historians writing and thinking about the environment and its relation to human beings. It seems that over time, these humanities scholars were pushed aside and took a back seat to natural scientists and economists who were at the front of the environmentalist movement. However, in contemporary society, people are still shaped by cultural values and political and religious ideals, each of which is a humanitarian, and not necessarily a scientific, issue.

So far, approaching climate change from a purely scientific or economic standpoint has not been successful in changing human behaviors, which is fundamental if we hope to protect the environment. Anthropogenic environmental degradation and climate change are specifically human issues, so we need to learn, think and talk about them from a humanitarian perspective as well as a scientific one.

As historian and environmentalist Sverker Sörlin (2012) writes, "After half a century of putting nature first, it may be time to put humans first." He summarizes the idea that because drastic climate change is caused by humans, it must also be solved by humans, and cannot be solved by nature itself. This is the moment that environmental science depends on the humanities in order to understand how humans think, behave and respond to one another and society as a whole. As Sörlin argues, environmentally relevant knowledge is changing because what environmentalists have found is necessary to save our planet is a better understanding of human behavior, an idea that is at the core of humanitarian studies.

Sörlin, S., 2012. Environmental humanities: why should biologists interested in the environment take the humanities seriously. BioScience 62, 9, 788-789.

Psychology and Sociology of Climate Change

The Climate Change Challenge and Barriers to the Exercise of Foresight Intelligence
by Ellen Broaddus

In Ross *et al.* (2016), experts from various academic fields assess some of the barriers that aid today's denial and inaction combating climate change, even with overwhelming evidence from the scientific community. This hesitancy is traced back to a combination of cognitive shortcomings and the difficulty to work collectively on an issue so complex and seemingly indirect. However, the authors provide examples of strategies used to combat said inaction and their efficacy.

In addition to the sheer magnitude of climate change and its indistinct effects, mankind's natural self interest creates barriers for action. Because the destructive effects of climate change are long-term, it's difficult to motivate people to change when they are not directly impacted. The authors draw a distinction between intrinsic human traits and the role of society in influencing goals, noting that societal traditions such as those of Native American tribes can counter our evolutionary resistance to needed permanent changes. Meaningful action is further deterred by the "absence of payoffs", when people refuse to make personal changes without participation from those around them. This is a self-fulfilling prophecy and leads to a gridlock, despite evidence that "communities of cooperation fare better than communities of noncooperation". Inaction is also justified by humanity's ability to deny and rationalize both the extent of the issue and its ability to make an impact. Ross emphasizes that the doubt is not fostered independently, but rather by "interest groups with powerful motivations" and resources, showing how economics and politics play a large role in the discussion.

Despite these barriers, Ross *et al.* AL.present some "small but nontrivial" psychological tactics, especially playing with norms and default options. By promoting the idea of a collective effort, via information distribution, opt-out rather than opt-in options regarding eco-friendly practices, and stigmatizing waste through negative branding, collective change can be established.

The media's portrayal of different subjects is also vital; such as shows with characters seeking family-planning information increasing the family-planning-clinic enrollment by 33% in Mexico. This "do what your neighbors do" approach engages agencies, business and religious communities, clubs, blogs, and schools and has proven successful ("building sea walls, widespread insurance plans offering protection"), putting a positive narrative on the issue.

The article also addresses some key necessary changes; not only obvious steps like limiting air conditioning, but redefining our current form of consumerism. The tactics above need to shape societal "norms" and foster grass-root support before effective policy changes are possible. The authors cite other social movements like car safety standards and gay rights where the shift in norms was much more effective in creating momentum than mandating steps that may have been counterproductive and created resistance.

Ross, L; Arrow, K; Cialdini, R; Diamond-Smith, N; Diamond, J; Dunne, J; Feldman, M; Horn, R; Kennedy, D; Murphy, C; Pirages, D; Smith, K; York, R; Ehrlich, P. 2016. The Climate Change Challenge and Barriers to the Exercise of Foresight Intelligence. BioScience, 66, 363-370. https://academic.oup.com/bioscience/article/66/5/363/2468623/The-Climate-Change-Challenge-and-Barriers-to-the

In America's Heartland, Discussing Climate Change Without Saying 'Climate Change'
by Ellen Broaddus

Hiroko Tabuchi (2017) analyses the paradoxical relationship between agricultural communities and the support of environmentalism and belief in climate change. Though they depend on a stable and prosperous ecosystem to survive, farming communities in the Midwest are overwhelmingly politically conservative and often deny climate change. Tabuchi sights a 2013 survey that "found that just 8 percent of farmers in the Midwest believed that 'climate change is occurring, and it is caused mostly by human activities'". However, farmers in the Midwest are still aware of environmental changes and challenges, but simply respond to them in a different way.

Tabuchi followed Doug Palen, a 4th generation farmer, who despite believing that the E.P.A's "Clean Water Rule", a regulation "to protect streams and other waterways", is a regulatory overreach, is an environmentalist himself. For example, Mr. Palen is adamant about no-till farming, a practice that saves 1.7 billion tons a year of topsoil from being washed away and reduces up to 80% of evaporation. This disparate approach to environmentalism is applicable on a larger scale, as politicians and leaders in the Midwest often "speak of pursuing jobs that clean energy may create, rather than pressing the need to rein in carbon emissions".

These differences go beyond policy, however, and have caused deep divides between Midwest farmers and the liberal scientific community. This divide may only deepen with the new Trump administration, as they've already made steps to remove climate change discussion and programs from their website. Trump himself has said that "many of our federal environmental laws are being used to oppress farmers instead of actually helping the environment" and that "farmers care more for the environment than the radical environmentalists". Despite this divide, Tabuchi emphasizes that it hasn't always been that way, citing the passage of the EPA and Clean Air Act under Nixon and the creation of the Montreal Protocol under the Reagan administration as evidence that bipartisan action is possible.

Tabuchi also presents strategies to continue climate change discourse without alienating the skeptics. These include getting support from a political standpoint, such as working with farmers and landowners that rely on solar and wind turbines. Most of all, he stresses the need to work toward establishing a common ground rather than starting by emphasizing the harmful role climate change has on the environment. By campaigning the benefits of eco-friendly practices, Tabuchi argues that a more open discussion can be possible.

Tabuchi, Hiroko. 2017. In America's Heartland, Discussing Climate Change Without Saying 'Climate Change'. New York Times. https://www.nytimes.com/2017/01/28/business/energy-environment/navigating-climate-change-in-americas-heartland.html?_r=0

Relating Climate Change and Gender Inequality

by Claudia Chandra

In 2016, Rebecca Pearse, a Postdoctoral Fellow in the School of Sociology at The Australian National University, conducted a study exploring the relationship between gender and climate change. Her study addressed issues such as whether men and women are impacted by climate change the same way, if governance over climate change is gendered, and if women can potentially take on a role in climate stabilization. These questions are increasingly significant, especially since it has been established that gender relations and inequalities contribute to the development of society in the context of climate change. This knowledge challenges the gender-blind way in which data regarding social changes brought about by changes in climate are collected. Pearse calls for deeper gender analysis in order to stop the omission of "key aspects of social life in a changing climate" in future research endeavors.

One of the study's findings is the existence of gendered vulnerabilities to climate change. Women have been found to be more affected by climate change than men. This vulnerability, however, is not caused by the intrinsic qualities of women but rather their socioeconomic conditions. For instance, research conducted by Tasokwa Kakota *et al.* in Southern and Central Malawi corroborates that more women compared to men in these regions have work that is dependent on water and wood fuel. From here Pearse deduces that climate change, which inextricably determines the availability of such resources, becomes central in determining the immediate factors (e.g. poverty and education) associated with "climate change-related burdens."

Pearse's studies also confirm the global persistence (and often intensification) of gender inequality with increasing climate change, and the differences in social responses to climate change between men and women. She notes that these disparities in responses are caused by differences in cultural and socioeconomic conditions. Pearse's report references Beth Bee's study of women living in drought in Guanajuato, Mexico, to exemplify this theory. Bee's study affirms that the knowledge of the women in Guanajuato were needed to ensure sufficient food supplies in an environment affected by climate change. However, because of the women's varying responses to being needed by their communities, Bee concludes that women cannot be defined as "virtuous environmentalists" or "victims of climate change." Pearse reminds us that the gendered impact of climate change is not merely a copy of gender inequality, but instead a reminder that disturbances to our personal lives may result in "new forms of gender inequality" and new "possibilities for resilience."

There is empirical evidence that suggests gender inequality as playing a large role in overconsumption in many Western countries. Marjorie Griffin Cohen found that on top of generally consuming more than women, more men also have jobs that contribute to GHG emissions. Unfortunately, the identification of gender inequality in the context of climate governance is rare, and successful action taken against this even more so. Due to this, Pearse believes that effective climate governance cannot arise only from equal representation of men and women, but more importantly from the goals and priorities that these policies seek to achieve.

Pearse's study draws many clear links between gender and climate change. It shows how society's understanding and responses towards changes in climate differ not only by gender, but also in a more complex manner determined by socioeconomic and cultural circumstances. More importantly, however, her study underlines the need for a better understanding of gender relations to create factual and current knowledge on climate change and gender inequality.

Pearse, Rebecca., 2016. "Gender and Climate Change." Wiley interdisciplinary Reviews: Climate Change. 2016 Wiley Periodicals Inc. http://onlinelibrary.wiley.com/woll/doi/10.1002/wcc.451/full

How U.S. Teachers' Knowledge and Values Hinder Climate Education
by Claudia Chandra

Although most American adults believe climate change is occurring, only about half believe that human activity is the main cause of global warming. This percentage is the lowest out of 20 countries studied in 2014. In an article for Science, Eric Plutzer *et al.* examine how the debate surrounding the causes of climate change affects science classrooms. They found that even though most U.S. science teachers teach climate science in their courses, their insufficient understanding of the subject hinders effective teaching. Moreover, due to the numerous perspectives surrounding this debate, many teachers inadvertently repeat scientifically unsupported claims in their classrooms. According to Plutzer *et al.*, "greater attention to teachers' knowledge, but

also values, is critical" to improve the current way climate
science is being taught to U.S. students.

Plutzer and his associates designed the first nationally
representative survey of science teachers focused on climate
change. The study found that three in four science teachers
spend at least an hour in their formal lesson plans examining
global warming. This includes 70% of middle-school science
teachers and 87% of high-school biology teachers. Most teachers
included explanations of observable consequences of global
warming such as the greenhouse effect (66%), and the carbon
cycle (63%), and also discussed mitigating their effects.

Nevertheless, median teachers spend only 1–2 hours of
their course on the topic of climate change. Plutzer *et al.*
acknowledge that the quality of instruction is more important
than the quantity, so they subsequently examine how students
are introduced to climate science. What they found was a series
of mixed messages from science teachers. For example, 30% of
teachers emphasize that current global warming "is likely due to
natural causes," 12% do not "emphasize human causes... or
avoid the topic altogether," 31% reported teaching contradictory
ideas, highlighting both the scientific consensus that climate
change is largely anthropogenic, and numerous scientists claim
that recent increases in temperature are natural. Plutzer *et al.*
conclude that this mixed approach occurs because teachers
wish to accommodate the differing values and perspectives that
students bring to a classroom.

Furthermore, they found three other underlying reasons to
explain the contradictory lessons that are being taught by many
U.S. teachers. First, some teachers experience "overt pressure
from parents, community leaders, or school administrators not
to teach climate change." However, cases such as this are rare,
with only 4.4% of teachers reporting to have experienced such
pressure. Second, teachers are not extremely knowledgeable
about the evidence of climate change and how climate models
function. Fifty percent of teachers surveyed stated that they
would prioritize unrelated topics such as pesticides, ozone layer,
or impacts of rocket launches, over climate change. Third, many
teachers, themselves, are unaware of the extent of the scientific
agreement. When asked: "what proportion of climate scientists
think that global warming is caused mostly by human activities?"
only 30% of middle-school and 45% of high-school science
teachers said the correct answer of 81–100%. Among those who
answered correctly, only 52% knew the percentage of scientists
who shared their view.

Plutzer *et al.* hypothesize that if most science teachers believe that more than 20% of scientists disagree that human activity is the primary driving force of climate change, "it is understandable that many would teach "both sides" by conveying to students that there is legitimate scientific debate instead of deep consensus." Thus the researchers conclude that the combination of limited training and understanding of the scientific consensus affects the teachers' acceptance of anthropogenic climate change. Furthermore, teachers' assessment of the scientific consensus is also dependent upon their own personal conclusions about global warming and its causes.

To improve the current way climate science is being taught in U.S. schools, Plutzer and his associates suggest that furthering teachers' understanding of climate science is essential. Two thirds of teachers surveyed said that they "would be interested in continuing education entirely focused on climate change." The aim of climate change education is to help teachers distinguish "what is scientifically uncertain" from "what is well supported." Plutzer adds that it will also help teachers to expect and be prepared to counter "specific misinformation and misconceptions about climate change likely to be voiced by students." This is crucial as teachers who are prepared for such debates are more likely to have the facts and confidence to "provide scientifically sound instruction."

Plutzer, Eric., McCaffrey, Mark., Hannah, A. Lee., Roseneau, Joshua., Berbeco, Minda., Reid, Ann H. 2016. "Climate confusion among U.S. teachers." Science. Vol 351, Issue 6274, pp. 664–666
http://science.sciencemag.org/content/sci/351/6274/664.full.pdf

Overcoming The North-South Divide in Climate Change Research and Policy
by Claudia Chandra

Nature Climate Change published a research paper in January 2017 by Malgorzata Blicharska and her associates from countries including Brazil, Kenya, Sweden, South Africa and India. The paper discusses the global North-South divide in climate change research, policy and practice, which originates from the Southern countries' smaller capacity to undertake research. Countries are categorized into either "Northern" (members of the Organization for Economic Cooperation and Development such as Europe, North America, East Asia and Australasia) or "Southern" (lower income economies such as

Asia, Latin America and Africa.) The report highlights how the disparities that exist between Northern and Southern countries, in terms of science and knowledge, will become a greater hindrance to the development and practice of effective climate change reduction actions and policies. The researchers explore the extent of this particular North-South divide, study the underlying issues associated with it, and examine the potential consequences for climate change policy development and implementation.

The North-South discrepancy in climate change research is in need of significant development as this divide leaves developing countries and small island developing states (SIDS) most vulnerable to the effects of global warming. As these countries contribute the least towards climate change data and research, they are often unable to respond to its effects appropriately. The extent of the North-South divide is substantial, as exemplified by the World Bank's data which states that expenditure on R&D in Southern countries was 0.38% of their GDP and 1.44% in Northern countries. Additionally, the number of scientific and technical journal articles published in 2011 by Northern countries was 10,442, a notable difference to the 1,323 published by Southern countries that same year.

The study also points out the underlying issues associated with the North-South divide; it is much easier for Northern countries to collect information and form knowledge on climate change as they have more resources and better chances of securing funding. Moreover, there is a prejudice regarding the ability of Southern research institutes to lead North-South partnerships in research, which additionally hinders Southern scientists' ability to become lead authors in their work. Blicharska and her associates reference a previous study by Barrett *et al.* which suggests that further collaboration between Northern and Southern researchers is required so that Northern countries can better understand the social and environmental differences that a Southern country has if they wish to implement effective action plans to reduce climate change. This is because, at the moment, most studies on global assessments are more focused on climate issues affecting Northern countries with results that are not transferable to Southern countries.

In order to address the North-South divide and its effects, the researchers have provided practical solutions based on the United Nation's Sustainable Development Goals (SDG). These solutions emphasize the need to strengthen the technological and scientific capacities of Southern countries, ensure policies conducive to fostering their development, and foster international cooperation in science and innovation. Some of the suggested solutions include the establishment of North-South research programs, funding projects where the lead researchers are from the country that the research focuses on, and increasing the representation of Southern researchers in the media. These actions are beginning to take place as evidenced by the many Northern programs that sponsor Southern researchers such as the Wellcome Trust, which launched in March 2016 and assists scientists from non-G7 countries who have previous experience in the UK or US but wish to pursue their work in their country of origin.

The scientists note, however, that some limitations exist for their suggested solutions. One is that empirical evidence of the underlying causes of the North-South divide is lacking, which therefore makes it hard to develop appropriate plans and policies to suitably address this divide. Another is that Southern countries have a bigger need for socioeconomic development before they are able to allocate more resources into research. Thus, as suggested by T. Edejer, "only the development of national capacity [of Southern countries] will eventually put the South on an equal footing with its northern partners."

Blicharska, M., Smithers, R.J., Kuchler, M., Agrawal, G.K., Gutiérrez, J.M., Mshinda, H.M., ... Mikusiński, Grzegorz., 2017. "Steps to Overcome the North-South Divide in Research relevant to Climate Change Policy and Practice." Nature Climate Change.
http://www.nature.com/nclimate/journal/v7/n1/full/nclimate3163.html

The Relationship Between Climate Change and Violence: A Case Study of Rice Crops in Indonesia

by Claudia Chandra

The Journal of Peace Research explores the connection between climate change and violence by investigating Indonesia between 1993 and 2003 in a study by Raul Caruso, Ilaria Petrarca, and Roberto Ricciuti published in 2016. Rice is the staple food for Indonesians and the researchers look at whether increases in its scarcity because of increasing temperatures affects the level of violence in the surrounding area. Indonesia was chosen for the study because it is considerably affected by climate change, has a history of social unrest, and a "disproportionate dependence on a single crop." Between 1994 and 2003, 46% of the total population was employed in agriculture. Not surprisingly, the reduction of rice production per capita in many provinces substantially increased the frequency of violent occurrences.

The data used in the study were obtained from the United Nations Support Facility for Indonesian Recovery (UNSFIR), the National Oceanic and Atmospheric Association (NOAA), and by compiling 3,608 events of social violence reported in each of the 14 provincial newspapers. Variation in minimum temperature is used as a variable factor as higher minimum temperatures increase the maintenance respiration requirement of rice crops, shorten their time to maturity, and reduces net growth and productivity. The data showed that the minimum temperature from 1993–1996 was higher than average, and an additional +0.9°C above average in the winter months of these years. The study also showed that the warmer temperatures reduced harvests. As the size of a harvest is a function of temperature, the researchers also confirmed a "negative and significant association" between the frequency of violent incidents and rice production per capita; when food was abundant, violence decreased.

The mechanism that drives the relationship between climate change and violence varies across different regions and societies. From an economist's point of view, climate change causes "exogenous shocks that affect agricultural production, affecting the set of opportunities, and thereby the incentives and opportunity cost of individuals." This occurs in numerous ways; first, scarcity increases rice grain prices and thus reduces living standards, and second the lower levels of rice output lead to a lessened demand for labor and lower wages. These results, occurring simultaneously, reduce the opportunity cost of violence (as poorer people have a smaller opportunity cost of committing violence compared to wealthier people) and therefore triggers it.

As violence in Indonesia is also linked to the country's transition to democracy during this period, the exact role of poor harvests is unclear. Furthermore, there were fewer than 100 observations, and other confounding variables were identified but not included. It is also unclear whether these results can be extrapolated to other crops. The researchers believe, therefore, that it is necessary to explore "other combinations of climate change crops, and violence in different countries" to be able to cross-analyze the different results and produce more conclusive information.

Caruso, R., Petrarca, I., Ricciuti, R., 2016. "Climate change, rice crops, and violence: Evidence from Indonesia." Journal of Peace Research. Vol 53(1)., pp 66–83.

http://journals.sagepub.com/doi/pdf/10.1177/0022343315616061

A Look Into Climate Change Neoskepticism
by Claudia Chandra

In 2016 Paul Stern, John Perkins, Richard Sparks and Robert Knox published a research paper, "The challenge of climate-change neoskepticism," in Science. The study focused on people who opposed policies that limit anthropogenic climate change (ACC). These are people who deny or question ACC's existence, its magnitude, rate of progress, risks it carries, and the benefit of current mitigation efforts. Neoskeptics define those who, within this group, strongly oppose action against ACC. Neoskepticism acknowledges the existence of ACC but do not believe that urgent mitigation efforts are necessary. Their reason for this varies; theories include climate models being "too hot" and results being too uncertain to come to any conclusions.

The researchers believe that neoskepticism may have derived more from ideological or economic interests than from scientific ones. Nevertheless, neoskepticsm's focus on the risks and uncertainties raises questions about the true impact of climate change and how best to respond to it. Additionally, the study argues that even though neoskeptics raise "legitimate questions," they also create "unjustified inferences." For instance, even though neoskeptics believe in ACC, they infer that mitigation efforts are not necessary. According to the researchers, this "seriously underemphasizes some well-established characteristics of ACC that are important for informing choices." These characteristics include, but are not limited to, the increasing risk for extreme damaging outcomes of ACC that indicates how waiting for uncertainty has increasing costs, and how insuring against worst case scenarios is sensible especially when future damage is likely to be worse than previously thought. In light of this, the study suggests that a better inference would be that efforts which seem overpriced now may, in retrospect, have been "low cost insurance."

Stern *et al.*, believe that to find accurate information on ACC, science cannot simply detect climate trends and make future predictions. It should analyze time and resources required for mitigation strategies, analyze the effectiveness of each of these strategies, and evaluate the financial costs and risks of delay.

By accepting the existence of ACC but simultaneously doubting mitigation efforts, neoskepticism underlines the necessity for greater risk analysis and management in climate change data. From this, the researchers suggest that climate science must consider known risks and uncertainties and adopt measures to reduce them. The science proposed by the study is "decision science" because there are uncertainties regarding risks, costs, and benefits, and because of differing information needs. Decision science is also appropriate because it integrates decision making with scientific analysis and considers trade-offs that may have been unaddressed. Furthermore, decision science also helps policymakers and the public assess potential actions and consequences of inaction, which happens to also be "the main challenge unaddressed by neoskepticism."

The study concludes by emphasizing that it does not presume that an analysis of risks, techniques for decision making with uncertainty, or better models will end climate change neoskepticism. This is because some of this skepticism is tied with ideological and financial interests. Nevertheless, a better understanding of the issues raised by neoskeptics will help decision making in the presence of climate change risks and uncertainty. If this happened, climate change policy may become more productive.

Stern, Paul. C., Perkins, John. H., Sparks, Richard. E., Knox, Robert. A., 2016. "The Challenge of Climate-Change Neoskepticism." Science. Vol 353, Issue 6300, pp 653 – 654.
http://science.sciencemag.org/content/353/6300/653.full

The American Misconception of Climate Change
by Claudia Chandra

In 2016, Patrick Egan, an Associate Professor of Politics and Public Policy at NYU, and Megan Mullin, an Associate Professor of Environmental Politics and Political Science at Duke University, published a paper about the United States' misconception of climate change. The researchers wondered why it is difficult to make more climate-friendly decisions even though science has continuously described and predicted the detrimental effects of global warming. They created a study to help understand this phenomenon. Through an analysis of domestic migration patterns in the US, Mullin and Egan found that the effects of climate change to this point in time are perceived as positive by American citizens. This implies that unless climate-related threats are better recognized by the public, climate change mitigation may continue to be delayed until it is no longer useful.

The study recognizes that models which project the consequences of future climate change cannot fully determine and include the severity of changes. Mullin and Egan refer to economist Nicholas Stern, who believes that "it is these hard-to-predict impacts that are the most troubling potential consequences of inaction." Through this, the researchers elucidate why potential climate-related threats have not been enough to provoke the public to substantially lower carbon emissions. Moreover, it is unknown whether attitudes towards climate change can induce greater public action. There is also uncertainty about the level of public action if attitudes were to become increasingly negative.

Egan and Mullin's study used a weather preference index (WPI) that measures "the extent to which US migration patterns are associated with weather at different locations" to estimate its citizens' weather preferences. They found that America's domestic-migration patterns show that its citizens disliked warm, humid summers, but preferred warmer winters. Their results were largely unaffected when data from other studies were used to calculate the WPI. This helps explain why the effects of climate change since the 70s have been perceived as positive improvements; it also highlights how this misconception could potentially undermine support for climate change reduction policies.

The researchers note that although there is a generally positive outlook on climate change as the US is currently enjoying warmer winters, this outlook may change in the future. Hotter summers that are predicted to come will probably shift the public's opinion on climate change, especially in areas that will be impacted more greatly by global warming.

A strength of Egan and Mullin's study is that the effect of long-term changes in daily weather on behavior is isolated. However, they did not consider or incorporate the effects of weather extremes that could have resulted in different findings. This is because public opinion, and ultimately their actions, are affected by extreme events (i.e. flooding, wild fires, hurricanes) that could potentially encourage eco-friendly action. Another limitation of the work is that it only uses data collected in the past 40 years. As this is a very short time period in climate science, naturally occurring climate variability can easily be confused with the actual effects of climate change.

Through their research, Egan and Mullin demonstrate how hard it is for Americans to comprehend the negative and potentially dangerous effects of climate change when its currently perceived changes seem to make life better. They also point out why it is globally significant if the US citizens feel that climate change is beneficial; living in one of world's largest economies with nearly the largest emissions of greenhouse gases, they have a large influence over global policy-making and stimulating greater action.

Egan, Patrick. J., Mullin, Megan., 2016. "Recent improvement and projected worsening of weather in the United States." Nature. Vol 532, 357 – 360. http://www.nature.com/nature/journal/v532/n7599/full/nature17441.html

How are Travel Plans in Germany Affected by Climate Change?
by Chris Choi

Claudia Schwirplies and Andreas Ziegler (2016) examine the effects of climate change on German tourism and the demand on the tourism market. For example, climate change can lead to higher temperatures and may threaten the attractiveness of certain holiday attractions. To make holiday activities more diverse, investors must shift where they put their money. However, this will result in multiple costs to the investment sector. Overall, Schwirplies and Ziegler seek to improve the comprehension of the multiple effects and defects of adaptation to climate change and tourism by conducting a study examining the German population's travel habits.

Four hypotheses regarding how tourists would react to climate change were made. The first hypothesis examined whether higher awareness to climate change would cause tourists to adjust their travel behavior. The second looks at risk aversion and how it plays a role in changing travel plans. The third hypothesis tries to determine if health risks related to higher temperatures are more likely to change travel behaviors. The last hypothesis questions whether tourists who are more able to cope with climate change are likely to change their plans

The study mainly targeted German tourists, and it strongly confirmed the first hypothesis. German tourists who were previously exposed to severe weather events caused by climate change (heat waves, heavy rain, floods, etc.) were more likely to change their travel plans. The second hypothesis, however, could not be confirmed. Some indicators for risk aversion such as taking risks concerning financial investments and health were found not to be correlated with tourism-related adaptation. The third hypothesis could not be confirmed either. Having many children less than 18 years of age is negatively correlated with choosing certain travel times and positively correlated with a lack of desire to travel. Though it can be said that having multiple children is an indicator for health risk due to climate change, it could also mean that these families do not have as many opportunities to travel. As for the last hypothesis, the results were slightly ambiguous. There are many factors such as the amount of income that the tourists make that may alter the data. Because they have the funds to travel, their travel plans may not be entirely swayed by the effects of climate change. However, this higher income may also allow them to choose other travel destinations, so it is hard to confirm the last hypothesis.

The results of this study reveal that future demand shifts in the tourism industry can lead to massive impacts to regional economies. This shift in demand could create more economic problems for some countries such as Spain and Greece. While only the first hypothesis was confirmed from this study, Schwirplies and Ziegler conclude that they need more specific information about tourism-related adaptation to climate change to make more specific deductions regarding their four hypotheses.

Schwirplies, C., Ziegler, A., 2016. "Adaptation of future travel habits to climate change. A microeconometric analysis of tourists from Germany". Sage Journals http://journals.sagepub.com/doi/abs/10.1177/1354816616683053

Climate Change and its Effects on Mental Health
by Chris Choi

Eva and Robert Gifford (2016) examined how climate change has had an impact on mental health. Victims of climate change-induced events have been afflicted with various mental health disorders such as PTSD or depression. It was also found that climate change-related heat waves led to increased aggression ranging from homicide to suicide. The goal of the article was to analyze the various impacts that climate change has had on mental health, how it could potentially lead to global social change, and to figure out possible solutions to buffer its effects on mental health.

Climate change-related incidents can still influence mental health before they even occur. Eva and Robert Gifford used the term 'eco-anxiety' to characterize severe worry about insignificant risks related to ecological worrying. This could elicit dramatic responses such as a decrease in one's appetite or panic attacks. After the climate-related event, they found that initial stress reactions including shock and grief could eventually become long-term psychological trauma including depression and PTSD. After Hurricane Andrew, 38% of children in Southern Florida experienced symptoms related to PTSD. Ten months later, 18% of those children still experienced symptoms of PTSD. After Hurricane Katrina, a quarter of the evacuees reported sever symptoms of PTSD while approximately 40% still experienced moderate symptoms. In addition, increasing levels of carbon dioxide may be responsible for reducing the nutritional value of some foods which may cause fatigue and depression.

Eva and Robert Gifford went on to examine how social factors could affect people's susceptibility to climate change, finding that people who are poorer are more vulnerable to the effects of climate change. They argued that this greater vulnerability is linked to feelings of social inequality and lower levels of social cohesion among communities. The poor do not have as much access to resources that buffer the effects of extreme climate events. These social factors could be applied on a global scale. For example, Dan Christman, the VP of International Affairs for U.S. Chamber of Commerce, stated that climate change could become the cause of conflict globally and may be why the U.S. goes to war in the coming decades.

Eva and Robert Gifford thought of several solutions to mitigate the effects of climate change on mental health and to prevent negative social impacts. One solution is to provide more funding and support for structures and systems that promote mental health. Another solution is to analyze the effects of mass evacuation and how the attitude towards climate change influences psychological coping as well how the media's presentation of these events affect viewers' mental health. The last solution could be to change how people view climate change. It should be viewed as a challenge to be met and overcome to buffer climate change's negative impact on mental health.

Gifford, E., & Gifford, R. (2016). The largely unacknowledged impact of climate change on mental health. Bulletin of the Atomic Scientists, 72(5), 292-297.
affects #mentalhealth such as #PTSD and how to lessen its effects.

Is Climate Change Wreaking Havoc on our Mental Health?

by Joshua Dorman

Climate change has long been seen as a serious threat to our natural environment, our lakes, our oceans, and our cities. But few have considered the mental effects of the phenomenon. In an article for the Huffington Post, writer Eleanor Goldberg explores how climate change is threatening the minds of individuals around the world.

In April of 2017, the American Psychological Association, in combination with an environmental group called eco America, published a report warning of the impending dangers of climate change on our mental health and sanity. The report, titled "Mental Health and Our Changing Climate: Impacts, Implications and Guidance," concludes that "people living in a number of regions could become more susceptible to [PTSD], anxiety, depression, suicide and other mental health issues as a result of climate change."

The predicted mental repercussions of climate change are expected to stem from a variety of supernatural events linked to global warming. For instance, in the year 2014, National Geographic reported that humans played a role in "at least 14 extreme weather events" and people who endure such events are often left to deal with the psychological consequences. In fact, after a sample study of individuals affected by Hurricane Katrina was taken, it was found that 1 in 6 had PTSD, suicidal thoughts more than doubled in frequency among the group, and about 50% of the individuals were found to have developed serious anxiety or depression.

Additionally, when temperatures rise, a whole different set of mental issues among the people affected begin to develop. Studies have found a clear positive correlation between rising temperatures and increased aggression and suicide. Moreover, individuals who are forced to relocate due to a global warming-induced disaster often experience solastalgia, a condition marked by persistent and prolonged feelings of intense loss and desolation. Furthermore, loss of land frequently leads to feelings of loss of identity. Unfortunately, it is estimated that by 2050, over 200 million people will be displaced from their homes by climate change. If the world community doesn't quickly move to halt global warming, the sheer volume of mental health issues amongst our population could prove catastrophic to our species.

Goldberg, Eleanor. "Climate Change Could Have A Serious Impact On Mental Health: Report." The Huffington Post. April 03, 2017. Accessed April 22, 2017.

Using Empathy to Fight Climate Change
by Bryn Edwards

In an article published by the Economist, written by an anonymous source calling itself Erasmus, the author argued why data is not enough to engage the public's interest in climate change. He used two international gatherings on climate change to add to his argument: the Copenhagen summit in 2009 and the Paris summit last year in 2017. Prior to Copenhagen, the main tactic scientists used to grab the public's attention was scaring people with facts. But before Paris, environmentalists realized that they needed more powerful messages, that people could connect to and empathize with. Even Francois Hollande, the president of France encouraged a strong spiritual connotation associated with the Paris summit.

This is not a new tactic, it has been used for thousands of years, beginning with the "prophets of old." Alex Evans, one of the U.N. organizers behind both both summits described this movement in one of his recent books, tracing all powerful human movements to a narrative as powerful as the movement itself. The woman's suffrage movement, the Civil Rights movement, even the Women's March on Washington in January all have this in common. He attributes Trump's victory to the fact that his campaign simply had a better narrative than that of Clinton's. He believes that the climate change movement cannot simply rely on negative stories of extinction, or habitat loss, but also needs positive success stories. He cites the success story of China's Loess Plateau, once called "the cradle of Chinese civilization," that became so degraded by unsustainable farming techniques that desertification took its toll and the land became unusable. After 30 years of conservation work, silt levels in watersheds have been greatly reduced, and green is slowly returning to the plateau. Evans asserts that world needs empathetic stories such as these to inspire people, and remind the audience that there is hope for the future if people can unite and work together.

Erasmus. 2017. Fighting climate change may need stories, not just data. The Economist.http://www.economist.com/blogs/erasmus/2017/01/climate-change-myth-and-religion?zid=313&ah=fe2aac0b11adef572d67aed9273b6e55

Resilience in Narratives: Building Stories, Creating Change

by Rachel Ashton Lim

How can small local communities take action in the face of the 2015 Paris Agreement's failings? Citing a lack of accountability and ambition as a key source of the aforementioned failures, Irish community worker Jamie Gorman suggests a two-pronged response, one of resistance and resilience. He mentions resistance efforts by Irish communities to projects such as fracking, and spends the majority of his paper discussing the importance of the latter part of this approach: building resilience.

Gorman first lays the foundation for why the Agreement was a failure. Firstly, while the agreement acknowledges that increases in global temperature must be kept below 2°C, the actual collective pledges of different countries show a 2.7–3.7°C increase in temperature, because the agreement merely invites countries to voluntarily pledge mitigation efforts. Secondly, it "falsely includes" the need for climate justice in its non-binding preamble, and Gorman claims that the state of emergency which was enacted in response to the Paris terrorist attacks enabled the government not only to place climate change activists under house arrests, but also, to ban demonstrations by human rights groups. This allowed the following social injustices to be committed: the insufficient redistribution of climate change benefits and burdens, the failure to recognize the differential impact on communities based on race, gender and weather, as well as the false participation of marginalized communities.

Gorman attributes the insufficient redistribution to the blame for environmental degradation being shifted from the West to China and India without taking due historical responsibility, as well as industrialized nations committing less than their fair share of action to cut carbon emissions. Gorman states that because differential impact is not clearly recognized in the agreement, not enough is being done to ensure that renewable energies, organic local food, and sustainable building materials are made available to all communities regardless of socio-economic class they are in, and there is an insufficient support system for those who will lose their jobs as the fossil fuel industry declines. Finally, the false participation of marginalized communities justified market-based solutions to climate change such as carbon trading and the UN REDD+ scheme. These economic responses promote land-grabbing from indigenous peoples and the creation of carbon markets which allows pollution to continue at an "acceptable" rate.

Gorman suggests that a narrative shift must happen for effective climate change action to take place: The anthropocentric Enlightenment narrative which privileges white men must change into one that promotes a participatory dialogue with a sense of urgency, acknowledging the lived realities of different communities. By engaging in dialogue, Dorman argues, individuals will be better equipped to internalize the issues faced by local communities and realize the need for social conviction in areas of food security, energy and jobs, and thus grow their own resilience against climate change.

Gorman, Jamie. 2016. "Stories of resistance and resilience, developing a community work approach to climate change and climate justice". Journal of Radical Community Work, 2.

Climate Change Segmentation in Singapore
by Rachel Ashton Lim

A nationally-representative census by researchers from the Nanyang Technological University has identified the different ways in which Singaporean citizens regard climate change, grouping them into three distinct segments: the concerned, the disengaged, and the passive. Expanding from pre-existing models of data-collection and analysis from the West, the paper not only offers insight into the impact of Asian cultures on climate change attitudes, but also makes targeted recommendations for national policy makers in affecting change within the Singaporean community, where the success rate of public campaigns is often quite low.

The study reports a consensus between Singaporeans on the science of climate change, with the majority of Singaporeans accepting the seriousness of the issue, its anthropocentric causes, and the need for mitigation measures. This consistency in belief is attributed to the fact that most, if not all, of Singapore's mass media outlets are state-owned and thus align with government policy, unlike in the United States, where citizens receive a lot of conflicting information about the issue. And because the national newspaper of Singapore, the *Straits Times*, is a founding partner of the global Climate Publishers Network, it aims to promote awareness of climate change. Where, then, do the distinctions in belief between the different segments in Singapore lie?

It is in answering *who* is responsible for affecting climate change mitigation, the study argues, that individuals begin to disagree. Singapore's strong and effective system of central government and public administration is cited as a key reason for citizen apathy, with many Singaporeans placing a high level of trust in the ruling government to manage resources and infrastructure effectively and efficiently, solving problems such that citizens themselves do not need to. Although Singapore is a small tropical island vulnerable to increases in flooding, heat stress, and other climate change-related impacts, not all of its citizens believe they will personally be affected by climate change.

The study found that those in the disengaged segment, consisting of 35% of the population, have below average education and income levels, do not believe that climate change will harm them personally, and are the least likely to believe that citizen action is crucial to addressing climate change, or that climate change should be of high importance to public policy. They also hold neutral beliefs about whether or not citizens and governments are able to address climate change effectively.

On the other hand, the concerned segment, 50% of the population, is younger, more educated, and better paid than the national average. This segment believes that citizens, and not governments, play the primary role in addressing climate change, although global warming must remain a priority of public policy. This is reflected in their consumption habits, too: they are the most likely of the three segments to seek out information about the products they purchase. The concerned also were the most likely to say that the majority of scientific researchers agreed that climate change was a real issue.

The last 15% of the population, the passive, are the oldest, least educated, and least wealthy segment. While this segment holds a similar level of belief as the concerned segment regarding scientific consensus, it strongly emphasized the role of governance in mitigating climate change. However, since the passive segment is on average the oldest, the paper argues, these individuals are in the unique position to influence family members. This is because Asian values assign a high level of respect to the elderly, thus giving them a lot of power in the family unit.

Interestingly, the study claims that it is the passive segment, and not the concerned, that pays the most attention to global warming in traditional news media, and which has engaged the most with pro-environmental communication. The study suggests that this figure reflects the *way* in which media users engage with content; those who rely on the media for active surveillance of issues and for social utility may not necessarily engage with the media as much as those who passively absorb the information, but they may be more likely to apply the information they absorb to their own lives. The concerned segment may have learned about climate change from non-media sources, such as from their friends and families, but recognize the value of the media as a source of information in the future should they need it.

In light of these findings, the paper recommends that efforts affecting climate change action should highlight government initiatives that make it easier for citizens to take action, such as the provision of easy access to recycling bins and energy-efficient products, and teach them how to best use these initiatives (*e.g.* how to sort out household products for recycling), since the majority of the population is in the concerned segment. Efforts targeted at the passive segment should be norm-based, to try to shift their perceptions, so that they believe the majority of Singaporeans engage in pro-environmental behaviors. Finally, the disengaged segment must be targeted as non-media users, but the study states that the challenges about accessibility and a lack of clear collective values necessitates further communication research.

Detenber, B.H., Rosenthal, S., Liao, Y.Q., Ho, S.S. 2016. "Audience Segmentation for Campaign Design". International Journal of Communication, 10, 4736-4758.

Climate Change Games
by Rachel Ashton Lim

Climate change Role-Playing Simulations (RPS) offer meaningful insights for policy-makers on how conflicts of interests, future uncertainties and capacity limitations may be overcome, argues a 2016 paper published in *Nature*. The paper, which has quantified the effectiveness of such games, states that the safe, low-cost environment of such simulations allows policy makers and diverse stakeholders to improve their climate change adaptation literacy. These simulations assign participants roles outside of their real-life circumstances, giving them confidential, role-specific information, and are based on real-world scientific information and institutional arrangements. They do not promote a specific management strategy, thus allowing participants to navigate this sphere of complexity of their own accord. In order to evaluate the role of climate change games in our political decision making processes, the paper assessed the engagement and understanding of participants in two simulation projects: The Institutionalizing Uncertainty Project (IUP) in the coastal cities of Rotterdam, Singapore, and Boston, and the New England Climate Adaptation Project (NECAP), a two-year research project based in four coastal New England communities.

In the IUP, 76 participants across the three cities were tasked with the decision of whether they should build a new highway in light of potentially significant, but uncertain climate change risks, and if so, how they would reform such plans. Overall, participants in this simulation reported a significant increase in their understanding of uncertainty as a complicating factor in adaptation planning, but also reported surprise that the many sources of these uncertainties stem from matters of governance and not science. Additionally, they reported increased confidence in the prospect of climate change adaptation.

In NECAP, 110–170 participants in each community were involved in simulations of their own towns, based on real-world, downscaled climate change projections. There was a significant increase in the participants concerns about climate change and the urgency that their town must act against it, and the simulation helped participants understand exact local actions that are necessary in the fight against Climate Change, avoiding solely "top-down" approaches. Participants also reported an increase in their understanding of the complexity of climate change and the scale at which it will affect different areas.

Beyond the main function of increasing climate change adaptation literacy, the RPS games were critical conversation starters that allowed participants to integrate climate change projections into real-life development projects. By getting policy makers "outside their comfort zone and talking about adaptation planning as a normal part of their duties", Climate Change Role Playing Simulations can play a key role in improving the effectiveness of everyday policy making and planning, and must be utilized more often in stakeholder engagement.

Rumore, D., Schenk, T., Susskind, L. 2016. Role-play simulations for climate change adaptation education and engagement. Nature, 6, 745-750.

Climate Change Education in Singapore
by Rachel Ashton Lim

Although room for improvement still remains in Singapore's formal education system with regards to integration of the pressing and complex modern issue of climate change, a paper in the Journal of Environmental Education has presented its geography syllabus as a model for improving climate literacy, both locally and worldwide. Faced by the issue of rising sea levels and blistering heat, Singapore, a strong, pragmatic nation which has utilized schooling as an effective tool for economic and social growth, must educate not only its workforce, but also its young. Although its three National Communications to the UNFCC has not made this explicit (focusing instead on training private sector players, public awareness campaigns, and on improving its energy efficiency and investing in research and development), the Singaporean National Climate Change Secretariat does a better job of this in its strategic document, discussing the use of school subjects such as the Sciences, Economics, Geography and Social Studies.

How well, then, is climate change integrated into the course objectives and outlines of these named subjects? An analysis of the PSLE, "O" level and "A" level national examinations syllabi has shown that out of these, only the Sciences and Geography include climate change in their course outlines; other subjects include peripheral mentions of other environmental concerns such as land use and "the tragedy of the commons". In the Sciences, concepts such as carbon sinks, the atmosphere and pollution are introduced, but not under one uniform topic. It is in the subject of Geography that "Variable Weather and Climate" becomes a key topic. Under this overarching theme, students learn about atmospheric and hydrologic processes, extreme weather patterns through the study of floods, responses to climate change and cyclones.

The study cites the input of former class teachers into syllabus revisions as a key factor to the successful integration of climate change into Geography classes. As former teachers, the curriculum specialists and officers are highly knowledgeable not only about the subject matter, but also, about best pedagogical practices and the diverse array of student needs. Students were also given the opportunity to express climate change as a key issue of interest through a series of Focus Group Discussions. Once the syllabus review has been completed by the curriculum specialists and student focus groups, the Cambridge International Examinations (CIE) is consulted to ensure the rigor and compatibility of the syllabus with that of international standards.

A study by the National Climate Change Secretariat has indicated that Singaporeans are keen to learn about climate change, but not everybody studies geography as a subject. The paper thus calls for wider epistemic access to climate change education across formal education subjects, using the format of the Geography syllabus review as a model for improvement.

Chang, C.H., Pascua, L. 2017. The curriculum of climate change education: A case for Singapore. The Journal of Environmental Education, 0, 0-10.

Climate Change Self-Dependency in Kiribati
by Rachel Ashton Lim

Going against the grain and resisting the image of small developing countries as being entirely dependent on stronger foreign economies, one island nation in the Central Pacific has taken steps towards creating climate change security for itself, reports *The Economist*. Kiribati, made up of 33 "wafer-thin" islands and atolls with a population of just 111,000 people, faces the risk of flooding completely; a mere 2 m sea level rise would put a large part of the nation underwater, and IPCC predictions pitch sea level increases to almost a meter by 2100. In light of these statistics, the 2°C limit set in the Paris Climate Change Agreement may not be enough to save the country.

In response, one of the country's political leaders, Anote Tong, has not only lectured many richer countries on the impact of rising carbon emissions on smaller developing populations, but also has developed plans to support the country should developed nations fail to act, carrying out better vocational training programs and buying 6,000 acres of land in Fiji using $7m of government funds. While this property investment will make money for the state, the land can be used also to gain food security through self-sufficient agriculture, and offers a possible location for mass migration should rising waters consume Kiribati. This, combined with the increase in vocational training, will enable the people of Kiribati to migrate with "dignity", and not as "climate change refugees".

However, Tong's presidency has ended after his three-term limit, and the future of such policies remains unclear. While many educated young people support Tong's approach, the older generation has proven more resistant. Opponents of Tong have accused him of ignoring local issues of unemployment and healthcare for the sake of building an international brand, of intentionally allowing some villages to flood in order to create a false perception of Kiribati's climate vulnerability (albeit with little proof), and of challenging divine authority in a staunchly Christian country.

The Economist concludes that the fate of Kiribati's climate change policy lies in the hands of newly elected Taaneti Mamau, whose home village has been affected by drought since 1995.

Politics in Kiribati: Making Waves (2016). The Economist.
http://www.economist.com/news/asia/21694548-south-pacific-climate-change-animates-presidential-election-making-waves

Identity and Urban Spaces
by Rachel Ashton Lim

Faced with the issue of climate change, urban planners have become increasingly concerned with the environmental sustainability of the spaces they design, beyond the creation of energy efficient landscapes. This approach, which encourages heightening the presence of natural environments within urban cities, is what sparked a study from the 4th Annual International Conference on Architecture and Civil Engineering. Investigating the shifting policy-making paradigm which considers Nature as its own entity, to one where Nature is integrated into the cities we live and play in, the paper examines the policies of four "Biophilic Cities" across continents, defined as those that "look for opportunities to repair, restore and creatively insert nature wherever it can"; namely, Curitiba, London, New York, and Singapore. The study also contextualizes the importance of creating, and enhancing access to, natural spaces in the age of digital media, where we no longer need physical spaces to interact with one another. With this point of view in mind, the paper ties the significance of nature not only to having ecological value, but also, of being critical to national identity and community building.

The policies implemented by these four cities can be organized into two main themes: Those aimed at infrastructure, and those aimed at increasing public involvement by incorporating nature into public spaces and into citizens' lives.

Examples of the former include the creation of public parks, such as in Curitiba, Brazil, where by 1982, the amount of green area was about 10 m^2 per inhabitant, close to the 2012 UN recommendation of 12 m^2. Large reservoirs were also built inside the perimeters of these parks in order to mitigate the local flooding crisis. Additionally, this type of policy includes the transformation of degraded areas into preservation and wildlife observation regions, including the WWT Wetland Centre in London. In New York, public transportation infrastructure was improved, so as to reduce the city's carbon footprint, and in Singapore, "green corridors" were created so that citizens could access parks more democratically, and so that wildlife migration became easier, aiding biodiversity. The study notes the uniqueness of Singapore's green corridor approach, in its attempt to link different neighborhoods through one overarching system.

For the latter policy, nature caretaking programs were implemented across all four cities. In Curitiba, citizens were encouraged to water and take care of trees in their neighborhoods, prompting the slogan "We give shade, you the fresh water". Over 60,000 trees on average were cared for each year through this program. In London, abandoned urban segments were restored, and the unemployed were offered educational programs so that they could use the area for small agricultural projects. The study cites the benefits of local food production as going just beyond the reduction of costs and CO_2 emissions, to include the revitalization of social interactions between citizens. In New York and Singapore, tree planting programs were implemented, "The Million Trees NYC" and annual "Tree Planting Day" respectively. Another interesting initiative was the development of phone applications in London to advise citizens on how to mitigate their carbon footprints (for example, by showing them the quickest routes to reach their destinations). Through their PLANYC program, New York also aims to increase the "walkability" factor of their parks so that every New Yorker need only walk for 10 minutes to reach a park, based on research that claims people go to parks more when they can walk to them even though public transport may already make it accessible.

The study concludes by stating the value of these cities as models for the global transformation of cities from current conditions into one of ecological urbanism.

Costa, M.M., Lazos, A., Oliverida, R.R.d., 2016. The Role of Public Parks in the Creation of an Urban Identity. 4th Annual International Conference on Architecture and Civil Engineering, 212-216.

Apocalypse Fatigue: Losing the Public on Climate Change
by Kele Mkpado

In an article published by Yale Environment 360, two writers Ted Nordhaus and Michael Shellenberger looked for answers as to why after almost two decades of scientific discovery and general acceptance of climate change, people still continue to deny it. As in this sort of subject, it is easy to get caught up in political nonsense, and that is exactly what happens.

First, climate change tends to be a low priority for most people. When polled and asked what problems faced our county many people responded with "jobs" or "debt" or "terrorism". The threat is too distant for Americans to worry about. It rarely affects daily life so most aren't worried about its effects. The first thought is that there are more pressing matters at hand, which honestly is hard to argue with. Second, there seems to be an illusion that society works so well that it will figure itself out. Psychologists have noted that people need to continue to believe in social order to obtain a sound mind and sense of security, despite a false narrative. Thirdly, many climate change activists are set on promoting doomsday-like scenarios, some that are so apocalyptic that ordinary people decline to recognize them as possibilities. Most scientists do not believe that tsunamis will rush across the land and volcanoes will spontaneously all erupt at once. If you morph these three ideas together, you end up with a society that is hard to educate to/or sway in opinion.

Ironically however, as of late more people are coming to observe climate change as a real and important issue. One poll states that 70% of Americans do agree that the climate is changing. Unfortunately, there is a lack of action on the part of the climate change acceptors. This is due in part to the fact that drastic change is distant, but more importantly that fixing climate change would force us to change our way of life. Our way of life revolves around money and is sustained through cheap pleasure, mainly at the expense of the environment. It would seem that our materialistic nature is too much a part of our identities to give up, thus halting progression.

More and more people do believe that something needs to be done, but either don't want to pay for it or see troubles elsewhere. Maybe it is true that we only need a few bright minds to take action against climate change. Throughout human history it is the few that advance society forward, and the faith that they will figure it out somehow should be taken with some credit.

Nordhaus, Ted, and Michael Shellenberger. "Apocalypse fatigue: Losing the public on climate change." Yale environment 360 (2009): 16.

The Spectator: Why Climate Change is good for the World

by Kele Mkpado

In an article by Matt Ridley of "The Spectator", he makes the opposing claim that climate change is going to do a lot of good before it does harm. Yes, he does believe that in the end it will end up being a bad thing, but the data he has compiled shows that he and his children will most likely be long gone before anything catastrophic happens.

It was hard to take his claims seriously at first, but if the data he has compiled is sound it does make some sense. His first claim is that warmer temperatures will bring about fewer deaths. This claim is fairly accurate due to the larger amount of deaths from sickness in the winter than in the summer. Data shows that there is a spike in deaths during the winter months, something that is absent in the summer. His next point is that the increased carbon dioxide in the atmosphere will spark an increase in biodiversity and cause certain plants to flourish as they are able to absorb mass amounts of a main input to their growth. He brings up data that shows that this is already occurring in parts of the world, whereas 31 percent of the world has become more green, and only 3 percent has become less green in the last 3 decades. He continues his argument by disputing the claim that climate change will hurt the poorest parts of the world the most. This claim is true, but he makes the point that because the progression of climate change is so slow, if the world's population continues to grow at the standard rate wealth wise, most of these poor people will be nine times as rich and have the infrastructure built up to defend themselves against the negative effects of climate change that are to come far down the road.

The author does lay down some ideas that do spark some interest and should be discussed. Why do we continue to implement so-called "green" policies when there could be net benefits of climate change for the next 70 years? In my opinion, if you give the human race 70 years to figure a problem out, no matter how difficult or improbable, we will find a way.

Ridley, Matt. "Why Climate Change Is Good for the World." The Spectator. The Spectator, 06 Feb. 2014. Web. 13 Feb. 2017.

Rejecting Climate Change: Not Science Denial, but Regulation Phobia

by Kele Mkpado

In the Journal of Land Use & Environmental Law, a 2016 research article published by Edward Rubin alludes to the fact that our attitudes toward climate change may not be totally in sync with outright denial. The problem may stem from a series of other causes that make denial the easiest road to take in achieving the actual goal of the whole thing.

In his study, Rubin sought to discover why the U.S. played such a counterproductive role in combating the effects of climate change. Was it purely because our citizens denied its existence, or is there another issue more fundamental to American society? He finds the argument that the American public does not agree with scientific findings to be rubbish due to the fact that the majority of other scientific findings are widely accepted in American society. He also believes that thinking it is a conspiracy theory is not warranted either, as conspiracy theorists use science to debunk certain conclusions that were arrived at by other means. He states "climate change deniers do not condemn their opponents for using science, but rather endorse or even glorify science and condemn their opponents for using it incorrectly". The conclusion he comes to instead is that with climate change and its effects come major policy and lifestyle changes that the american public is not so keen to invoke. This is mostly apparent in conservative sphere of the Nation, where Republican-driven politics revolve around less regulation and modifications to the traditional American way. Instead of stating that climate change is real but that they don't wish to implement policy to prevent it, they instead just flat out deny it altogether. Realizing that a rational policy would demand a major alteration to American society, they and their supporters who oppose such an alteration instead paint the narrative of climate change as fiction.

Rubin, Edward L., Rejecting Climate Change: Not Science Denial, but Regulation Phobia (January 16, 2017). Journal of Land Use & Environmental Law, Forthcoming; Vanderbilt Public Law Research Paper No. 17-3. Available at SSRN: https://ssrn.com/abstract=2900352

The Independent: Climate Change Increases the Risk of War, Scientists Prove
by Kele Mkpado

In an article by Ian Johnston of the independent, he explains that climate change will have drastic alterations to our landscape and cause natural disasters, forcing certain populations to be involved in relocation, inevitably leading to war.

Researchers conducted a study between 1980 and 2010 that there is already a correlation between climate related disasters and conflict breaking out in the region. They noticed that this was more apparent in ethnically fractionalized societies, where there is a constant struggle for power and land. It just so happens that the equator is the hottest place on the planet, and home to many ethnically diverse nations. If climate change were to have a large enough effect on these regions without quick adaptation, groups of people will be forced to migrate elsewhere, surely to cause some conflict with neighboring populations. It was cited that with ethnic divides comes an already high stress situation, and something like a climate disaster could be the factor that sets of armed conflict. The author notes that climate disasters like the drought in Afghanistan prolonged the armed conflict that arose there due to a lack of natural resources. In other places like Somalia and Syria, conflict arose in the form of crime, an increased spike only destabilized the region even more.

When thinking about climate change we cannot only discuss the natural disasters that might occur from the planet. We must also recognize the effects and consequences of those disasters. When thinking about floods, droughts, storms, heat waves, and sea level rise, we must add war to the list.

Ian Johnston Environment Correspondent. "Climate Change Increases the Risk of War, Scientists Prove." The Independent. Independent Digital News and Media, 25 July 2016. Web. 06 Mar. 2017.

Effect Specific Climate Information Has on the Public
by Bradley Newton

It is commonly agreed that the partisan media plays a major role in influencing the beliefs of its viewership. Conservative media outlets push the idea of the absence or unimportance of climate change, as opposed to the information disseminated by more liberal media entities that support its existence. Carmichael *et al.* (2017) does not argue that that media outlets do not influence the public, but rather that this idea is basically speculative. Their study is meant to provide empirical evidence on how much the news and other sources influence the public.

The authors studied the effects of media coverage, extreme weather, issuance of major scientific reports that can be easily understood by the general public, and changes in economic activity and foreign conflict. The study supported the seemingly obvious notion that partisan media strengthened the beliefs of like-minded individuals. However, it also found that the same material, when presented to those of opposing beliefs, proceeded to push them further away from agreeing with climate change views of liberals, causing them to see climate change as even less of an issue. Another observation from the data collected was that when scientific evidence for climate change was presented, concern for the issue increased among those of Democratic affiliation, whereas Republicans were relatively uninfluenced by the information. The appearance of extreme weather had no notable increase in concern among either Democrats or Republicans. As for how economic situations affected the concern of the public towards climate change, it was found that both Republicans and Democrats became less concerned during weaker economic periods, however, in slightly different fashions. Democrats viewed climate change as more of an issue with the onset of economic expansion, whereas Republicans only lost interest during an economic downturn. The way the two sides react sounds like what we would expect, but what the authors are trying to say is that the views of each side shift on opposite sides of whatever the economic climate is.

Carmichael, Jason T., Robert J. Brulle, and Joanna K. Huxster. "The Great Divide: Understanding the Role of Media and Other Drivers of the Partisan Divide in Public Concern over Climate Change in the USA, 2001-2014." Climatic Change (2017): n. pag. Web.
http://link.springer.com/article/10.1007/s10584-017-1908-1#Sec13

Climate Change Knowledge of First Year College Students
by Bradley Newton

Shealy *et al.* (2017) based their research on the idea that the average high school student has a warped or false understanding of climate change. This is damaging because a false understanding will affect the actions that students take pertaining to climate change. The fewer people who believe climate change is of concern, the less action will be taken in trying to prevent or slow it down. By accessing data from a national survey of first year college students—to assess students who completed the entirety of their high school curriculum—the authors found specific high school activities that correlated with the belief that climate change is caused by human activities. Accordingly, the hypothesis for their research was, "How do high school science experiences correlate with climate change beliefs?" The survey was called the Sustainability and Gender in Engineering (SaGe) survey, and was administered in introductory English classes in randomly selected colleges so as to provide the survey with a wide range of students of different majors. At the end of the study it was found that high school students' views towards climate change were affected by social factors such as school culture and peer education. Academic performance and courses taken were less of a predictor for whether or not a student believed that human activities are a major cause of climate change as opposed to outside-of-class activities such as clubs or other extracurricular activities. This basically means that covering climate change in class did not necessarily encourage students to align their beliefs with the scientific consensus. An interesting detail the article points out is that this aligns with another study that states that the beliefs of students are more strongly correlated with their student activities than with the beliefs of their professors.

Shealy, Tripp, Leidy Klotz, Allison Godwin, Zahra Hazari, Geoff Potvin, Nicole Barclay, and Jennifer Cribbs. "High School Experiences and Climate Change Beliefs of First Year College Students in the United States." Environmental Education Research (2017): 1-11. Web. http://dx.doi.org/10.1080/13504622.2017.1293009

Social Norms and Climate Change
by Bradley Newton

Those in charge of educating the public and enforcing new habits to help combat climate change are constantly looking for better methods for reaching out to the public and convincing them of its validity. Such outreach is needed on a large scale for the effects to be felt, which is why media outlets are usually the main tool for information dispersion. However, an effective way to utilize the media in explaining climate change is yet to be found and as of right now the majority of Americans perceive the issue with uncertainty due to low levels of knowledge on the topic. Because of this, most people associate the issue as being more impersonal, or rather as something that does not directly affect them. Nowadays people usually gain a lot of their pro environmental information from such media platforms as YouTube or Facebook. An article written by Spartz *et al.* (2017) focuses on the implications of social norms that go along with YouTube. The article states that there has been evidence found that supports the idea that "perceived social norms can act as determinants of individuals' motivation to engage in larger group actions related to climate protection." This basically means that people are followers, and if a large enough group of people is interested in a certain idea or topic, the likelihood of others joining in rises substantially. Spartz *et al.* seek to widen this idea with the notion of whether or not this same concept applies to people's perception of validity or prominence of climate change in their own life based of social cues provided by social media. The study was run using data collected from a large public university in the American Midwest. Participants were given a link to a controlled YouTube video in which the independent variable was the number of previous views the video had when shown to each of the participants. The results of the study showed a positive correlation between the number of views the video showed, and the "perceived importance or salience" the viewer saw in the video's content on climate change.

Spartz, James T., Leona Yi-Fan Su, Robert Griffin, Dominique Brossard, and Sharon Dunwoody. "YouTube, Social Norms and Perceived Salience of Climate Change in the American Mind." Environmental Communication 11.1 (2015): 1-16. Web.
http://www.tandfonline.com/doi/full/10.1080/17524032.2015.1047887?scroll=top&needAccess=true

Disproportionate Policy Making
by Bradley Newton

Maor *et al.* (2017) focus on the idea of disproportionate policy making in their article, believing that it is something the could be intentionally used to effectively reach a certain goal. The article defines disproportionate policy making as being when a policy in question poses greater costs than derived benefits, which can pose itself as either an overreaction of a policy or an underreaction. A policy can be described as an overreaction if the decision-makers imposing it invest too many resources into its sustenance, and at the opposite end of the spectrum it can be described as an underreaction if the benefits minus the costs are lower than if an alternative route had been taken. The article applies this idea to the current situation of climate change as an "intentional and strategic" policy response. Maor *et al.* acknowledge the rise of climate change on the agendas of national and international entities, but believe that most of the policies that have been enacted so far can be described as an underreaction. Governing bodies have had and are having trouble with what climate policies to adopt, and how exactly they should be molded to be most effective. More specifically, whether policies should lean towards the mitigation of human pollution or adaptation to the changing climate. Maor *et al.* use the concept of disproportionate policy making to describe how decision makers are currently creating policies for climate change. It is recognized that humans are emotional creatures, and that they tend to use simplified heuristics to come to conclusions as to how things should be done. A certain policy could gain a high level of traction with the public, but in the end, may not have the exact outcome the public may have had in mind due to the poor allocation of resources used to push the policy forward. For example the public may want preventative measures to be taken to help assuage a certain problem, but the extent to which they might want resources to be used may be an overextension of what is really needed. However, politicians and others alike would be more than happy to push such policies forward if it will help them get re-elected, regardless of the consequences. There are also the existence of other politicians who are not so blind, and impose over reactive disproportionate policies with the goal for it to eventually crash and burn. The reasoning for this is that its failure could be used as an example for why that type of policy should be discouraged, leading to the creation of other under reactionary disproportionate polices or no policies at all that pertain the issue in question. The article concludes saying that the spotlight placed on the climate change has not been all good for the issue. Due to its popularity, it has been filled with manipulative policies that do nothing but advance the agendas of self-centered politicians, and it calls for greater attention to be paid to the underlying reasons for why and how policies are being made that pertain to climate change.

Maor, Moshe, Jale Tosun, and Andrew Jordan. "Proportionate and Disproportionate Policy Responses to Climate Change: Core Concepts and Empirical Applications." Journal of Environmental Policy & Planning (2017): 1-13. Web. http://www.tandfonline.com/doi/full/10.1080/1523908X.2017.1281730?scroll=top&needAccess=true

Social Scientists Needed

by Alejandro Salvador

In a letter to the editor of Nature Geoscience, Professor Reiner Grundmann from the University of Nottingham discusses the approach given to climate change and its solutions. Grundmann states that climate change should be seen as a social problem rather than as a scientific one. He begins his analysis by comparing climate change to the 'ozone hole' problem, which drove the international community to pursue policymaking from a scientific standpoint thirty years ago. Scientific consensus established targets, timetables, and measures needed to reduce pollutants. The measures worked. Consequently, when the perils of climate change threatened the international community, the scientific approach prevailed. The problem lies in the notion that the ozone layer case and climate change are different in substance; climate change is a social problem, while ozone layer protection was not. Furthermore, the author uses a distinction made by urban-policy experts: there exist tame problems—those that can be solved—and wicked problems—those that have no clear solution and ought to be constantly re-solved. The ozone problem falls in the tame category, climate change in the wicked.

Dr. Grundmann argues that climate change has been misclassified as a tame problem and given a scientific attitude when it comes to policy. However, there is no scientific consensus on how to solve or manage climate change. As a wicked problem, it does not have a stopping rule. And in the absence of scientific consensus, social scientists—other than economists—have been left aside.

This has led policy makers to derive climate policy without considering the complex social elements familiar to social scientists. Also, if climate change policy is justified by science, the detractors of such policies will attack the science behind them. The author states that climate change needs pragmatic solutions that consider society's behavior and cultural values. Several solutions have been proposed, but many would have intricate effects on our social reality. For this reason, the insights needed to solve climate change come from the social sciences, not from climate science.

Grundmann, R., 2016. Climate change as a wicked social problem. Nature Geoscience, 9(8), 562-563.
http://www.nature.com/ngeo/journal/v9/n8/full/ngeo2780.html

Risk Perception and Climate Change
by Alejandro Salvador

In an article published in Nature Climate Change in 2016, researcher Paul C. Stern analyses citizens' perception of climate change risk from a sociological perspective. He begins his analysis by presenting the results of a 2012 paper by Daniel Kahan and colleagues about climate change risk perception. The paper states that risk perception is not altered by increased scientific knowledge or numeracy, but rather by citizens' world-views. In this sense, people with a collective and collaborative world-view perceive greater risks from climate change than people with a more hierarchical and individualistic world-view. This happens because those with a hierarchical world-view do not believe that collective action should be involved in authorities' decisions, in contrast to the beliefs of people with a collaborative view. These differences in ways of looking at the world go in line with the cultural theory of risk: risk perception is more indicative of people's world-views, rather than actual risk. Furthermore, current research suggests that citizens with altruistic values are more concerned about climate change than those who hold self-centered values.

However, Stern claims that studies such as Kahan's could potentially paint a pale picture if considered on their own. International comparison has shown that risk perception goes beyond self-entrenched universal values; it is also cultural. The cultural aspect is seen in the acceptance of climate change consensus. For example, US political differences correlate to whether individuals reject climate change consensus or not—conservatives tend to disregard climate science. Furthermore, social movements—in favor of and against climate change consensus—play an important role in the polarization of risk perception.

Paul C. Stern argues that given that climate change affects people in different manners, challenging different world-views and values, research needs to give more attention to its social effects—rather than just producing physical facts. Also, there must be space for reasonable dialogue, that acknowledges some degree of uncertainty in climate science, and voices different viewpoints.

Stern, Paul C., 2016. Impacts on climate change views. Nature Climate Change, 6, 341–342.
http://www.nature.com/nclimate/journal/v6/n4/pdf/nclimate2970.pdf

Women and Climate Change
by Alejandro Salvador

In a paper published in Productivity, researchers N. B. Chauhan and H. M. Vinaya discuss the role of gender in climate change. The authors state that climate change necessarily affects women and men differently. This is not only because of the different roles that gender plays in society, but largely because of the limited representation of women in important climate change decisions. It is for this reason that climate change responses must be targeted at different genders.

The key difference between men and women, when it comes to climate change, lies in their role in the economy. The authors argue that women in developing countries are mainly food producers and contributors. Nonetheless, they have inadequate access to the administration and control of the resources with which they work. This difficulty is exacerbated by their lack of political representation, as they cannot influence the decisions that directly affect them. Furthermore, a vicious circle is created. As women are affected by climate change, the inequality between men and women increases, and the more affected they are.

The authors continue to state factors that impact the risk women face in a changing climate. These include location, women are more likely to be poor and therefore live in areas more vulnerable to climate change; social aspects, women tend to have fewer access to social rights than men; economic factors, women are generally poorer and have limited access to financial institutions; and education, women tend to be less educated and have fewer access to information than men. For all these reasons, the authors believe that decisions regarding climate change should take into consideration the different position of women. If they are present in the crucial decisions that shape climate change development, they would be able to offer their distinct perspective. Climate change puts different hurdles in women's lives, and their knowledge and experiences are key in solving them.

Chauhan, N. B., & Kumar, V. H. M., 2016. Gender responsive climate change strategies for sustainable development. Productivity, 57(2), 182-186. http://ccl.idm.oclc.org/login?url=http://search.proquest.com/docview/1824517294?accountid=10141

Loss Research

by Alejandro Salvador

In a changing climate, we must be aware of loss. Whether it's a water-borne illness or a hurricane, losses will arise from climate change. Learning to manage and avoid them is a necessary step we must take as we look ahead to increasingly hotter temperatures. In a commentary in *Nature*, Jon Barnett, Petra Tschakert, Lesley Head and W. Neil Adger discuss the science of loss and its relationship to climate change.

The authors begin by defining loss, and identify different types of it. Loss exists when a person is disposed of something valuable to them, to which there is no commensurable substitute. One category of loss—and perhaps the most important—is defined as primary goods; these are necessary items for a "free and dignified life", such as health, safety, sense of belonging, esteem, and relative freedom. There are also different types of losses that can't be measured by usual metrics.

The authors argue for the necessity of a science of loss, that focuses its research in three main areas: what do people value highly—and why, what drives change and loss, and what to do once losses arise.

The nature of things valued by people is a research topic that spans across multiple disciplines from the social sciences. Research has shown that climate change endangers items that go from homes, to knowledge and social relations. The authors argue for a knowledge of loss that includes the nature of loss, and how it varies across social contexts. This knowledge would allow us to further explore loss with a solid base of what is endangered.

Once we understand the risks at stake, a science of climate loss must consider the climatic elements that drive change—and loss with it. It must not try forecast when and where loss will occur, but try to recognize the variability of loss across social contexts and engage with people from places where loss is more likely.

Finally, though haunting, the prospect of loss must be accepted. This would allow us to better plan, manage, and possibly prevent it.

Barnett, J., Tschakert, P., Head, L., Neil A. W., 2016 Nature Climate Change 6, 976–978
http://www.nature.com/nclimate/journal/v6/n11/full/nclimate3140.html

Climate Change Offenders
by Alejandro Salvador

Climate change impacts different dimensions of our existence, ranging from environmental to economic systems, but not much has been studied about its impacts on our social systems. In *Nature Climate Change,* Rob White examines the impacts that climate change has had on our judicial and criminal system.

Recent papers have identified three areas relating climate change and crime: individuals, how extreme weather triggers criminal violence; place-based activities, how biophysical changes alter the propensity of criminal behavior; and communities and climate, which considers problems such as survival and migration strategies due to a changing climate. Furthermore, environment-related offences can be classified as offences that contribute to climate change, offences due to the consequences of it, offences concerning turmoil and organized crime, and offences of regulation and law enforcement.

In this context, there are two players that can't be overlooked: governments and big multinational companies. They tend to be key committers of ecocide—an anthropogenic extensive destruction of the environment. While government intervention is key to tackling the critical challenges that climate change poses, state support for business can result in a net outcome of little effect of climate change regulation.

While climate change can bolster crime, it can also alter the way it's prevented and enforced. For example, institutions of criminal justice could diminish carbon emissions, or sentence offenders to help in ecologically beneficial projects. Judicial agencies are key to regulating climate change and they must not tolerate ecocide.

Rob White argues for research on the intersection of crime and climate change. if we want to combat and respond to climate change, it is imperative to regulate environmental-related criminal activity with theoretically informed responses and a solid foundation on prevention strategies techniques.

White, Rob., 2016 Nature Climate Change 6, 737-739
http://www.nature.com/nclimate/journal/v6/n8/full/nclimate3052.html

Gaps that Need to be Closed, not Bridged
by Alejandro Salvador

Change requires adaptation. One of the greatest challenges that climate change presents us is coming up with adequate responses and adaptation practices. In this context, according to researcher Debra Davidson in a 2016 commentary in *Nature Climate Change,* input from the social sciences is crucial. And although its value and necessity has been acknowledged, we need more of it. Debra Davidson discusses the existing gaps in agricultural climate adaptation research. Agriculture is a key sector in need of adaptation, and current research is not producing comprehensive knowledge about it.

To evaluate current research on the topic, Dr. Davidson analyzed content from peer-reviewed journal articles on agricultural climate adaptation published in 2007 and 2015. Some of the results are encouraging: there is a significant increase in the amount of literature produced on the subject, more attention is being paid to developing countries, and input from the social sciences has increased. Nonetheless, this input presents notorious gaps, and tends to miss the social factors that enable (or not) systemic change in agricultural practices.

The author identifies three key factors that tend to be overlooked: gender differences in agricultural climate adaptation, the role social networks play in it, and the influence of governments and institutions.

Gender roles in agriculture are significantly distinct, especially in developing countries. Women tend to be more vulnerable to the impacts of climate change, and their limited access to resources and financial institutions limits their adaptation capabilities. Current research doesn't reflect these differences, disregarding a crucial aspect of climate adaptation. When it comes to social networks, researchers tend to rationalize human behavior, yet farmers do not always behave that way. They exist within a cultural and interconnected framework, in which social networks greatly influence adaptation outcomes. Finally, our local and global agricultural systems function under the influence of different laws and institutions, where external actors can affect farmers' adaptation success.

Debra Davidson argues that research must take this into consideration, and that more collaborative research between the social and natural sciences is desirable. The gaps in existing research must be closed, and input from the social sciences is necessary to do so. To promote collaboration, more funding for the intersection of social and natural sciences is needed, and norms and practices from both fields must accommodate each other.

Davidson, Debra. 2016 Nature Climate Change 6, 433-435: Gaps in agricultural climate
adaptation research
http://www.nature.com/nclimate/journal/v6/n5/full/nclimate3007.html

Helping Policymakers
by Alejandro Salvador

When it comes to climate change, scientists conduct the research needed—crucial to determine possible outcomes and risks—but it's ultimately up to policymakers to act on the available knowledge. In a commentary in Nature published in 2016, Stéphane Hallegatte, Katharine J. Mach and colleagues encourage researchers to shape their results to the necessities of policymakers, making their research more evidently relevant to the crucial decisions they must make if we are to limit climate change to a 2°C increase in global temperatures.

Hallegatte and Mach propose four aspects on which researchers should work to delineate their research for policymakers: they must integrate disciplines from the start, explore multiple dimensions, consider uncertainty, and inform holistic solutions.

Knowledge is limited by existing research, and currently, this knowledge says little about key aspects that policy-makers should look at. Climate change assessments should incorporate a range of disciplines that are relevant for policymakers. For example, they should look at the impacts and risks of climate change and contrast it to possible development outcomes.

Furthermore, climate change assessments must look at a broader range of possible scenarios. Climate change risks and responses are different depending on location, time-scopes, and mitigation. Assessments should explore these outcomes, instead of characterizing only a few, and compare the risks that different mitigation pathways offer for different locations. This would help policymakers choose responses from a more informed standpoint. Also, assessments should consider both the winners and losers of climate change. While climate change may affect fishing communities by destroying vital resources for them, it could improve agricultural yields; policymakers need to be aware of the different interest groups at stake.

Another topic for consideration is uncertainty. Decision-makers need to be aware of the multiple sources of uncertainty present in the climate change discussion. Starting from unknowns coming from a deep lack of knowledge, corrigible through more research and funding, to probability ranges that have an inherent degree of uncertainty. Other areas of uncertainty that must be considered are societal reactions, and the random features of the climate system.

Finally, assessment should inform holistic solutions. Climate change affects multiple aspects of our existence, and multiple aspects that policymakers need to be aware of. Assessments must compare the risks arising from climate change, and their interplay with other aspects and interests of society, such as poverty, energy costs, and political and economic impacts to name a few.

Hallegatte, Stéphane., Mach, Katherine. 2016 Nature 534, 613-615
http://www.nature.com/news/make-climate-change-assessments-more-relevant-1.20155

A Lack of Foresight
by Alejandro Salvador

The existence of anthropogenic climate change is now widely acknowledged by the broader scientific community. It has been so for several years. However, the perils that an unregulated scenario poses are yet to be correctly tackled and lessened. In an article in *BioScience,* scholars from a broad range of interdisciplinary disciplines discuss this thoughtless lack of foresight intelligence—the ability to act in accordance to a sustainable future—with a psychological framework in mind.

The authors begin by providing an overview of the psychological barriers to foresight intelligence. The first of these is the "noisy-signal problem". Climate change does not manifest itself with a clear identifiable signal—the increase in global temperatures can be obscured by variable temperatures world-wide. Another problem arises from the evolutionary characteristics of human beings. We evolved to be focused in short-term survival and needs, opposing the long-term approach needed to combat climate change. The existence of "free-riders" poses another problem. Communities are less willing to act and accept short-term costs for long-term benefits if they know that other communities will equally benefit without incurring in the costs. Related to this is the "drop-in-the-bucket" problem. People understandably believe that their own individual efforts will not make a difference in the grand scheme of things, prompting inaction. Finally, the human inclination of denial and rationalization hinders climate action efforts.

But in the realm of psychology, not everything is discouraging. The authors provide three success stories of "psych-wise interventions" that could potentially aid in the fight against climate change: the power of norms, default options, and the role of the media. Group norms affect people's behavior. If they perceive that people around them are acting on climate change, they will be more likely to adopt their surrounding's norms. On the other hand, setting climate-friendly default options on electronic appliances, for example, makes people more likely to accept them, even if they can change them. Finally, the media plays a huge role in people's attitude towards climate change. The spurge of collective concern following Al Gore's "An Inconvenient Truth", a book and documentary on climate change, serves as a prime example, albeit the media can also promote climate change denial and inaction.

The authors discuss different ways to assist the fight against climate change. Visual signals, such as LEED signs and solar panels, can inspire action. Climate education from young ages can help people understand the science behind climate change and prevent dangerous denial. Not only must we raise public awareness about climate change, but also change social norms that impede the practice of foresight intelligence.

Lee Ross, Kenneth Arrow, Robert Cialdini, Nadia Diamond-Smith, Joan Diamond, Jennifer Dunne, Marcus Feldman, Robert Horn, Donald Kennedy, Craig Murphy, Dennis Pirages, Kirk Smith, Richard York, Paul Ehrlich. BioScience (2016) 66 (5): 363-370: The Climate Change Challenge and Barriers to the Exercise of Foresight Intelligence
https://academic.oup.com/bioscience/article/66/5/363/2468623/The-Climate-Change-Challenge-and-Barriers-to-the

Inoculating the public
by Alejandro Salvador

Despite widespread scientific consensus on the existence of anthropogenic climate change, the public has still not reached the same level of agreement. The reasons for this are multiple, from disinformation campaigns claiming science's inherent degree of uncertainty means consensus is uncertain, to political polarization. In an article published in the interdisciplinary journal *Global Challenges,* researchers Sander van der Linden and colleagues investigate whether inoculation theory can protect people from deceptive information about climate change.

Inoculation is a method used to impact people's perception. It consists of forewarning readers that some information about to be presented may contradict their beliefs. A false statement is then highlighted, and refuted, before readers are presented with a counterargument. As the authors explain, it acts as a sort of vaccine against misinformation. A small dose of a virus generates resistance to the virus itself.

The question lies in whether inoculation theory can be used to combat misinformation about climate change. In particular, the authors investigated public perception of the scientific consensus about anthropogenic climate change. They conducted two different experiments. The first one consisted on a survey looking to identify the most influential counterarguments against climate change. The statement "there is no consensus on human-caused climate change" was identified as the most convincing one. The second experiment consisted of testing whether inoculation can shield people against these statements. Inoculation worked as follows: respondents are warned that some information might contradict their prior beliefs. Then, the statement saying that there is no consensus on human-made climate changed is briefly refuted. Only then are the respondents exposed to the counter-message—denying scientific consensus on climate change. Contrastingly, the control group is directly exposed to the misleading message. Both groups respond to a series of questions about their perceptions before and after reading the message.

As expected, inoculation was successful. People who had been previously "inoculated" tended to negate the misleading message, and their perceptions on scientific consensus didn't change much before and after the experiment. On the other hand, scientific consensus perception was undermined in the control group when presented with arguments supporting this claim. In an era of information, and misinformation, inoculation theory could be useful to protect climate change believers, and combat deniers.

S. van der Linden, A. Leiserowitz, S. Rosenthal, E. Maibach, Global Challenges 2017, 1, 1600008: Inoculating the Public against Misinformation about Climate Change http://onlinelibrary.wiley.com/doi/10.1002/gch2.201600008/full

Can Psychology Mitigate Climate Change?
by Tanisha Sheth

In 2011, Paul C. Stern, currently a principal staff officer at the National Research Council of the National Academies of Science, wrote an article regarding the contributions of psychology to limiting climate change. The article drew an interesting parallel regarding how human activities that are directly responsible for global warming, are in turn related to various human activities such as migration of human populations, technological advancements and most importantly, the behavior of individuals and households as consumers. Stern then writes about how psychologically targeted action can change an individual's perspective and behavior regarding climate change. He cites various research papers proving that previously made interventions to modify attitudes towards the environment have shown progressive results.

In retrospect communication, specifically through persuasion campaigns and circulating information through mass media have been popular however, ineffective solutions at tackling the issue. This is because studies have found that information can increase knowledge but has minimal effects in changing behavior. However, campaigns which have yielded positive results are the ones that have taken advantage of psychological knowledge regarding the framing of information such as vivid, personalized messages and structuring energy choices as avoiding loss rather than achieving gain. Other strategies include comparison of return rates from energy efficient investments to those of returns from a stock or a mutual fund. Also, a feedback mechanism with services inclusive of tailored recommendations or motivational elements. Behavioral psychologists have vouched for this as such a mechanism is closely related to receiving tangible rewards rather than a typical monthly energy bill. Feedback techniques can be equipment like miles per gallon monitors or "smart" utility meters. Other tactics include financial incentives such as by time-of-use electricity pricing and benefits of reduced energy use. Non-financial factors would also take into account persuasiveness and convenience of a program. Combined approaches that integrate financial incentives and targeted market strategies have found to increase plasticity by more than 20% in adopting eco-friendly means.

Psychological research is also vital for public support. That is the risk perception regarding nuclear energy has made individuals more favorable to implementation and expansion of large wind and solar energy projects for limiting climate change. In conclusion, psychological research can potentially change the current idea of consumption and identify ways to satisfy peoples' needs while simultaneously reducing greenhouse gas emissions and in this manner predict behavioral changes in sustainable environment.

Stern, P., 2011, Contributions of Psychology to Limiting Climate Change, American Psychologist 303-14.

Can Studying Human Behavior Contribute to Climate Change?

by Tanisha Sheth

In 2011, Janet K. Swim, currently Professor of Psychology at the Pennsylvania State University; Susan Clayton, a professor of Environmental Studies at College of Wooster; and George Howard, who currently teaches at the University of Notre Dame and is part of the Psychology Department wrote a paper in the American Psychologist, stating that the rapid changes caused in the climate are attributable to human behavior. By examining patterns of consumption and reproduction they were able to identify and distinguish individual, societal and, behavioral predictors of environmental impact.

They cited various research papers proving that current levels of human consumption, together with the exponentially increasing population are having an adverse impact on the environment, causing climate change. Using Psychology, one is able to determine what aspects drive population growth and consumption and also derive a relation between the two and climate change. Logically so, they found that the potential impact of population growth on climate change is greater in countries with high per capita emissions. They also inferred that change in the number of households is a better unit of analysis, in the area of energy consumption, than change in the number of individuals. Interestingly, after much experimentation the Professors realized that the perceived links between an individual's behavior and specific environmental problems could potentially encourage contraceptive use. Studies showed that procreation decisions are influenced by perceptions regarding the economic and emotional value of children which vary inter-generationally.

Furthermore, an individual's consumption choices can reflect people's knowledge and concerns regarding consumption and GHG emissions, for example, whether he or she tries to buy products that use less energy or use products in an energy-efficient manner. The professors wrote about consumerism as a cultural value and how demographics, ability (income, knowledge and health) and motivation lead to certain type of behaviors determining consumer choices.

Human activity is largely responsible for trends in climate change. Although the socially perceived view is that climate change has stemmed from ignorance or lack of consideration for the environment, psychological research attributes it to seemingly irrational behavioral decisions. Explicit and implicit decision-making is a gateway between cultural contexts and behaviors that contribute to climate change. On one hand of this decision-making process lie cultural and social contexts that encourage or discourage population- and consumption-relevant decisions, and on the other, behaviors that contribute to climate change. In conclusion, this paper serves as a call-to-arms for psychologists to bring in their skills to apply regarding the environmental challenges the world is facing.

Swim, Janet K., Susan Clayton., and George S. Howard., Human Behavioral
Contributions to Climate Change. American Psychologist 66.4, 251-264

A Climate Scientist Is Smeared for Blowing the Whistle on 'Corrected' Data
by Charlie Thomson

In an article written by Julie Kelly, a columnist for the National Review, the issue of whistleblowing and scientific data was discussed. Not even 72 hours after a federal whistleblower exposed acts of misconduct at a key U.S. Climate agency, the CEO of the nation's "top scientific group" was already dismissing the claims as erroneous. On February 7th, the head of the American Association for the Advancement of Science, Rush Holt, told a congressional committee that allegations made by a high-level climate scientist were nothing more than a mere "internal dispute between two factions", insisting that the issue was "not the making of a big scandal". Three days prior to this, on February 4th, a former official with the National Oceanic and Atmospheric Administration (NOAA), John Bates, who was in charge of that agency's climate-data archive, posted a lengthy, detailed account on how a 2015 report on global warming was grossly mishandled. In a blog entitled *Climate Etc.*, Bates wrote his 4,100 word expose which accuses Tom Karl, an ex colleague of his at the NOAA, of influencing the results and publication of a crucial paper that offers an explanation to the pause in global warming.

Mr. Karl's study was published in *Science* in June of 2015 — just months before world leaders were to meet in Paris to agree on the costly climate change pact. The international community and media hailed Karl's report as a final word disproving the global warming pause. Despite this, Bates, an acclaimed expert on atmospheric sciences, claims there is far more to this story than just that. According to Bate's reports, agency protocol to properly archive data was not followed, and the computer used to archive the data had suffered "a complete failure," according to Bates.

This will not cease anytime soon. As Bates explained later, climate alarmists and profiteers will only intensify their smear campaign as the story unravels further. Congress is now expanding its investigation of NOAA, Bates has indicated that more information and evidence is coming out, and NOAA is saying that they will now bring out experts to review Karl's report. Regardless, there needs to be some more transparency and accountability in regards to these hot issues in the scientific community.

Kelly, Julie. "A Climate Scientist Is Smeared for Blowing the Whistle on 'Corrected' Data."National Review. National Review, 17 Feb. 2017. Web. 19 Feb. 2017. <http://www.nationalreview.com/article/444942/john-bates-whistleblower-climate-scientist-smeared-global-warming-advocates>.

Is Anything Wrong With Natural, Non-Man-Made Climate Change?

By Charlie Thomson

Mario Loyola — a senior fellow for the Wisconsin institute for Law & Liberty and author of "Twilight of the Climate Change Movement", poses the question of whether or not humanity is responding in an adequate manner to the issue of climate change. In his opinionated article, Mr. Loyola asked this question to an environmentalist colleague of his: "If we found out that the planet was warming for purely natural reasons, would you be in favor of climate engineering to stop it, because the current temperature and sea level are the right ones for humans?" Loyola's colleague answered curtly: "No, of course not, man". This response satisfied Mr. Loyola because his colleague had just made a compromise to the fundamental argument that favors the reduction of carbon emissions — the risk of catastrophic and irreparable climate change. In his article, Mr. Loyola insists that climate alarmists are solely concerned with human impact on the world's climate and that most people are not in fact alarmed about climate change itself. Furthermore, Mr. Loyola proposed that nothing Climate alarmists have offered up as solutions for climate change would do anything to protect humanity from naturally occurring climate change. Likewise, if climate change were purely natural and the rising sea levels had nothing to do with man's carbon footprint, most scientists and environmentalists would likely be against doing anything to prevent it, just as Mr. Loyola's colleague conceded in their conversation quoted above. Despite this, it goes without saying that not all climate alarmists agree with this hypothesis. Many believe that rising temperatures and sea levels are cause for alarm regardless of their causes. People such as the latter hold opinions in the minority, however policy prescriptions that arise from their concerns have nothing to do with carbon emission reduction. If the planet is more concerned about global warming regardless of its causes, then the correct policy prescriptions must be about both adaptation to this change and legislation that promotes prevention of further climate change.

As explained from Mr. Loyola's point of view, the best course of policymaking for this planet's climate are policies that include climatological and ecological adaptation methods alongside preventative policies that impede or halt humanity's carbon footprint wherever possible. In this day and age, as Mr. Loyola claims, most alarmists are solely concerned with the human footprint aspect of climate change and readily disregard that fact that our planet's climate has been changing in radical and unexplainable ways for millennia. While humans have undoubtedly impacted this change for the worse, there needs to be a more balanced discussion about climate change so that all things stay considered when agreeing upon and implementing costly policies — policies that have not taken the various uncertainties of climate into account. Such policies, like the Paris Agreement on climate change, would affect the world's poorest and least developed countries the most. The proposed result of this agreement? According to Mr. Loyola, the results would include a reduction in climate change that today's scientists would not be able to measure or attribute to the implementation of this policy. As in nature itself, the answer to the ongoing debate over climate change must be balanced, considering past and present data and the cost-benefit of such policies to everyone, not just the fortunate lot living in the first world.

Flows, Capital. "Is Anything Wrong With Natural, Non-Man-Made Climate Change?" Forbes. Forbes Magazine, 04 Feb. 2017. Web. 05 Feb. 2017. <http://www.forbes.com/sites/realspin/2017/02/03/is-anything-wrong-with-natural-non-man-made-climate-change/2/#608a24ecd8ea>.

Ecocide: Climate Change Criminality
by Kelly Watanabe

White (2016) seeks environmental justice through defining criminality as committing a harmful act, even if it is not defined as illegal by law. Environment-related criminal activity causes climate change which encourages more criminal activity. White provides examples of offenses that cause climate change: pollution, abuse of non-renewable energy sources, and manipulation of energy subsidies. Climate change triggers responses of more delinquency: water and land theft, overfishing, organized criminal activity such as food riots, and carbon trade fraud. Additionally, White provides a criminological perspective on crimes associated with natural disasters. Pre-disaster offenses include improper construction standards, such as weak steel reinforcement. After the disaster, crimes such as insurance fraud and sex trafficking can be exacerbated by climate change consequences. White suggests that viewing environmental degradation as a serious offense with severe charges can help to mitigate the effects of climate change.

Most ecocide—significant damage to an ecosystem due to human actions—relates to improper allocation of limited natural resources. The most common perpetrators of ecocide are powerful corporations "concerned with maintaining economic status quo." White provides the example of the Alberta tar sands project—a joint conspiracy of the Canadian government with big oil companies that caused the destruction of forests and is the most significant contribution to Canada's global warming.

White presents barriers that inhibit prevention of ecocide and climate change mitigation. Social perceptions of climate change as a non-human-related activity relieves corporations of direct blame. In politics, climate change reforms are not fully supported. Hence, corporations ignore efforts to mitigate greenhouse gas emissions. White also offers crime prevention suggestions for institutions of criminal justice. He calls for a push toward more ecology enhancement projects for offender rehabilitation. In the future, research must be done in the criminology field to develop a classification of climate change crimes. Accurate prediction and prevention of ecocide starts with a database that can specifically reference different types of ecocide.

White, R., 2016. Criminality and climate change. Nature Climate Change 6, 737-739.

Dealing with Climate Change Deniers
by Annette Wong

In light of Donald Trump's presidency, there is a growing presence of climate change deniers in The White House. Cognitive psychologist Rolf Reber, professor at the University of

Oslo, and writer for 'Psychology Today', attempts to explain how climate change deniers deliberate.

Firstly, Reber explains that it is because climate change is an abstract idea that people become skeptics. Most people, especially in America, claim that because they observe no less snowfall, there is no reason to believe that climate change exists. They believe solely in their observations, even though statistics show that there are subtle increases in average temperatures during the last few decades. Furthermore, since the human eye cannot see the concentration greenhouse gases, nor are the oceanic damages in plain sight, people easily ignore the changing climate.

Secondly, the devastating consequences of climate change are not likely in the immediate future. The large and more dire concerns will take effect in a few decades. Since there is a relatively large time difference between the present and the time climate change's full effects will come into play, people simply do not care about their environmentally unconscious actions.

Thirdly, many climate change deniers doubt the motives of scientists. They assume that climate scientists only want to be honored, become influencers, and receive grant money. Deniers believe that climate scientists thus create "lies" about environmental issues for their own personal benefit, and therefore deem climate change a myth.

Reber suggests two ways in which society and governments can deal with climate change deniers. The first method is that we can try convincing people that climate change is real, but this is likely to be ineffective because people are innately stubborn. The second, and more effective way that Reber suggests is that we should emphasize the short-term impacts on the environment and on humans' health. For example, the public should promote the idea that using fossil fuels in cars affects health negatively, and may increase cases of asthma. We could also increase the awareness that eating red meat is correlated with high blood cholesterol, and perhaps even cause cancer.

In a time of denial, to fight climate change, we cannot solely try to persuade stubborn people that climate change exists. It may be more promising to mitigate climate change by convincing people to act in ways that are in their own interests, and simultaneously can help mitigate environmental damage.

Reber, Rolf. "Fighting Climate Change in a Post-Factual Age." Psychology Today. Psychology Today, 10 Nov. 2016. Web. 31 Jan. 2017. <https://www.psychologytoday.com/blog/critical-feeling/201611/fighting-climate-change-in-post-factual-age>.

Ethics, Religion, and Climate Change

How Climate Change Science can Benefit from Religion
by Claudia Chandra

In 2016, Professor Daniel Sarewitz at Arizona State University published an article in Nature, which discussed the need for scientists to adopt an inclusive approach to climate change. Sarewitz noticed that science and the church are currently "walking hand-in-hand" on one of the most significant issues of the twenty-first century: climate change. The person responsible for this reconciliation is Pope Francis. In his encyclical letter of May 2015, the Pope had "called for changes of lifestyle, production, and consumption to combat climate change." This evoked a growing need to mitigate the effects of global warming among his followers. In 2016, he achieved great successes in the COP21 global warming conference in Paris. This success fostered the growth of concern over the issue of global warming.

Sarewitz believes that the church's concern over climate change is remarkable because not only does it agrees with scientists' views, it also could, because of its conservative ideals, potentially challenge these views. Sarewitz hypothesizes that this may be because the Pope's "moral logic" leads him to prioritize a political environment where all belief systems are welcome over a widespread agreement on the science of climate change.

The COP21 agreement is viewed as a significant breakthrough because all countries involved signed up to its aims. The effectiveness of this agreement, however, depends upon each country's ability to reduce carbon emissions while simultaneously increasing their citizen's quality of life and well-being. Consequently, the progress made on climate change reduction will be determined by the political decisions about "how to best pursue both goals." Sarewitz claims that effective politics will "demand constructive engagement among multiple voices to achieve solutions that all can live with." He also quotes

Pope Francis who believes that answers "will not emerge from just one way of interpreting and transforming reality."

Nevertheless, as pointed out by Sarewitz, America's initial mistake in climate-change policy was that such pluralism had always been ignored. It was the role of scientists and environmental activists to "frame action" in such a manner that "alienate[d] economic and social conservatives." For example, policy proposals often demand government intervention in markets and incentives to regulate production; such policy ambitions are naturally viewed negatively by US conservatives. Furthermore, because scientists claimed that their agenda was driven by scientific data, conservatives found good reason to doubt the scientists' motives and credibility of their work.

Sarewitz observes, however, that the Pope carries a link between climate change science and "conservative US touchstones such as 'family values.'" Pope Francis has previously called family, "the basic cell of society," as it is where "we first learn how to show love and respect for life" and "respect for the local ecosystem and care for all creatures." Moreover, the Pope also argues that "concern for the protection of nature is also incompatible with the justification of abortion." He believes that we cannot genuinely teach the importance of empathy if we fail to protect human embryos. In these ways, the Sarewitz sees ways in which Pope Francis has acted as bridge between climate change science and conservative scepticism.

For the optimism gathered at the COP21 agreement to turn into actual progress, climate change politics must be able to influence the fundamental values that lie behind conservatism. As demonstrated by the Pope, these values can be compatible with climate change science. In his recognition of current climate change, Pope Francis has also shown that, now, "conservative voices and belief systems can begin to enter constructively into the climate debate" after being absent in the two previous decades. Nevertheless, Sarewitz notes that even if science and religion are in sync, there may be hurdles that remain in the politics. This is also where, logically, "science can learn a thing or two from religion."

Sarewitz, Daniel., 2016. "Constructive engagement is the key to climate action." Nature. Vol 529, 6 – 7.
http://www.nature.com/polopoly_fs/1.19103!/menu/main/topColumns/topLeftColumn/pdf/529006a.pdf

Traditional Religious Beliefs and Their Effect on Climate Change Adaptability.

by Chris Choi

Conor Murphey researched the relationship between religion and climate change and how it demonstrates rural populations' ability to adapt to these disturbances. Many areas of Sub-Saharan Africa still retain their traditional belief systems which continue to influence the lifestyles of different populations. The populations' traditional beliefs are usually linked with Traditional Ecological Knowledge, which is used to describe the indigenous traditional knowledge regarding how to sustain local resources. To prevent climate change, TEK management policies have been created, however, a change in belief or adhering to multiple beliefs makes it difficult to follow them. Murphey conducted case studies in Malawi and Zambia to study how TEK, traditional beliefs, and the introduction of Christianity exist together in communities while determining how practicing multiple beliefs affects their ability to adapt to climate change.

The people of Bolero, Malawi, mainly a Tumbuka community, relied on rain-fed farming. The Tumbuka community believe in Chiuta (God) who determines the amount of rainfall. Chiuta either can bring good rainfall or disease if the ancestral spirits are angered. In terms of livelihood vulnerability, this belief interferes with dealing with issues such as environmental degradation, climate variability and erratic rainfall, droughts and land constraints. In Bolero, 95% of the modern-day population is Christian. Scottish Presbyterian missionaries came to Northern Malawi during the colonial period, and the Tumbuka community willingly accepted the new teaching.

As for the population of Monze, Zambia, 87% of the population is Christian and 12 % practice other religions which include traditional beliefs. They believed in the Monze, a rain spirit. The Lwiindi ritual is a rain ritual where they pray for a good season of rain. During the early 20th century, the Monze shrine where they prayed for Lwiindi lost religious appeal and instead became a more political structure due to colonial influence. The British South Africa Company placed local chiefs to govern people, but they did not have as much influence as the real leaders who inherited the souls of their ancestors.

For both populations, following Christian faith has affected their ability to uphold TEK management policies. For Bolero, staying Christian and adhering to the practices makes it hard for them to fully acknowledge their own traditions. One such tradition is to keep a certain tree species from being cut, yet the younger generation is bringing them down. In Monze, the younger generation was blamed for the recent failure in rain rituals due to the younger generation's lack of practicing their traditional beliefs. However, while Bolero's belief systems co-exist better than Monze, there are still concerns of a weakening of traditional beliefs. Murphey concludes that it is still necessary to further understand the importance of traditional beliefs to fully comprehend a population's willingness and ability to adapt to climate change.

Murphy, C., Tembo, M., Phiri, A., Yerokun, O., Grummell, B., 2016. "Adapting to climate change in shifting landscapes of belief". Climatic Change, 134. 101-114. http://link.springer.com/article/10.1007/s10584-015-1498-8

Difference in Religious Views Alters the Stance on Climate Change
by Chris Choi

Nancy E. Landrum, Connor Tomaka, and John McCarthy (2016) examine how the words used by two religious organizations affect people's views on climate change. The Cornwall Alliance (CA) and the Evangelical Environmental Network (EEN) are two organizations that in their religious approaches towards the relationship between humanity and the environment. CA believed in dominion, or mastery over nature while EEN believes in stewardship, or unity with nature. CA refutes the idea of climate change and believes that the science is not true. EEN in a stark contrast, acknowledges human-caused climate change. The researchers examined texts from each group and used rhetorical analysis to see how their stories depicted humans and climate change differently. They first analyzed the literary genre used when describing the story, then they looked at the classical framing categories which include metaphors, slogans, and contrast. After using these two frameworks, they looked at the ethos, pathos, and logos of each text and then analyzed the use of fear and hope in them.

They found that CA believes people who are alarmed by the effects of climate change are misguided. These people were depicted as buffoons in comedy or antagonists in tragedy while humans and gods were depicted as the protagonists of the story. CA believed that current methods to mitigate climate change would lead to increased poverty in the future. Members of the EEN believed the opposite. They believed that those who were uninformed were the buffoons. Most of their stories are centered around climate-related disasters, and they argue that poverty is a result of environmental degradation.

After examining both organizations, Landrum *et al.* concluded that climate change is a commons problem in which members of a population make decisions regarding common resources for individual gain at expense of the group while neglecting the group, and also make decisions for short-term gain at the expense of long-term consequences. They believe that a resolution can be found by encouraging cooperative behavior between the two organizations. They found that people tend to surround themselves in an echo chamber, or a place where people only converse with others who share the same belief. Overall, they found that an increased sense of cooperation between the two spectrums of Christianity is necessary and that each side must be less biased and more open to other opinions to make more progress in mitigating climate change.

Landrum, N. E., Tomaka, C., & McCarthy, J. (2016). Analyzing the Religious War of Words over Climate Change. Journal of Macromarketing, 36(4), 471-482.

The Catholic Church and the Polarization of Climate Change Belief
by Rachel Ashton Lim

In 2015, Pope Francis released an encyclical which declared climate change action a catholic moral imperative of environmental stewardship, while aligning the disproportionate effects of climate change on poorer communities with catholic beliefs. The question to be asked, then, is did this encyclical affect concerns among American Catholics about anthropogenic climate change? The data from a peer-reviewed study in the *Climatic Change* journal certainly implies so, although not in the manner that you might think.

Using over-the-phone interviews with a nationally-representative sample, researchers assigned numerical scales to anthropogenic climate change belief, belief in whether or not climate change has disproportionate impacts on the poor, as well the scientific credibility assigned to the papacy, in order to compare beliefs before and after the encyclical's publication, among both Catholics and non-Catholics alike. The study found that political leaning (i.e. whether people identified as conservative or liberal) had a very large, polarizing effect on the reception of the Pope's encyclical. In other words, in both

Catholic and non-Catholic populations, liberals who were aware of the Pope's encyclical reported higher rates of climate change concern, perceived climate risks for the poor, and perceived papal credibility than those who were not aware of the encyclical. However, on the other end of the spectrum, conservatives were more likely to report lower climate change concern, climate risks for the poor, and papal credibility than those not aware of the encyclical.

While Catholics and non-Catholics produced highly similar linear correlations between political leaning and both climate change concern and perceived climate risks to the poor, Catholics attributed overall higher credibility to Pope Francis' scientific credibility than non-Catholics. Yet somehow, despite the implication that Catholics should be more receptive to the Pope's messages, political leaning remained a dominant factor in beliefs about climate change.

Why was this so? The study cites other research papers to explain possible reasons for such findings. One reason involves confirmation bias, where people accept messages that align with their pre-existing beliefs and reject those which threaten them. Another reason was that for some Christians (and in fact, the majority of evangelicals), climate change has been attributed to an apocalyptic worldview in which God's power and wrath, rather than human consumption patterns, is responsible for climate change.

The paper knowledges that while the observed effects are statistically significant, they are usually very small, and that the results are centered around the United States and should not be extrapolated to other countries. However, the researches still stress the need to take their findings into account and become aware of our possible biases, to come to more accurate conclusions regarding climate change, as well as for large-scale organizations to think carefully about their methods of communication.

Li, N., Hilgard, J., Scheufele, D.A., Winneg, K.M., Jamieson, K.H. 2016. Cross-pressuring conservative Catholics? Effects of Pope Francis' encyclical on the U.S public opinion on climate change. Climatic Change, 3, pp 327-380.

Using Culture to Adapt to Climate Change
by Alex McKenna

In 2016, Rory Walshe, PhD student at King's College London, along with Alejandro Argumedo, director of the ANDES Association, conducted research in the Cusco Region of Peru in order to study the cultural values of indigenous groups that enable them to adapt to climate change. Focusing on communities in The Potato Park, a cultural conservation area where the negative impacts of a changing environment are becoming more and more prevalent, they identified four values that form the basis of adaptation: *ayni* (reciprocity), *ayllu* (collectiveness), *yanantin* (equilibrium), and *chanincha* (solidarity). While these values support making natural and local adjustments to manage climate change, they conflict with the prevailing science based policy, creating a dichotomy that I intend to explore in future articles.

Nonetheless, the many ways these indigenous groups use their culture to adapt to climate change is fascinating. For example, because of *ayllu*, a desire to achieve equality for all, the inhabitants use land collectively, allowing them to share the crop varieties that best withstand changes in the environment. Similarly, *yanantin,* which emphasizes equilibrium, allows them to shift cultivation zones upwards or downwards depending on the temperature of the air, thereby balancing nutrients in the soil. Perhaps the most interesting adaptation is founded on their belief in *ayni,* a reciprocity that promotes synchronizing labor with agrarian cycles and sharing products grown in neighboring communities with others. C*hanincha,* which champions solidarity and equality, recently led communities in the Park to collaborate on and equally divide profits from cultural tours, sources of income that supplement the dwindling opportunities in agriculture.

So, what exactly can these communities in the Park tell us about adapting to climate change? While many cultures across the world have deep ties to nature, most live by a set of values that are unique to them and their specific environment. Thus, I doubt a global, one-size-fits all approach will ever be effective. Rather, we should explore utilizing small scale community-based policies that are specific to individual needs and that not only preserve culture, but complement it as well. Although Walshe found no evidence of cultural value erosion in the Park, studies show that younger generations across the world are increasingly rejecting traditional culture in favor of "technology and outside knowledge". Maybe, as this research in Peru suggests, cultural values can be used as tools to combat and circumvent the repercussions of climate change. If this is the case, then society may be moving in the wrong direction.

Walshe, R., Argumedo A., 2016. The cultural values enabling adaptation to climate change in communities of the Potato Park, in the Peruvian Andes. Ecological Perspectives for Science and Society, 166-173. http://tinyurl.com/hm2y922

Religion and Climate Change: Interesting Take of an Evangelical Conservative

by Kele Mkpado

There are many things today that divide our country on a daily basis. Whether it be religion, politics, or where we live, these traits define our ideology and shape our ideas. Usually in society, it is likely to be clustered with people of the same religion, race, and political views. As I discovered each group's general stance on climate change, it was surprising to see that every Christian denomination has put out a statement regarding climate change as a truth and a call to action from God to take responsibility for the earth. After this discovery, I found an interesting blog post by Dr. Scott Rodin who states his changed stance on climate change, but also his thoughts before his change of mind and why he believed the way he did.

Dr. Rudin explains that he and those with his same views have been conditioned ever since the environmentalist movement gained roots to despise and discount their ideas due to the image of earth-loving hippies. He states his 5 reasons for his discount of climate change, and realized that they didn't make any sense. For him, it was more of a Me vs. Them sort of debate. People who care for the environment couldn't care less about those losing their jobs due to climate change policy; hard working Americans. And the fact that these people are portrayed as super-hippies who chain themselves to trees did not help their image. After analyzing that his claims were completely invalid, and did not have any provable science behind it, he came to the conclusion that his denial was unfounded and his assumptions were wrong.

I found that religion plays an even larger role in politics than it does in its own religion. Being of a certain political stance is causing some people to completely deny their religious beliefs to further advance their political sides. I think if the church's stance on the climate intensifies, more and more believers will discover climate change as something that cannot be denied any more.

Rubin, Scott, Dr. "Why Climate Change Can't Be True (Even Though It Is)." The Stewards Journey. N.p., 19 May 2015. Web. 04 Apr. 2017.

Arts, Public Media, and Climate Change

Communicating the Science and Human Significance of Climate Change
by Ellen Broaddus

Seidler and Stevenson (2017) review two books dealing with the psychological factors that impact the personal and societal undervaluing of humanity's role in causing climate change and its effects on them. They stress that this is not a new issue: even in 1988 the Intergovernmental Panel on Climate Change (IPCC) emphasized the need for a systemic change in energy production and consumption. Almost 30 years later, CO_2 emissions have more than doubled, and it is still unclear whether current efforts such as the Paris Conference (COP) will lead to meaningful action.

The two books, *What We Think About When We Try Not to Think about Global Warming* and *Stolen Future, Broken Present: The Human Significance of Climate Change* suggest that our inaction is caused not by a data gap or lack of understanding of the risks but our "psychic habits, social dynamics, and ethical quirks". In the first book, author Stoknes discussed the need for effective marketing. While studies show that "scary" emotional marketing tactic is successful among almost all audiences, Stoknes poses some important questions about the role of marketing and persuasion: is the societal denial of climate change a result of too few messages? What is the balance between sufficient advertisement and evoking denial and rationalization? Are we presenting enough range of marketing tactics to engage everyone?

Author David Collings discusses climate change as an unavoidable, unaccommodating issue, stressing that the idea of "compromise between free market ideology and inescapable environmental imperative" is not feasible; it is us, not nature, that must change. However, he cites society's resistance as stemming from to our inability to alter the intrinsic vision we hold of ourselves and of society. This is not a new phenomenon; the shift to coal-powered grain production caused immense social anxiety as the customary structure of labor was shifted, and realization of humanity's insignificance in the Earth's colossal timespan threatened our fragile social fabric and was met with backlash. This reaction is caused by our inability accept complete awareness of our situation: something that would cause an unequivocal response that we aren't ready to accept. Overall, both authors stress that "understanding the human response to climate change is becoming at least as important as understanding climate change itself" and call for steps to balance the intellectual and emotional approaches to combating resistance to the acceptance of climate change.

Seidler, R; Stevenson, R. 2017. Communicating the Science and Human Significance of Climate Change. BioScience. https://academic.oup.com/bioscience/article/doi/10.1093/biosci/biw174/2900180/Communicating-the-Science-and-Human-Significance

Dying to defend the planet: Why Latin America is the Deadliest Place for Environmentalists
by Ellen Broaddus

The Economist (2017) discusses the prevalence of violence against activists in Latin America. In 2015, 185 environmental activists were murdered, a 59% increase from the year before. This issue is especially prevalent in Latin America, where more than half of the murders took place. With so many environmental activist deaths, such as 50 in Brazil alone in 2015 and 123 in Honduras since 2010, the article analyzes reasons for such uncontrolled crime. The biggest component causing violence is the abundance of natural resources throughout Central and South America. The prevalence of fertile soil, gold, and rainforests draws many large businesses and mafias to the area. Additionally, new technologies in agriculture and mining practices have made land even more profitable, increasing tension between corporations and activists.

Although there are many activists operating under the philosophy of environmental conservation, many of the resisters are indigenous people, accounting for up one-third of the activism-related murders. Rather than working towards global sustainability, many of these "protesters" are simply defending their traditional livelihoods, such as tropical forests that contain up to a quarter of the world's carbon.

The indigenous mission often complements the larger global climate change campaigns and has led to more attention on the issue, but unfortunately has not decreased the violence. This is largely because many Latin American countries, especially in the rural areas, lack effective policing and judicial support. In many cases, such as that of Berta Cáceres, an indigenous leader and anti-dam activist in Honduras, the murders are simply written off as "attempted robberies" and never seriously pursued. This is even more prevalent for foreign victims, who's attackers are hardly ever brought to trial.

This issue goes beyond individual greed, as often times governments fail to help (and often hinder) the pursuit of justice. Despite institutional programs such as the "International Labor Organization that 'requires them to consult groups affected by development projects'", Latin American governments often take the side of the attacker. The influence of money also exacerbates the issue, as politicians linked to environmentally costly industries and projects have often been linked to attacks on activists. The complexity and depth of this issue means it is not easily solvable, but is very important for the future of both natural resources and indigenous communities throughout Latin America.

2017. Dying to defend the planet: Why Latin America is the deadliest place for environmentalists. The Economist. http://www.economist.com/news/americas/21716687-commodities-technology-and-bad-policing-why-latin-america-deadliest-place

Hot and bothered: The Sundance Climate Film Festival
by Ellen Broaddus

The Economist (2017) explores the convergence of film and environmentalist worlds at this year's Sundance Film Festival. Sundance, located outside of Salt Lake City, often draws independent film producers and directors and pushes the boundaries of Hollywood's social and ideological norms. This year, however, there was a large presence of environmentally themed non-fiction films. The most prominent was "An Inconvenient Sequel: Truth to Power", the sequel to Al Gore's 2006 movie "An Inconvenient Truth" which has been said to "have spawned the genre of climate-change films". The 2006 film covered the shocking data of climate change, and received criticism from many climate change sceptics for being too "alarmist". The sequel, however, addresses these critics by showing that the calamities ("melting icepacks, rising temperatures, severe flooding") of the first movie are not only true but have emerged more quickly than predicted. The film also crosses into political territory, covering Gore's training and lobbying efforts with the Paris Climate conference. Additionally, he mentions his meeting with President and climate-change-denier Donald Trump in December of 2016, revealing only that there will be "more conversations to come". Despite the seemingly sober tone, which shows how much worse things have gotten in just 10 years, the film does show the minor progress. Gore, who has been championing action towards mitigating climate change for more than 25 years, noted that "the will to act is a renewable resource". The presence of so many environmental documentaries "had a powerful effect, depressing audiences with stark visual proof of destruction wrought on the environment, while managing to inspire them a little with humanity's ability to respond". Films like "Rancher, Farmer, Fisherman" showed the work of traditionally unlikely environmentalists toward systemic change. The festival was also a "triumph of visual and narrative storytelling", overcoming the technological challenges of documenting places like glaciers and coral reefs and revealing the earth's natural beauty. In the midst of such political controversy about the presence of climate change and what we should do about it, the Sundance Film Festival stood as proof that this issue extends past scientific and political bounds.

2017. Hot and bothered: The Sundance Climate Film Festival. The Economist. http://www.economist.com/news/books-and-arts/21715633-years-movie-fest-utah-featured-al-gores-inconvenient-sequel-and-other?zid=313&ah=fe2aac0b11adef572d67aed9273b6e55

Communicating the Science and Human Significance of Climate Change
by Ellen Broaddus

In Live Science, Megan Gannon discusses an often overlooked known harmful effect of global warming: the reemergence of (formerly underground) nuclear waste. It is commonly known that increasing global temperatures have catalyzed the melting of glaciers, but recent photo maps posted by NASA's Earth Observatory show the expected changes to Greenland's ice caps. In addition to affecting the ecosystem and animals, this change also risks uncovering Camp Century, a "once-secret U.S. military base built in 1959 primarily to test the possibility of launching nuclear missiles from the Arctic to the Soviet Union". Although the camp is currently buried under more than 100 feet below a crust of snow and ice after being abandoned in 1967, a study published in August 2016 by the journal "Geophysical Research Letters" predicts that the site could change from net snowfall to net melt by 2090. Once this happens, the damage would be irreversible and would cause Camp Century to eventually be uncovered. This would become an extremely large environmental hazard, as the site houses more than 53,000 gallons of diesel fuel, 6.3 million gallons of wastewater, and various other "unknown volumes of low-level radioactive coolant and polychlorinated biphenyls (PCBs)". As the ice melts, the pollutants will be released, seeping into marine ecosystems and severely damaging the animals that live in them. The eventual necessary clean up would create a first in political disputes regarding climate change. The pollution that will eventually be released from the melting of ice surrounding Camp Century raises questions regarding the accountability for climate change disasters created in the past. Because the impacts of the Industrial Revolution are only recently amounting to tangible change, it will take immense international collaboration to create action towards mitigating problems that have little connection to the countries needing to solve them. For this reason, among others, researchers stress that this situation is an example of why it is vital that we start trying to mitigate climate change as soon as possible.

Gannon, M. 2017. Maps Show Where Melting Glaciers Will Reveal Cold-War-Era Nuclear Waste. Live Science. http://www.livescience.com/57694-melting-greenland-ice-revealing-nuclear-waste.html

The Role of Museums in Communicating Climate Change
by Claudia Chandra

In 2017, Morien Rees of the Varanger Museum in Arctic Norway published a commentary on the critical role of museums in combating our current climate change. In an article for Nature Climate Change, Rees expresses how an international alliance of museums could have a pivotal role in coordinating "more effective public communication on and engagement with climate change." Rees doubts that current channels used to communicate climate challenges are adequate because he finds that the public's response to this issue is largely indifference. He believes that scientific reports providing an "objective view of climate change and its political and economic impacts" are aimed at the media, and are insufficient in overcoming the public's "state of inaction." According to Rees, scientists and climate activists are "like the orchestra playing bravely on as the Titanic approaches an iceberg."

Indeed, to initiate political action on climate change the public must be engaged to a higher degree. Rees believes that how and where communication occurs is as important as the information communicated. He also noticed that museum projects prioritize communication over information, and engaging dialogues over one-way lectures. Due to their nature, Rees claims that in museums, "the language of science can be translated and given a more accessible form." This is bolstered by the fact that museums do, in fact, transcend the boundaries of space and time.

Furthermore, museums have already shown evidence of successful international cooperation, which Rees views as a prerequisite for meeting the inherently global challenges of climate change. Museums can also "erase borders" between global warming and other sectors of society, enabling them to present climate change as a cultural, ecological, and technological challenge. And finally, to maintain the policy of "think globally, act locally" in the context of climate change mitigation, museums become useful institutions as they inherently bridge the gap between the global and local.

An initiative based on this policy is being developed by Rees' own Varanger museum. The museum is in the Arctic climate zone and its tundra is predicted to be impacted by climate change more than any other terrestrial biome. Using this as a source of inspiration, the museum initiated a project on how climate change is impacting the Varanger Peninsula National Park. Using an interdisciplinary approach, as well as collaborating with NGOs, Varanger aims to "provide an area that encourages an awareness of the ethical nature of global climate change by presenting local impacts on bumblebees, salmon smolts, migrating birds, and the Arctic fox." This approach of using a museum as a place for global thinking while focusing on local climate issues can involve many target groups, sites, and formats, that could substantially help communicating global warming and its implications.

Museum professionals from countries including America, Australia, Norway, and the Coalition of Museums on Climate Change have created objectives that can be used as starting points to encourage public action. They believe that, first, museums should have a voice on the international stage, more specifically in forums such as the paris conference and UN presentations. Second, we should encourage museums to develop as places for dialogue with NGOs and other community organizations on a local level, and governments and international organisations on the global level. And third, all museums, not only specialist or science museums, should promote wider engagement on climate change issues. Through these objectives, museums can become catalysts for climate change mitigation by increasing public awareness and inspiring action.

Rees concludes that museums, because of their nature and international infrastructure, must be exploited to help combat global warming. As global public participation is a necessity to meet the climate change goals set by the international community, museums can facilitate this goal through their "unique dissemination skills and accessible local arena."

Rees, Morien., 2017. "Museums as catalysts for change." Nature Climate Change. Vol 7, 166–167.
http://www.nature.com/nclimate/journal/v7/n3/pdf/nclimate3237.pdf

How Visual Communication Creates a Climate Change Divide
by Claudia Chandra

In an article for Nature Climate Change, Alfons Maes discusses a visual divide in the field of climate change. Maes hypothesizes that advancements in visual technology are linked with a clearer and more realistic communication of global warming. For example, the spread of adaptable and interactive visual mediums suggest that scientists can reach wider audiences. He then describes climate change as "a playground for visualization," using examples of documentary film producers who "immerse us in... realistic images of changing realities all over the world," and climatologists who "reduce natural phenomena into visually appealing data visualizations." However, he also asserts that innovations in visual communication, especially in climate science, do not account for audiences with low levels of literacy. This is concerning as populations with low literacy levels are equally, if not more, affected by and ignorant of climate change.

Maes argues that although pictures and visual codes contain relevant information, there is a "conventional code" that the viewer must understand to make sense of an image. He compares understanding visual codes to language and points out that visual codes have the advantage of being easily understood by "exploiting resemblance with the outside world." For instance, arrows are used to suggest causal relationships and clouds or speech bubbles are used to express thoughts. He claims that current visual communication such as these requires learning and literacy to be successful in conveying their intended messages.

Furthermore, Maes adds that there is little study on the extent to which audiences with low levels of literacy understand visual graphs and representations of climate data. He believes we should work to create "simple, robust, broadly accessible visuals to stimulate understanding and awareness" of global warming for illiterate populations. These visual conventions will be useful in communicating important data or information that "go beyond mere representations of the real world."

To achieve this, Maes suggests that visuals should reflect common learned conventions and avoid "features that require interpretation." He turns to the field of health as an example. Maes states that health is "arguably the only domain in which scholarly attention has been devoted to visual literacy in audiences with low levels of literacy," and adds that it demonstrates the utility of ensuring that such audiences understand visual codes. Looking at visual codes behind medicine bottles for example, helps improve comprehension and recall for future use. Visual codes in health are effective and easy to understand because they have simple designs, resemble well-known concepts as much as possible, and are tested locally using participatory design methods.

Maes believes that visual communicators of climate change should adopt the same approach that the field of health has towards designing visual codes. For this, it needs "continuous attention from different expert fields." Scholars should continue creating symbols/ codes that allow in-depth and accurate comprehension of climate change processes. More data should also be sought for understanding how climate change visualizations affects human behavior and their approach to the issue. And mostly, Maes believes that researchers "must devote more effort to understanding visual literacy in vulnerable audiences."

Maes, Alfons. 2017. "The Visual Divide." Nature Climate Change/ Vol 7, pp. 231– 233
https://www.nature.com/nclimate/journal/v7/n4/pdf/nclimate3251.pdf

Networks Ignoring Climate Change
by Ethan Lewis

Angela Fritz, a writer for the Washington Post, wrote an article bringing up the issue of the lack of climate change coverage by the media. Fritz starts the article by stating that there is more than enough climate change news to cover.

Twenty-fifteen was the hottest year ever recorded, the Paris agreement was signed by dozens of countries, and California had its worst drought in decades. Unfortunately, if one gets their information via news networks, there is a high chance you didn't hear about any of the above. Networks like ABC, NBC, CBS, and Fox dropped their climate change coverage by 66% in one year. In 2015, networks spent 146 minutes on the topic of climate change while in 2016, it was a mere 50 minutes.

Fritz offers one explanation of why the media doesn't cover climate change; EPA's scientists say that the chemical chlorpyrifos can cause memory decline in young children and is showing up in our food and water at unsafe levels. The chemical was banned but is still used at 40,000 different farms. Pruitt's response to the accusation was that we need to be "certain" that the chemical is causing defects. Fritz continues by saying that the U.S. judicial system understands that 100 percent certainty in science is almost impossible to come by. Fritz says she is not surprised that the networks don't want to talk about climate change, it's a hot-button topic in politics because politicians made it that way.

Despite the lack of coverage in 2016, half the country thinks that climate change is human caused and believe that it is a problem. The media has a responsibility to report the facts, and if scientists agree an extreme weather event was made worse by climate change, viewers have the right to know. Fritz ends her paper by stating she doesn't know whom the networks and Congress are serving to turn a blind eye to climate change, but according to the national poll's, it's not the voters.

Fritz, Angela. "Analysis | The networks all but ignored climate change last year. That's bad news for science." The Washington Post. WP Company, 30 Mar. 2017. Web. 02 Apr. 2017.

Hyperlinking Climate Change
by Rachel Ashton Lim

By mapping the hyperlinking behavior of climate change stakeholders across the web in 1998, a study in the Journal of the Public Understanding of Science has given us historical insight into the beginnings of the climate change debate. Situating itself in the late twentieth century, the study contextualizes the debate in the age of the Internet's maturation, where access to public opinion was no longer limited to the approval of editors and investors; leading to "a new web pluralism". However, the study also highlights a major issue with this system: involved parties *can* use the internet to post their opinions and request information from others, but many engage only in discussions which adhere to their pre-existing beliefs or their political agendas, which the authors of the study dub the "neo-pluralism" of the web. The authors also criticize the limitations of search engines in filtering relevant URLs according to credibility, worsening the effect of neo-pluralism. In pluralistic use of the web, organizations began to yield a new type of power in the online realm; By choosing to hyperlink (or by choosing *not* to), organizations can decide who they want to acknowledge and recognize as valuable players in various debates, and who they want to delegitimize through active exclusion. Thus, the study examined the presence — or absence — of hyperlinks that different organizations used to steer visitors in the direction of similar or alternate viewpoints in the discussion on climate change.

The study found three distinct overarching hyperlinking behaviors, which correlate to their domains: .org sites belonged primarily to NGOs including Greenpeace, .com sites belonged primarily to corporations including Ford and Mobil, and .gov sites belonged to government-linked organizations including the IPCC. Anomalies to these hyperlinking behaviors were called "delegates". In order to determine which organizations to include, "central players" were chosen from each of these three groups, and in order for other actors to be considered in the study, a central player must have hyperlinked to its website. The three central players that were chosen were Shell, Friends of the Earth, and the UNFCC.

The study found that .org actors had the densest network of "interlinkings", or links to websites of the same type (in this case, those of other NGOs). "Extralinks" to leading governmental organizations were also present, but extralinks to .com actors were rarely found on .org sites. It was noted that most organizations which crosslinked often were also on the receiving end of a high number of hyperlinks from other websites, with the exception of Greenpeace, which rarely had hyperlinks external websites. The study called this behavior one of "privileged self-sufficiency". On the other hand, .com actors showed almost complete abstinence from interlinks. These organizations did, however, engage in external linking, but to a lesser extent than did .org actors. Almost oppositely, .gov actors linked much more to internal actors than they did to external ones, affirming the view that governmental organizations form a single operating body, without acknowledging other stakeholders in the discourse. Two all-round linkers were also identified by the study: Friends of the Earth, a grassroots NGO from the UK, and British Petroleum, a multinational gas and oil corporation.

Three other outlier "delegates" were identified by the study. The first, the Global Climate Coalition, a corporate lobby group, linked exclusively to its governmental opponents. The second, Shell, linked also to external opponents, including Greenpeace and other NGOs. In light of this fact, the study points out that Shell was one of the first multinationals to hire an Internet manager, who was also an advocate for open dialogue. The third was the UN-affiliated Global Environmental Info Center, linked to the groups who they were committed to supporting, namely, NGOs and GOs, thus deviating from the usual .gov behavior.

The study concludes by stating how its findings are significant; by learning the "debate-mapping logic", it argues, organizations may enter and make themself relevant in the online debate on climate change. Actors should request linkage from a leading participant to the debate, an action which poses low barriers to entry, and practice reciprocal "hyperlink diplomacy" by doing the same for others. In this way, groups and individuals may therefore better contribute to a more accurate and pluralistic representation of the state of climate change.

Rogers, R., Marres, N. 2000. Landscaping climate change: a mapping technique for understanding science and technology debates on the World Wide Web. Public Understanding of Science, 9, 141-163.

Eco-friendly Fashion in Death
by Rachel Ashton Lim

Modern funeral conventions now widely practiced contribute massively to greenhouse gas emissions and fossil fuel use, as well as the pollution of our soils and water —and fashion designers are taking notice. Advocating for environmentally friendly green burials (as opposed to cremation and burials of toxified embalmed bodies), the work of three fashion designers identified in a paper by the *Fashion and Textiles* journal is part of a larger movement pushing for the acceptance of death which will allow for the de-institutionalization of toxic funeral customs. The paper has evaluated the current eco-friendly offerings in the funeral industry using the "5 Steps of Eco-effectiveness" as proposed by McDonough and Braunngart: Firstly, by getting "rid of" known culprits; Secondly, by following informed personal preferences; Thirdly, creating a "passive positive" list; Fourthly, activating the positive list; And lastly, Reinventing the relationship between consumer and the product. As defined through this framework, it is not enough to be merely "eco-efficient". Products must be "eco-effective", not only removing dangerous materials but inserting ones that can change our negative effect on the environment into positive ones.

The three designers analyzed in the paper hail from Australia and the US. The first, Mark Mitchell from Seattle, used a background in theatrical costume to inform his aesthetic in creating his Burial 1 collection, referencing old Hollywood and nineteenth century Parisian couture. He created a collection of one-of- a-kind custom burial ensembles using heirloom, hand-stitching techniques. The materials he used were mostly fine fabrics, predominantly undyed and unbleached natural fibers and fabrics from mostly silk and wool. Mitchell stated that he chose to design burial clothing as a way to deal with the trauma of his survival guilt as many of his friends died from the AIDS epidemic. Because this was primarily a personal project and not an environmental one, Mitchell has stated that he will no longer make burial clothing, unless by commission. The Fashion and Textile paper states that, in light of this, Mitchell's design fulfilled the first two steps of eco-effectiveness, because he got free of the known culprit of synthetic fibers, and he chose the best natural fabrics according to his particular aesthetic sense. However, he did not achieve the next three because he prioritized his aesthetic over the eco-friendliness of his design, and so, whilst it was eco-efficient, it was not eco-effective.

The second designer, Pia Interlandi, is an Australian scholar, artist, and funeral celebrant. She is in the process of combining fashion design, fiber science, forensics, and practicality to use of water-soluble fibers in creating her line, called "Garments for the Grave". To determine the best material to use in her collection, she dressed 21 slaughtered pigs in burial garments of her own design, later exhuming them at 50-day intervals over the course of a year to examine decay of different fiber types such as hemp, hemp/silk blend, polyester embroidery, nut shell, and casein. She found that hemp disintegrated the most quickly, followed by silk. Polyester remained unchanged. She has not yet finalized the materials she will be using, but her clothes are designed to be more like kimonos and cocoons, rather than usual clothes, to make it easier to dress the dead. She does not bleach and dye her pieces. If she gets a special request to dye the fabric, she would do it by hand. Like Mitchel, the paper states that Interlandi fulfilled steps 1 and 2 of eco-effectiveness.

The last designer, Jae Rhim Lee of Boston melded both art and science in her creation of the Infinity Burial Suit for both people and pets launched by funeral start-up, Coeio, in late 2015. Lee was inspired to create the Infinity Burial Suit after watching how hurricane Katrina victims rehoused in FEMA (Federal Emergency management agency) trailers were become ill from the trailers' formaldehyde off-gassing. The suit is made of unbleached or black cotton, and is lined with an added specially cultivated fungal culture to aid decomposition underground and break down toxins in a process called mycoremediation. Again, Lee's design passes the first two steps of eco-effectiveness, but not the last three.

The paper concludes by stating that although the work of these offer better options than traditional burial clothing, there is more room for improvement to make the products eco-effective. For people who may not invest in these clothing lines, the paper suggests that past research has indicated the use of white, unbleached cotton may be a suitable transition choice, laundered many times to weaken the material and aid its decomposition.

Michel, M. Gwendolyn, Lee, Young-A. 28 March 2017. Cloth(ing) for the dead: case study of three designers' green burial practices. Fashion and Textiles, 4:4, 1-18.

Music and Climate Change
by Tanisha Sheth

Musicians have resorted in song to protests ranging from civil rights to apartheid. However, the world is yet to see a popular song on one of today's most pressing issues—Climate Change. For most of the past year, the United Nations has been desperately trying to get the public to listen to songs such as 'Love Song to the Earth' featuring almost everyone from Paul McCartney to rapper Sean Paul, and about a dozen more—one sung by Native American schoolchildren and another by middle-aged farmers. There have been SoundCloud uploads and YouTube videos, lyrics translated into multiple language in a vain effort to gain popularity. But, chances are that one has not even heard of them and the general consensus to this surprising result is that all of them are unanimously awful. The most toe-curling of all is Sean Paul's rap in Love Song to the Earth: "Mama Earth is in a crazy mess, it's time for us to do our best, from deep sea straight up to Everest." The hearts of these singers might be in the right place that is they are singing in hopes to motivate people but they are so adversely earnest, they make one wonder if anyone is capable of writing a popular song about the issue.

Toby Gad, who co-wrote Beyonce's 'If I Were A Boy' said writing 'Love Song to the Earth' was indeed, challenging. He could not figure out a way to write the lyrics so as to resemble a thought-instilling song instead of a preaching sermon. The experience also made him realize that he could not resort to any scientific material in it, or even use the words 'global warming' or 'climate change' as "half of America would turn it straight off".

Strangely, the closest anyone has come to writing a popular song on Climate Change is the British dance act Orbital who, in 1996, released 'Impact,' which tried to get the message across through techno music and its subtitle, The Earth is Burning. Paul Hartnoll of the band, suggested a few ideas as to why only a handful of songwriters have tried to tackle the subject and it's because of the issue's scientific nature. "We will not get a stream of good climate change songs until climate change starts affecting people when they get up in the morning, and people's relatives start dying from it," he said. Which makes us think— Do we have to reach such an extreme before people start taking initiative?

Mackay, Emily., 2015 'Where are all the Climate Change Songs' BBC

Media Inaccurately Dramatizes Climate Refugees of Carteret Islands
by Kelly Watanabe

Media reports on the sinking Carteret Islands—Pacific atolls of Papa New Guinea—portrayed the islanders as the first direct victims of climate change; rising sea levels forced the population to migrate to Bougainville Island. John Connell (2016) puts the situation into a perspective unfiltered by the misleading media. Due to recent emphasis on climate change, the public media quickly blamed global temperature increase and rising sea levels for the lack of sustainability on the Carteret Islands (CI). Current media reports sourced their information from previous inaccurate media reports, not the actual story; the media ignored the inherent scientific evidence showing that other geographic factors were more influential. Dangerous tidal waves (tsunamis) are caused by natural recurring tectonic plate movement and violent El Niño wind patterns, not climate change. According to Connell, the brackish water and flooding created by the tides are a more pressing problem than the rising sea levels. Inadequate fresh water supply depletes crops and fish, making the land inhabitable. CI households began migrating long before evidence of climate change emerged. In reality, economic opportunity, not climate change, incentivized islanders to migrate.

Why does media ignore the true reason for CI migration? Connell maintains that an apocalyptic island makes a more attractive story. Since climate change is linked to emissions from industrialized nations, the media evokes sympathy from the public by portraying CI islanders as victims of a problem they did not create. The media reports give CI islanders an excuse for the problems which actually lie in CI government. Even with the geographical and climate threats, most CI islanders do not migrate due to unattractiveness of developing a new identity, inadequate government funds, and political conflicts with Bougainville. CI islanders themselves were hoping that the media reports would help islanders gain support for migration. However, less than ten CI households have migrated to Bougainville.

Connell, J., 2016. Last days in the Carteret Islands? Climate change, livelihoods and migration on coral atolls. Asia Pacific Viewpoint 57, 3-15.

The Motion to Mitigate Climate Change through Emotional Stories
by Annette Wong

As the environmental advisor to the British Government, and a co-organizer of the UN climate change summit, Alex Evans has a unique theory on why the Paris environmental summit far exceeded the success of the Copenhagen summit.

Evans suggests that environmentalists and green activists in the Danish summit attempted to present climate change issues with "pie-charts, acronyms and statistics", what he thought was a boring and unengaging approach. When the Paris summit begun, it seemed that environmentalists understood that the most effective way to promote the urgency of climate change was through narrating personal stories in hopes of evoking emotion.

Even politicians seemed to understand that emotion was the most effective method in which to spread the message on climate change. French president Francois Hollande "encouraged a strong spiritual input in the summit". Personal stories about loss, sacrifice, and pain, created "morally compelling narratives" that provided engagement from the population.

Evans coined his theory, "The Myth Gap", claiming that all social movements that were successful because both small and large communities could be held together by common stories both from the past and about the future. This includes not only climate change, but also the movements that capsized slavery, and even the political shockwave that was Brexit.

Evans was particularly interested in stories relating to Israeli rituals and religion. Many pieces of Israeli literature are written to inspire people, rousing strong moral values in their readers. Evans believes that to inspire people, stories must encourage "restoration and redemption" rather than solely focus on evils and failures. In terms of climate change issues, this would mean a "greater emphasis on success stories". He uses the example of China's Loess Plateau and their miraculously well-repaired ecosystem.

Alex Evans' theory of reaching out to passionately engaged communities with stories, extends to religious communities. However, unique religions have different religious narratives, which may often cause conflict between groups. Evans draws from the example of Sunni and Shia Muslims in Iraq who still are at war due to their beliefs. This is where Evans believes at least one of the challenges lies. It will be difficult to fashion stories that draw strong conclusions and morals that transcend different large and small communities. It is thus important to encourage tight-knit communities, no matter what size, to listen to each other's stories without hate.

ERASMUS. "Fighting Climate Change May Need Stories, Not Just Data." The Economist. The Economist Newspaper, 08 Jan. 2017. Web. 21 Jan. 2017. <http://www.economist.com/blogs/erasmus/2017/01/climate-change-myth-and-religion>.

The Media is Failing Our Climate Change Movement

by Annette Wong

Marcia G. Yerman, a freelance writer, artist, and avid climate activist, discusses the media's failure in engaging the audience with pressing climate issues.

Mainstream television news has been steadily covering fewer stories on climate change in the past five years. In *Media Matters for America*'s research on the subject, it was found that coverage on climate issues on FOX, ABC, NBC, and CBS collectively fell by $5 between 2014 and 2015. The only network to have examined specific issues ranging from the Paris Climate Summit to the Clean Power Plan was PBS. They were also the only news station to cover the methane emissions issues that ExxonMobil faced.

Yerman stresses that the media should be concerned about climate change, and should be covering topics relating to climate and health, and the economy, as well as national security. It was worrisome to see that President Obama's Clean Power Plan had been basically ignored by most national media outlets, considering it was the "first federal statute limiting carbon pollution from power plants".

Perhaps it is because climate change seems like a phenomenon with distant consequences, and thus is not considered a pressing or interesting story, compared to as breaking news sections related to world politics. However, the truth is that climate change is an ever looming and increasingly dangerous threat that we, as a global community, all face.

Yerman brings up the point that major networks often try to present climate change in a more palatable way by offering a "softer approach" to its issues. For example, creating stories on how nature (animals, plants, birds) is being effected by climate change. However, this is not sufficient in a world where the public must understand the urgency and the impacts of our daily actions on the environment.

In terms of international science and math rankings, America is only ranked 28th out of 76 countries, proving of how science-phobic the media can be. Yerman thus pushes that the news needs more science stories. The major threat of the climate crisis is not being properly informed by the scientific facts. There are too many news anchors that are not willing to challenge statements or fact check their sources. This just isn't acceptable in a time where scientific truth must prevail.

The importance of climate coverage on national prime-time television is evident. The media is in part responsible for not showing the real consequences of climate change on our lives. The media must keep us informed, and making sure that the urgency for us to act against the destruction our planet is placed on the same level as other political and social issues that are given the spotlight in the status quo.

Yerman, Marcia G. "Climate Change And The Media." The Huffington Post, TheHuffingtonPost.com, 29 July 2016, www.huffingtonpost.com/marcia-g-yerman/climate-change-and-the-me_1_b_11207298.html. Accessed 23 Mar. 2017.

Trump's America and the Media's Climate Change Coverage

by Annette Wong

Oliver Milman, author for the guardian on media-related climate topics, discusses the American media's failure during the presidential elections. He criticizes the media's inadequacy in questioning Trump on matters relating to climate change. According to Milman, this is the "single greatest rebuke to the idea that power should be help account for the benefit of this and future generations."

What Milman says makes sense, because in the long run, climate change will be one of the biggest issues faced by the entire world's population. America, being one of the world's leading nations, should have a president that knows what he is doing, and is accountable for the increasing environmental damage that will come in the near future. The media's failure to hold him accountable, or to clarify his intentions through their coverage is highly unsettling. This lack of coverage is apparently due to the presidential election itself having been fiercely debated. Society was so focused on Trump as a personality, that they forgot to pay attention to his role as the president, particularly with regards to climate change issues.

The failure to cover climate issues was most evident during the presidential debates between Trump and Clinton. Within the 4.5 hours of debate, only one question came close to any climate issues, and that was a question about coal mining. Trump essentially attempts to deny that the problem of climate change exists, to promote factory jobs in America. The Press has allowed the environmental issues in the United States to be dwarfed by every other issue during the election period. Even emails were more discussed than the more pressing and dangerous issues of water shortage, pollution, and rising sea levels.

One would assume that cable television, where scientific journalism is more prevalent, would have better coverage of climate issues. However, even the cable networks were shying away from climate coverage during the election periods. The public was sometimes notified of the seas "eating away America's east coast", but that was about it. Climate Change have should been treated as a central issue to every economic, foreign policy, and energy topic discussed by both Trump and Clinton. Instead, it was being treated as a side issue and pushed aside.

Trump's decisions in the next 4 years are going to influence America's climate forever, and so the media should push for more climate change coverage. It should be of primary importance that the public urges the government to make decisions that will benefit the generations to come. If the media does not hold Trump accountable, and if the public is not reminded that climate change is the next century's greatest threat, then we can only blame ourselves for the terrible situations to come.

Milman, Oliver. "Why the Media Must Make Climate Change a Vital Issue for President Trump." The Guardian, Guardian News and Media, 13 Nov. 2016, www.theguardian.com/environment/2016/nov/13/climate-change-trump-presidency-environment. Accessed 10 Apr. 2017.

Economic Behavior and Climate Change

Green Finance for Dirty Ships
by Ellen Broaddus

The Economist (2017) investigates the problem of pollution in the shipping industry, one that carries more than 90% of the world's trade. Despite only contributing 3% of the world's greenhouse-gas emissions, ships burn heavy fuel oil, releasing exorbitant amounts of noxious oxides of sulphur and nitrogen into the atmosphere. While it is clear that changes need to be made, overcapacity, debt, and financial instability throughout the shipping industry create a big challenge.

The UN's regulatory agency in charge of shipping has recently "agreed to cap emissions of sulphur from 2020", and the European Parliament voted to "include shipping in the EU's emissions-trading scheme from 2021", but organizations such as the NGO "Carbon War Room" and consultancy "UMAS" stress the negative economic impact of these changes. Upgrading current ships will cost tens of billions of dollars, but the industry is struggling financially as it is. Due to the financial crisis and a lull in world trade, earnings have reached a 25-year low. There is also a decrease in demand for ship-lending, caused by the fact that those who would have to borrow for upgrading the ships, the ship owners, would not benefit from the more efficient ships. This is because it is the contractor who lease the ships who pay for the fuel. The payback time for upgrading ships is usually 3 years, longer than most contractors charter the ships for, so there is little incentive for them to invest in upgrades.

A possible solution is the development of green-lending structures that "share fuel savings between ship-owners and charterers over a longer contract, giving both an incentive to make the upgrades". With new technology that gives us the ability to measure and track exact fuel consumption, such schemes are now possible. Additionally, the financial sector is getting involved, such as the European Investment Bank announcing $282 million for ship retrofits and potentially billions more to come from other banks. The hope is that this green finance, which may be extended to green aircraft and trains in the future, may help resurrect these industries in financial trouble.

2017. Green Finance for Dirty Ships. The Economist.
    http://www.economist.com/news/finance-and-economics/21718519-new-
    ways-foot-hefty-bill-making-old-ships-less-polluting-green-finance

Climate Change: The Cause of Another Great Recession?
by Joshua Dorman

Hedge fund managers and investors are becoming increasingly worried about a possible second Great Recession caused not by mortgage-backed securities or the fall of major banks, but by an event seemingly unrelated to finance: global climate change. Katy Lederer (2016) attended the seventh annual Investor Summit on Climate Risk last year, a convention designed to tackle the issue of financing the transition to renewable energy that was established at the Paris Climate Talks and discusses the hypothetical effects of a prolonged shift away from fossil-fuel investments. At the summit, approximately five hundred financial professionals with a net sum of twenty-two trillion dollars under management convened in New York City to address this growing threat to the world economy. Under the façade of thousand dollar suits, diamond-studded cufflinks, and wine-and-cheese Hors d'oeuvres, the collective outlook was not an optimistic one. One analogy was repeatedly mentioned: the economic impact of remaining invested in fossil fuels was likened to the collapse of the economy when the housing bubble burst in 2008.

Financial professionals across the world are quickly accepting the possibility of a global financial crisis caused by delayed investor reaction to climate change. A panel at the last World Economic Forum polled its audience and found that about eighty percent of the attendees agreed that the business world should briskly prepare for a "fossil-fuel-free future." Moreover, Al Gore has ramped up his rhetoric, likening carbon assets to the perilous subprime mortgages that instigated the collapse of the economy in 2008 and imploring financiers to "divest altogether from their fossil-fuel holdings." Additionally, the financial ramifications of remaining invested in fossil fuels are bleak to say the least. At the investor summit in New York, Mark Lewis of British banking giant Barclays "estimated that if companies and investors don't adequately anticipate shifts in energy markets, roughly thirty-four trillion dollars in value at risk." In other words, if investors don't engage in an "orderly transition" to clean energy investments, climate change itself will not only decimate fossil fuel-based investments, but the entire world economy as a whole.

Nevertheless, a promising solution to avert catastrophe has emerged: create more investment opportunities in the clean energy market to draw hedge fund managers away from the fossil fuel industry. Unless action is taken quickly, those diamond-studded cufflinks on their wrists might soon be worth a whole lot less.

Lederer, Katy. "The Climate Summit of Money." The New Yorker. February 24, 2016. Accessed January 22, 2017. http://www.newyorker.com/business/currency/the-climate-summit-of-money

Is Climate Change Burning Up the Fashion Retailing Industry?
by Joshua Dorman

The impacts of climate change are well and truly numerous, even wreaking adverse effects upon an industry that has outlasted everything from drastic shifts in consumer tastes to epic financial downturns: fashion. Dr. Steven J. Hausman, a data scientist and president of Hausman Technology Presentations, recently observed that the climate of 2016—the hottest year on record according to NASA—has had a "direct effect on fashion and apparel retailing." And indeed it has, with the effects of the phenomenon being felt by the likes of fashion giants Levi Strauss & Co., VF Corp., L'Oreal, and many others.

One particularly salient ramification of climate change on the fashion industry is that shifts in weather patterns have begun to affect consumer browsing patterns. Owners of boutique fashion houses have started noticing that when temperatures reach between ninety and one hundred degrees Fahrenheit, people tend to remain cooped-up inside their air-conditioned homes. The result: a severe decrease in browsing time and, in response, plummeting sales revenue.

Moreover, producers and suppliers are beginning to anticipate a "retail environment with only two major seasons," foreseeably a long and scorching summer followed by a temperate winter and a "warmer-than-usual-spring." The repercussions of such weather patterns have, in effect, already been felt by numerous fashion firms. Most notably, the prolonged summer of 2015 caused a decrease in "sweater weather," thereby wreaking considerable damage to businesses that sell those long-sleeved knitted garments that so many of us adore and cherish. In the words of Rachel Tabbouche, founder and CEO of UnderCoverWaterWear.com, even though the "calendar might say it is fall, you're not thinking of down coats and bulky sweaters when it's 80 degrees out."

Furthermore, companies who could previously rely on cold winters to support their outerwear businesses are now being forced to adapt to dynamic consumer demands reflecting changing weather patterns. For instance, Saint James, an upscale boutique fashion firm which specializes in wool knitting, has been disconnecting their newest collections from seasonality, relying instead on lighter and airier fabrics to appeal to customers. Additionally, Fruit of the Loom's recent launch of their menswear line of "cooling boxer briefs" demonstrate that a vast range of clothing companies are pivoting away from seasonal collections and moving toward more flexible garment lines that can accommodate consumers in a warming climate.

However, John Opperman, the executive director of Earth Day Initiative, points to a "silver lining" to these alarming threats: as the world grows more aware of the debilitating effects of climate change, new individuals are beginning to take up the mantel and embrace solutions to combat this ever-increasing danger facing our planet.

Zaczkiewicz, Arthur. "Is Climate Change Killing the Seasonality of Fashion Apparel Retailing?" WWD. October 20, 2016. Accessed January 28, 2017. http://wwd.com/business-news/business-features/climate-change-impact-fashion-apparel-10525390/.

Global Warming and the Emergence of Plastic Slopes

by Joshua Dorman

What do you do if you run a ski resort and climate change is severely impacting your revenue from winter tourism? You introduce ski slopes made of plastic, of course. In an article in CBC News, Nicole Ireland explores how snowboarding and ski resort operators around the globe are "weatherproofing" their businesses.

For many winter-tourism-focused corporations, rising temperatures are severely restricting both the amount of snowfall and people's willingness to engage in winter activities. According to Peter Williams, director of Simon Fraser

University's Center for Tourism Policy and Research, there are two possible approaches ski resorts can take to deal with the toll of climate change. They can "adapt their operations to maximize what snow they have, and/or they can add other adventure or cultural activities that require less or no snow." For some companies, this may mean adding mountain biking trails, ecological tours, festivals, or even Iron Man competitions.

Unsurprisingly, corporations have already begun to adapt to the changing demands of an industry inextricably linked to the effects of climate change. Whistler Blackcomb, a ski resort in British Columbia, recently announced a $345-million plan to become "weather independent," making plans to add wave simulators, waterslides, rope swings, interactive caves, and other activities that can remain free from the toll of climate change. In fact, Williams claims that, for many companies, the "weather independent" business strategy has "proven to be pretty successful in not only filling empty rooms that would be there during the snow season, but also in expanding the season."

However, some mountain resorts are going to extreme lengths in an attempt to "hold on to skiing"; they are constructing arenas where guests can slide down a variety of surfaces with the absence of snow, using artificial materials to create "dry slopes." For instance, the Midlothian Snowsports Centre near Edinburgh, Scotland offers "year-round dry slope skiing and snowboarding" using plastic or carpet-like fabrics to imitate the effects of powder. As crazy as it may seem, such an option might have to be considered by businesses that face the brunt of global warming's impact.

In general, it seems like the winter tourism industry is managing to adapt to the demands of climate change. In fact, many resorts are also taking it upon themselves to make a visible environmental difference and lessen their fossil fuel emissions. According to official data, thirty resorts in Colorado recently participated in the state's Sustainable Slopes program and succeeded in reducing their carbon dioxide emissions by an aggregate 1,700 tons. Hopefully we have a few more years of snow ahead of us before indefinitely swapping powder skiing for skidding down slopes made of plastic.

Ireland, Nicole. "Hitting the plastic slopes: Climate change pushes ski resorts to 'weatherproof'" CBCnews. August 13, 2016. Accessed February 04, 2017. http://www.cbc.ca/news/business/ski-resorts-weather-proofing-climate-change-1.3715284.

Will Climate Change Push Property Values Under Water?

by Joshua Dorman

Ordinarily, realtors looking to sell coastal property focus primarily on how close a house is to the shoreline when putting it on the market. Now, however, buyers are increasingly asking a seemingly paradoxical question: how *far back* is it from the water's edge? In an article for the *New York Times*, investigative reporter Ian Urbina explores how the dynamic industry of waterfront real estate is adapting to the ever-increasing challenges caused by climate change.

As rising sea levels continue to weigh on the minds of individuals living in seaside areas, the data concerning coastal properties paints a bleak landscape, to say the least. On a national level, median home prices in low-risk flooding areas are up about 29.7 percent to what they were 10 years ago, while housing prices in high-risk flooding areas are down 4.4 percent over the same period. More specifically, home sales have increased by roughly 2.6 percent nationwide over the last year, while sales have dropped 7.6 percent in the high-risk flood areas of Miami-Dade County in Florida. Much of the reduction in real estate transactions has stemmed from a blatant change in buyers' priorities when looking for homes. Instead of scoping out houses with spectacular water-level views and close proximity to the sand, their primary concerns have transitioned to whether the house is a high enough above sea level, if it's fortified against storm surges, and whether it comes equipped with emergency power and sump pumps. Moreover, rising insurance premiums have become one of the most frequent deterrents for prospective buyers. For instance, a couple by the name of Roy and Carol Baker struggled for years to sell their home in Florida's Siesta Key because interested parties kept backing out when they discovered the $7,000 annual flood insurance expenditure. Yet insurance premiums are continually being priced in at over $10,000 per annum in high risk areas as the effects of climate change continue to cause record amounts of flooding. Waterfront homes, it seems, may already be on their way out.

Furthermore, the economic impact of a collapse in the market for oceanfront houses "could surpass that of the bursting dot-com and real estate bubbles of 2000 and 2008." Currently, about forty percent of people in the U.S. reside in coastal areas, and those who can afford it are fortifying their homes against the impending onslaught of continued flooding.

Nevertheless, Sean Becketti, the chief economist for Freddie Mac, predicts that "it's only a matter of time... before sea level rise and storm surges become so unbearable that people will leave, ditching their mortgages and potentially triggering another housing meltdown." The effects of such a crash would likely be felt by everyone from real estate lenders, to property owners, to the very financial organizations that create mortgage-backed securities. This time, however, the prices of houses near the water would likely never recover.

The beachfront real estate market is clearly in for onerous times ahead, and the world must quickly adapt their expectations to prevent another economic crisis. Brent Dixon, a resident of Miami Beach who is making plans to relocate further away from the ocean's edge, has issued his own dire proclamation: "the water always wins."

Urbina, Ian. "Perils of Climate Change Could Swamp Coastal Real Estate." The New York Times. November 24, 2016. Accessed February 25, 2017. https://www.nytimes.com/2016/11/24/science/global-warming-coastal-real-estate.html?_r=0.

Tourist Behavior Affected by Climate Change
by Bryn Edwards

A recent study from the 2017 Journal of Sustainable Tourism proposed a psychological explanation for tourist behavior, in particular the effect climate change has on vacation locations. This is a promising development in terms of changing future behavior to further minimize damage that tourism has on native environments and ecosystems. Tourist behavior associated with travel to threatened locations can be attributed to reactance theory, which tells us that people inherently put worth on their freedom, and do not want that freedom taken away. Threatened destinations are alluring because people are more motivated to visit a place if they will not have such freedom in the future. Some factors influence how reactive people are to threatened locations; for example, travel is less important to some people, and people's awareness and perception of climate change is different. There are four stages that people use to validate the impact that their travel has on the environment. The first stage is denial. People inherently act in their own best interests, and the paper mentions "extensive evidence" of exactly how far people are willing to go to deny the obvious truths in front of them. The second stage is the "consumer's need to reduce tension." Basically, a person goes out of their way to eradicate conflicting actions with beliefs. The third stage is people exercising their freedom to travel by demanding more of what they know they shouldn't, like traveling to disappearing and vulnerable locations. For example, tourist travel increased 32% to Svalbard, Norway, which corresponded with an increase in awareness of declining polar bear habitats. The fourth stage is "helplessness," the feeling that their actions are so small and insignificant that there is little to no effect. The paper effectively outlines the social implications of human psychology, and the negative impacts on the environment. As I read, the four stages mentioned above resonated on a more personal level, making me realize that I too am guilty of such negative travel practices.

Xavier, F. and Hindley, A., 2016. Understanding tourists' reactance to the threat of a loss of freedom to travel due to climate change: a new alternative approach to encouraging nuanced behavioural change. Journal of Sustainable Tourism, Vol. 25, No. 1, 26-42.
http://www.tandfonline.com/doi/pdf/10.1080/09669582.2016.1165235

The Cost of Climate Change for Alaska
by Bryn Edwards

A study recently published by the National Academy of Sciences predicted climate change related infrastructure costs for Alaska in the next century. If global warming continues at the same rate through 2099, costs of public infrastructure will be around $5.9 billion dollars. However, if the lowered emissions promised by the 2015 Paris Climate Change treaty come to fruition, Alaska could save $1.2 billion dollars. The agreement pledged to a global temperature rise at most of two degrees Celsius, and unfortunately for many parts of Alaska the warming is quickly approaching the threshold. The study does not include costs of docks, harbors or pipelines which are privatized. While the study shows that the impact would be centered around southern Alaska, this is somewhat misleading in that this is only so because the population is concentrated in the southern region, and very few people or infrastructure are in the northern areas that would require maintenance. The northern region–areas like the Aleutian islands–are much more dramatically affected by rising temperatures than the south, but costs are concentrated around cities. The Prince William Sound area is expected to incur the highest costs, since it receives the most precipitation a year. The root of the infrastructure-related issues is that most buildings and roads are built on permafrost. As temperatures rise, the permafrost melts and the ground becomes less stable. Landslides like the infamous 600 foot slide that occurred in Denali National Park in 2013 will be more common occurrences unless temperatures cease to rise in the next century.

Rosen, Yereth. Study: Climate change will be costly to Alaska's public infrastructure. Alaska Dispatch News. https://www.adn.com/alaska-news/environment/2017/02/09/ climate-change-to-be-costly-to-alaskas-public-infrastructure-study-says/

The Unfortunate Effects of Climate Change on Air Travel
by Joshua Dorman

By now, most individuals have become aware of the increasingly far-reaching consequences of climate change. Recently however, one more repercussion has been added to this ever-growing list of side effects. In an article for *The Washington Post*, writer Chelsea Harvey explores the troubling connection between climate change and flight turbulence.

According to a study conducted by atmospheric scientist Paul Williams of the University of Reading, flight turbulence could significantly increase under climate change, potentially resulting in a significant uptick of in-flight injuries—and anxiety—for passengers. Williams found that "an increase in atmospheric carbon dioxide concentrations could cause changes in the jet stream over the North Atlantic flight corridor, leading to a spike in air turbulence." The basis of this phenomenon is well known by the scientific community; as the planet heats up, warming surface-level air is estimated to alter the atmospheric slope between the poles and the equator. In his research, Williams used several climate models and found that these changes in the atmospheric slope will most notably manifest in a stronger jet stream, bringing an increase in the wind patterns that cause air turbulence. In his analysis, he focused on a specific area in the North Atlantic region where planes frequently fly, and conducted his simulations in the wintertime, when turbulence is at its peak. He examined 21 different "wind-related characteristics known to be indicators of air turbulence levels," such as air flow directional changes and wind speed.

The results of his study are troublesome to say the least; he found an increase in turbulence across the entire spectrum of categories. Light turbulence was estimated to increase by 59%, moderate turbulence was projected to increase by 94%, and severe turbulence was calculated to increase by 149%.

The ramifications of such evidence could prove to be truly far-reaching. For instance, not only will increased turbulence cause a higher rate of wear-and-tear on planes, it will force pilots to use extra fuel navigating the skies and maneuvering their planes around rough patches. Such consequences could potentially force airline manufacturers to completely change the designs of their planes, and will undoubtedly result in more jet fuel being left up in the atmosphere. However, perhaps most importantly for the regular consumer, it seems like that cushy five-hour flight from L.A. to New York that so many appreciate could disappear, replaced by a jolting, bumpy, and jarring journey through the skies.

Harvey, Chelsea. "How climate change could make air travel even more unpleasant." The Washington Post. April 06, 2017. Accessed April 09, 2017. https://www.washingtonpost.com/news/energy-environment/wp/2017/04/06/fasten-your-seatbelts-climate-change-could-increase-air-turbulence/?utm_term=.79a8a329e8c3.

Schneider and Louisville's Green Initiative
by Vikramaditya Jhunjhunwala

In the spring of 2011, the mayor of Louisville created a commission dedicated to planting more trees. This commission was to be co-chaired by none other than Katy Schneider, former deputy mayor of Louisville and advocate of environmental issues. Madeline Ostrander (2016) outlines Schneider's efforts in creating a healthier environment for her city, and reminds the people of urban America of the environmental dangers their concrete worlds face in the absence of greenery.

Ostrander recounts that Schneider's journey began in early 2012 when Schneider approached Brian Stone, a professor at the Georgia Institute of Technology, to find out the extent of temperature changes in Louisville. Stone proceeded to reveal that Louisville's temperature had increased by about 1.7 degrees every decade since 1960. Stone also noticed that urban areas were heating more than rural areas. He discovered that this situation was primarily caused by what meteorologists call the urban heat-island effect whereby dark and paved surfaces absorb solar radiation consequently causing the air temperature to rise.

Approximately 2 months after the formation of the tree commission, Louisville was hit by an intense heat wave that resulted in the demise of 86 people. This spurred the Louisville government and Schneider's commission, to commission Professor Stone to produce a finely detailed heat island map of the city. On the basis of Stone's study, Louisville citizens and government began laying down lighter-colored pavements and planting trees in open spaces. The government also began incentivizing the installation of cool roofs and recently launched a public information campaign to help residents fight harmful heat effects. Schneider, for her part, started a volunteering association by the name Louisville Grows that would, in four months, plant nearly fifteen hundred trees. Sadly, despite the monumental steps taken by Schneider's foundation and the Louisville community, Louisville is still threatened by the heat island phenomenon and is in need of nearly half a million more trees, according to Stone's study.

It is clear to see that initiatives like Schneider's are crucial in tackling the problem of urban heat, but Ostrander emphasizes the need for a sustained movement by citing a published study by a group of scientists in Columbia University, New York that illustrates how the rise in temperature could see three thousand American lives perish yearly from heat until 2080. Thus, it is imperative that citizens of America a take cue from people like Schneider and take steps in the right direction otherwise the future of the urban America could look very dim.

Ostrander M., 2016. As Our Cities Grow Hotter, How Will We Adapt?. The New Yorker. Elements section (September 2016).

The Middle Class and Climate Change
by Vikramaditya Jhunjhunwala

Policymakers have long been divided on the issue of the rising middle class. On the one hand, the middle class spurs economic growth by consuming more goods and services than any other section of society. On the other hand, such consumption leads to increased carbon emissions from factories and vehicles, which accelerates climate change. Therefore, communities concerned with the environment and those concerned with economic development have found it difficult to unite their approach towards the emerging global middle class.

Unfortunately for the environmentalists, efforts in halting middle class progress seem rather futile given the economic and political power of the now 3 billion strong middle class. Appealing to good sense does not constitute an effective tactic either; in the US, an individual's carbon emissions decrease by only 5% when the person is informed of his or her carbon footprint. Despite this, some evidence suggests that a larger middle class may not be harmful for the environment in the long run.

Almost all of the world's projected population growth is set to take place in countries with small middle class societies such as those in Africa. Whereas countries in Europe, where the middle class constitutes a large portion of the population, have an average population growth rate of a mere 0.2% per year.

This correlation between the strength of the middle class and population growth primarily comes down to the middle class' investment in education. The economic burden of sending children through secondary school and on to higher education makes middle class households more conservative regarding family planning decisions. Unsurprisingly, a woman devoid of a formal education has, on average, four to five more children than her high school graduate counterpart.

On a global scale, the impact of education and family planning can be significant. The United Nations estimates that global population in 2100 is set to reach 10.9 billion (compared to 7.4 billion today). However, demographers at the International Institute for Applied Systems Analysis in Vienna figure that with widespread education, global population in 2100 could be as low as 9 billion people.

This 2 billion reduction in human population can not only bridge the gap between the goals of the environmental and development communities but can also stymie the climate change wave that is harming the world's environment.

Kharas H., (2017). Middle class prosperity can save the planet. (2017). The Guardian. Retrieved 19 March 2017, from https://www.theguardian.com/the-gef-partner-zone/2017/feb/13/middle-class-prosperity-can-save-the-planet

Owning Up: The Countries Responsible for and Those Affected Most by Climate Change
by Matt Johnson

Global warming is now large enough that it is identifiable over regional cyclical cycles. Since preindustrial times, we have seem warming of a little less than 1°C. While this is quite small from a global perspective, the regional temperature changes are now quite noticeable in many areas: especially at mid and low latitudes. A study by James Hansen and Makiko Sato (2016) tracked the frequency of occurrences of local temperature anomalies, and found that the deviation from the mean of 1951 through 1980 to be quite stark.

Global warming in recent decades has resulted in a shift of

the "bell curve of local temperature anomalies" by about one standard deviation, indicating that conditions year round are unusually warm compared to prior decades, and extreme heat waves are now even more extreme. The study found that warming in regions like the Mediterranean and Middle East is now more than two standard deviations from the mean of 1951–1980, similar to the situation in the tropics.

The changes in climate are uneven over the seasons. The study found that "the summer bell curves for the United States and (North and Central) Europe are shifted more than one standard deviation, while the shift in winter is only about half of a standard deviation". Here, shifts in summer climate may be noticed by the perceptive public. The bell curve has shifted even more in China and India, adding about half a standard deviation in both the summer and winter. In the Mediterranean and Middle Eastern regions, the summer shift is around 2.4 standard deviations.

These data show that the countries historically responsible for CO_2 emissions, those in the western world, are less affected than developing nations in Asia and the Middle East. In all regions, global warming is increasing the coincidence of heatwaves and droughts, which is especially harmful to these developing nations, and those in already dry climates; as global warming progresses, wet regions are going to get wetter and dry regions are going to get drier. As the study points out: "Livelihoods are affected by higher temperature and associated absolute humidity, especially at latitudes with conditions already near the tolerance limit for outdoor work". Therefore "developing countries in the tropics are affected disproportionately" as more work occurs in non-air-conditioned indoor and outdoor spaces than in developed nations.

The United States and Europe are each responsible for about 25% of climate change, China about 10% and India about 3%. So, while developed nations have done the most to create climate change and along the way have indirectly prepared themselves to cope with increased temperatures, the lagging countries are the ones that have to pay the price in the years to come. As we approach the point of an uncontrollable spiral of warming, will developed nations make an equivalently large effort to stop it?

Hansen, J. and Sato, M., 2016. Regional climate change and national responsibilities. Environmental Research Letters, 11(3), p.034009.

The Blind Side of Climate Change Economics
by Rachel Ashton Lim

How accurate are the Intergovernmental Panel on Climate Change's (IPCC) economic estimates of Climate Change-induced damage? A post-Paris agreement review of its Fifth Assessment Report (Stern, 2016) calls for an imperative revision to its economic model. The review's main suggestion is for the social science to become better integrated with the natural sciences in order to accurately evaluate the economic consequences of Climate Change, which are direr than is currently estimated. However, the review also suggests that the benefits of transitioning to low-carbon growth are underestimated in the report and must be evaluated more holistically. Combined, these two factors will enable the public, private and non-profit sectors to make decisions that will drive the world into the net-zero carbon economy it must achieve within this century.

Stern's criticisms of the IPCC's Fifth Assessment Report stems from three factors: its understatement of the limitations to the research which it cites and analyzes, the lack of consideration for shocks to infrastructure, and its failure to account for possible mass migration of coastal communities due to rising sea levels. While the report currently estimates a 0.2 to 2% decrease in global GDP as a result of a 2 °C increase in the mean global temperature, the research's main limitation is its lack of certainty of data, which causes impact estimates to be highly variable, going upwards to catastrophic.

According to Stern, the benefits of transitioning to a low-carbon economy are not fully expressed in the report because it fails to evaluate the positive effect of learning process, economies of scale, effect of decreased pollution and the protection of biodiversity. Stern argues that although the initial investment into more sustainable technologies may be large, it may create an environment for innovation and efficiency that will enable greater long-term economic growth.

Stern recommends established models widely used by the finance industry as a replacement for the existing economic climate change model used by the IPCC which better account for human life and shocks to infrastructure. However, he also urges research teams across disciplines to continue to look for ways to improve economic methodology with respect to climate change.

Stern, N., 2016. Current Climate Models are Grossly Misleading. Nature 530, 407-409.

The Economic Impact of Climate Change on Fisheries
by Alex McKenna

Recently, scientists at the University of British Columbia made a shocking discovery; if climate change continues to accelerate, by 2050 global fisheries could lose over $10 billion dollars in annual revenue. Marine fisheries support nearly 10 to 12% of the world's population, and generate more than $100 billion in revenue each year. However, these numbers may soon fall. Climate change, specifically rising ocean temperatures, melting ice, high salinity, warm air, and decreased oxygen levels, is already causing major shifts in the distribution range and productivity of many fish populations.

In addition to a decrease in the amount of fish, a team of scientists at UBC thinks that warmer water temperatures may also reduce the maximum body size of marine fishes. All of these changes, however, will be regionally specific. The researchers predict that changes in fish productivity due to climate change will result in higher catch potentials for upper latitudinal regions, but a fairly significant decrease in the tropics. Thus, small tropical island countries that depend on fish, like Tuvalu and Kiribati, are projected to see a 70% decrease in catches, and these changes will have severe implications. Vicky Lam, a postdoctoral fellow at UBC's Institute for the Oceans and Fisheries, states that "developing" countries will be hit hardest— these people depend on fish for both food and income. However, at the same time, some northern countries such as Greenland and Iceland could see fishery revenues double as fish move towards cooler waters.

Lam and her team also used climate models to compare the economic impacts of climate change on fishery revenues under a high-emission scenario with a low-emission scenario where ocean warming was kept under 2°C. Not surprisingly, they found that global fishing revenue could decrease by an average of 10% and 7%, respectively. To improve their food security as global warming effects become more and more prevalent, some communities are resorting to fish farming. While this may be a valid solution, William Cheung, associate professor at UCB, thinks that rather than easing the financial burden of fishing losses, this method may further drive down the price of seafood and decrease fishery revenues.

In order to fully assess the effects of various greenhouse gas emissions on fish stock and fishery revenues, Gaworecki thinks that scientists must conduct "full-fledged" analyses and engage in further research.

Gaworecki, M., 2016. The economic impact of climate change on global fisheries could be even worse than we thought. Pacific Standard, 1-5.
https://tinyurl.com/j843lyn

Carbon Taxes, Path Dependency, and Directed Technical Change: Evidence from the Auto Industry
by Kele Mkpado

While there is little dispute that carbon emissions from internal combustion engines contribute to climate change, Philippe Aghion from Harvard, Antoine Dechezleprêtre, Ralf Martin, and John Van Reenen from the London School of Economics set out to discover if changes in policy affected major companies carbon output. Their curiosity sent them to the auto industry, in which cars produce 16.5% of all CO_2 emissions worldwide. They divided the firms into two groups, one which was considered "dirty" using internal combustion gasoline engines and one "clean", whose fleet comprised more electric, hybrid, and hydrogen innovations. Measuring over several decades, all car companies were deemed dirty to begin with. Research led researchers to three key findings. With rising oil prices worldwide, they saw many companies began to switch to clean energy to reduce their costs and remain more profitable. More importantly perhaps, the researchers noticed that there was a trend in companies who innovated earlier than others. These companies continued to move closer to alternative fuel sources other than oil. Lastly, researchers determined that local cultural and behavioral trends played a part in the decision making of the companies. They noticed that if nearby companies changed their energy habits the whole geographical area would respond in kind. Because oil prices have remained relatively low in recent years, there is little monetary motivation for companies to make the switch to cleaner energy. All of this research and data led the researchers to one conclusion. If they could somehow create a policy with the same effect as rising oil prices, they might have their solution. They believe that a tax or taxes on these so called "dirty" companies would motivate them to move toward cleaner energy, therefore setting a trend of innovation in which a tax is no longer needed.

Philippe Aghion, Antoine Dechezleprêtre, David Hémous, Ralf Martin, and John Van Reenen, "Carbon Taxes, Path Dependency, and Directed Technical Change:

Evidence from the Auto Industry," Journal of Political Economy 124, no. 1
(February 2016): 1-51.

Climate Change from the Perspective of an Emerging Economy
by Bradley Newton

Malaysia is a developing country, and in recent past has
experienced a burst of economic growth due to the expansion of
the consumer middle-class, increase in manufacturing, and the
continued export of primary commodities such as palm oil, all
leading to increased greenhouse gas production. The 2009
European Union Renewable Energy Directive pushed countries
within the European Union to have 20% of their energy needs
met using renewable sources by 2020, has increased demand
for palm oil which is used in certain biofuels. However, a surge
in the demand for palm oil is good for the Malaysian economy,
but the resulting increase in the number of plantations and
peatlands will cause a notable increase in Greenhouse gases
due to the deforestation needed to accommodate these
plantations, and the amount of carbon that the peatlands
contain.

We are used to looking at climate change through the
perspective of Western culture, media and the privilege that we
have that allows us to set aside resources specifically for
preventative measures towards climate change. Malaysia on the
other hand is in the process of developing and maturing its
economy, and having to scale back on palm oil production
would put a large damper on its economy. This is not to say
though that Malaysia is putting in no effort at all to combat
climate change, however, most of the media coverage and talk
about climate change is externally stimulated rather than
internally—meaning that participation in global events such as
international climate change conferences or World Earth Hour
are the main spurs for action. To put it plainly, Malaysia still
needs help from other countries to make any considerable
difference in its emissions.

Manzo, Kate, and Rory Padfield. "Palm Oil Not Polar Bears: Climate Change and
    Development in Malaysian Media." Transactions of the Institute of British
    Geographers41.4 (2016): 460-76. Wiley Online Library. Web.
    http://onlinelibrary.wiley.com/doi/10.1111/tran.12129/full

Evaluation Method for Assessing and Applying Sustainability

by Bradley Newton

Jabareen (2017) has created an approach for evaluating urban and community plans for sustainability. After studying many examples of planning literature, he came to the conclusion that most of the planning literature was very vague and overly simplistic preventing its leading to anything sustainable. One of the more notable plans of interest was the PlaNYC 2030, which is New York City's project for altering the city to be able to accommodate a rising population and to push down pollution.

The first aspect of Jabareen's framework is that the planning should be seen as a utopian vision of the future; i.e climate change should be at the center of the planning. Equity is the name of the next component of the framework, and it describes the idea that inequality in a community is a factor in environmental degradation. It says that in a society there are those who are unable to adapt to climate change, and that such things can be affected by approaches to resource redistribution and government institutions. The author thinks that planners need to respond to the inevitability of climate change and its effects by finding ways to better their infrastructure to help prevent risky events induced by climate change. Jabareen coins the name "uncertainty management" for the action that needs to be taken by planners. The fourth part of the framework is the act of sustaining the community's natural capital, which Jabareen defines as everything from the oil in the ground, the quality of the soil, and the stock of fish in the ocean, to the capacity of the globe to recycle and absorb carbon. The fifth measure of the framework focuses on the realization that planning with the added uncertainty of climate change is more complex than if it is disregarded. He stresses that all the institutions and entities in the planning process must be willing to adapt and be flexible to whatever situation that may present itself due to climate change. This is all to make sure that the expectations of the stakeholders are met to keep the project from falling apart. A central theme to Jabareen's framework is pollution reduction, and so it makes sense that the sixth part, ecological energy, states that whenever possible that new, clean, and alternative energy sources should be used. The seventh part of the framework goes hand in hand with the sixth, since it encourages stimulating the economy in areas that deal with clean energy. Jabareen calls it ecological economics. The final facet of the framework talks about the importance of being cognizant of the physical form of the city. This pertains to its spatial planning or compactness, architecture, transportation, population density, and many other physical aspects of the community that affect the activities of its inhabitants which in turn affects the environment.

Jabareen Y. (2017) A New Evaluation Method Applying Sustainability and Climate Change Concepts: The Case of Planning New York City 2030. In: Uyar T. (eds) Towards 100% Renewable Energy. Springer Proceedings in Energy. Springer, Cham
https://link.springer.com/chapter/10.1007/978-3-319-45659-1_31#enumeration

The Trump Budget Cuts
by Luis Salazar

The State comes together and discusses budget cuts. Almost thirty percent of its original budget is cut. The funding for core programs is proposed to lose nearly ten billion—eliminating foreign aid and climate change approaches.

Similarly, the Trump proposal would decrease the basic budget for economic aid by eleven billion. This would create friction between development programs and progress. Treasury International Programs are proposed to be decreased by $1.5 billion. These are only a few reductions in the Trump budget proposal; all the combined cuts add up to over twelve billion dollars.

The budget cuts illustrate Trump's idea of "Making America Great Again" by focusing more on programs that push the agenda of prioritizing the U.S. The author Carol Morello displays a brief chart—defense and homeland security budgets would be increased while the EPA and State budgets would be drastically cut.

Climate change organizations are in the middle of these attacks. Under this proposed budget, the Global Climate Change Initiative, aimed at the foreign investment of renewable energy sources, would lose all of its $350 million funding. SImilarly, the Green Climate Fund, an organization heavily supported by Obama, would also lose all of its funding.

The budget reduces the presence of the U.S. in the United Nations pushes for an increase in budgets from other members of the UN. Also, the U.S. is aiming to reduce the international development banks budgets. This negatively affects anti-poverty programs currently in place in other countries. Humanitarian relief is still an important part of Trump's budget, with the exception of the Emergency Refugee and Migration Assistance fund, which was eliminated.

One of the more terrifying proposed cuts is reduced funding for educational programs. These programs are heavily valued for the increased diversity in skill and talent that has been brought into the U.S.

The Fulbright Program, program for scholars, including members of Congress, was initially proposed to be eliminated. The Trump Administration aimed at eliminating the Bureau of Education and Cultural Affairs, but instead decided to reduce the budget and allow the Fulbright Program to continue.

Overall, the Trump Budget attacks the research of climate change, one of the most prominent issues of today. By slashing almost nearly all of the funding, Trump would make it hard to further develop and fight climate change.

Morello, Carol. State Department's 28 Percent Cuts Hit Foreign Aid, U.N. and Climate Change. The Washington Post. WP Company, 16 Mar. 2017

Response to Green Infrastructure
by Luis Salazar

Carmine Famiglietti battled a city crew ordered to construct a bioswale on the corner of his home as an attempt to relieve stress from the old sewer system. The sewer system has seen increasing damage as a result of climate change, so a bioswale—a ditch that helps the earth absorb excess water slowly—eases the effects of climate change on the sewer system.

Famiglietti successfully removed the workers by staring them down, as illustrated by his Facebook post. While some friends applauded his efforts of keeping the workers away temporarily, other friends critiqued his protest, citing that bioswales are intended to make neighborhood water cleaner.

In the past decade, nearly 3,000 bioswales have been created in New York, all raising discontent. Mostly, bioswales are unattractive, but they have also been built on public property without the consent of communities. The environmental cleanup work has been condemned by members of the community.

Bioswales are critical to the survival of sewer systems, and ultimately, cities. If a city is to remain strong, it must adapt to the adverse affects of climate change. The reaction to bioswales is similar to that of wind farms and solar energy rays; these environmental efforts have been critiqued for being ugly, despite the overarching purpose and their potential benefits in fighting the effects of climate change.

Eric A. Goldstein, an environmental director, disregards protestors of bioswales as community members that refuse to accept any change to the neighborhood. This means that people are protesting change even if it means added benefits and security. The city has invested $1.5 billion in green infrastructure. These investments have been made primarily in locations that lead to polluted waterways, preventing stormwater from being polluted in sewers. In New York, stormwater that reaches sewers is mixed with raw sewage from home. The goal of green infrastructure is to prevent the overflow of waterways.

Jeanette Romana, a resident near a bioswale, has a major complaint of the bioswale collecting garbage. The city, in response, plans to hire more workers to help maintain bioswales. Pennsylvania, like New York, began placing bioswales and consequently received similar feedback.

While the city does not intend to stop creating bioswales, a compromise seems to have been made—residents are now able to pick between several styles of bioswales. From patches of grass to concrete. These options have been created to battle the argument that bioswales are unsightly.

Nir, Sarah Maslin. To the City, a Pollution Fighter. To Some Residents, an Eyesore. The New York Times. The New York Times, 23 Mar. 2017.

Managing Climate Risks
by Luis Salazar

Annual Averages mislead people into taking what seems to be the "higher payout." When investors are deciding where to put their money, it is important to consider all of the risk options. For example, stocks pay off when the economy is expanding; similarly, stocks do not do well when the economy is not growing. Gold, on the other hand, may not pay off immediately, but it is beneficial to invest in gold in times of economic crisis. Investing in gold aids managing risks in the long run—this form of insurance policy is a risk many investors are comfortable making even though it provides a low average return.

Contrary to this theory, President Trump has signed an executive order in which the social cost of carbon—one of the most important measurements of climate change—is now hidden. The social cost of carbon is defined the monetary effects of an increase in carbon dioxide. This measurement is in charge of "cost-benefits analyses" of policy, such as the Clean Power Plan. As illustrated by Michael Greenstone, the social cost of carbon before the executive order was $40 per metric ton; after the executive order, the social cost of carbon is predicted to drop to no more than $5 per metric ton. The executive order predicts the dangers of valuing climate change risks less.

A discount rate is used to estimate what future damages are worth today. During President Obama's administration, it was decided that a 3% discount rate was reasonable. This means that $100 worth of damages happening in a century are valued at nearly $5.20. Under Trump's administration, the discount rate was increased to 7%, meaning that every $100 worth of damages in a century are currently valued at 12 cents. Discount rates are important because we can tell how much we value our future based on them. The long term effects of climate change are important consider because the damage will last for centuries. Lower discount rates means paying more today.

Financial markets illustrate the importance of matching discount rates with risk profiles. When the risk serves as tax, investing in stock and receiving an annual return of 5% is the best option. When the risk is high and recession-like, investing in gold is the best option. Financial markets highlight the importance of investing as a form of insurance.

Climate change is a risky investment. The uncertainty of temperature, greenhouse gas concentrations, and sea levels is disruptive. Though these changes are uncertain, the possibilities are open for damage. These risks encourage the use of a low discount rate as a form of investment.

Greenstone, Michael. What Financial Markets Can Teach Us About Managing Climate Risks. The New York Times. The New York Times, 04 Apr. 2017. Web.

Justice, Capitalism and Climate Change
by Alejandro Salvador

Although it took some time, and there are still some skeptics scattered around, there is solid scientific consensus about the existence of an anthropogenic climate change. Nonetheless, there isn't much consensus on what to do about it. Climate change has consequences and implications that span across multiple dimensions. Its politics raise questions regarding distributional justice, morality, what to do and what not to do, and so on. All of which foster heated discussions around these topics. In a recent paper, renowned historian

Dipesh Chakrabarty from the University of Chicago contextualizes all these conflicting viewpoints, which tend to center around capitalism and globalization, and argues that the debate is heavily influenced by the experiences from the West.

When it comes to climate change, there are two approaches identified by Chakrabarty. The first one is a quite straight forward one-dimensional challenge: We are emitting too much greenhouse gas, and must therefore reduce greenhouse gas emissions. The main solution proposed is to quickly transition to renewable energies. However, there are many debates surrounding this approach. Chakrabarty takes on issues of distributional justice between rich and poor nations and between present and future generations. There are also disagreements regarding capitalism, often blamed for stimulating climate change. Should we continue with a consumerist capitalistic society, replace it with some sort of egalitarian model, or completely scale back the world economy and go back to cleaner ways of living?

The second approach to climate change is multidimensional. Humans climbed too quickly to the top of the food chain, which didn't give enough time to the earth systems to adapt to new human practices. This brings up the idea of the Anthropocene, and the multiple ecological problems that it presents.

Chakrabarty discusses at length the relationship between capital and the Anthropocene. He fiercely stands against the idea that the rich are somehow protected from climate change; while in the short term, they may have better means to protect themselves—he argues—in the long term, a changing climate affects rich and poor alike.

The concept of justice is repeatedly mentioned. The politics of climate change must address multiple issues regarding fairness. An interesting issue raised by Chakrabarty is the less human-centered justice (or injustice) towards non-human forms of life. Climate change endangers a vast number of species; a Great Extinction seems frighteningly possible—some argue that it has already started. On top of that, the already mentioned issues of intergenerational justice, and distribution of carbon emissions between developing and developed nations, make the concept of justice a key element of the climate change debate.

Finally, Professor Chakrabarty reminds us that these discussions occur in a time and space. Inherently, they are shaped by current interests and future assessments. Different countries weigh climate change differently, and while it has a global effect, some countries seem to discuss climate change more consistently. Developing countries are particularly behind in the discussion, which shapes the debate on the experiences of the West.

Chakrabarty, Dipesh. 2017 Theory, Culture & Society 0(0) 1–13 DOI: 10.1177/0263276417690236
http://journals.sagepub.com/doi/10.1177/0263276417690236

It's Time to Act—Here's How
by Alejandro Salvador

The fight against climate change requires of an organized effort by local governments, media, and corporations to decrease emissions. The private sector plays an important role. If we are to achieve the levels of emissions necessary for a sustainable future, our industry has to be cleaner and more efficient. Considering the size of private industry, it can be easy to dismiss personal actions against climate change as insignificant. Yet, it is imperative for the population to take measures that go in line with a low-carbon future. Reuven Sussman, Robert Giord, and Wokje Abrahamse at the *Pacific Institute for Climate Solutions* present a report on how to encourage action on Climate Change.

Before tackling the question of how to encourage action, it's important to understand the underlying one of what discourages action in the first place. The literature on this topic consist of four main theories: rational choice theories, the idea that people weight the cost and benefits of a decision and act accordingly; theories of altruism, climate change action depends on people's values and beliefs; theories of multiple motivations, there are different interconnected drivers of behavior; and theories of psychological barriers, which pose different psychological arguments why people don't act on climate change.

What comes next is an overview of the different strategies—based on theory, that can shape behavior. These are to improve information channels, tailor information to different audiences, set goals and intentions, make pledges to reduce energy consumption, give feedback on the behavior of individuals, use social interaction to influence people, and finally, try to make energy consumption a sort of game for the population to engage in it.

The strategies posed are not intended to act as single infallible methods, but rather to act in conjunction with each other. Reinforcing the weaknesses of some with the strengths of others. They should also be applied in context, with careful consideration of the political, social and economic environment present. Furthermore, more research is necessary. It's crucial to understand that behavior changes might be subject to change with time. The persistency of behavior change that this policies promote might not be indefinite. Research should bridge this gap in our knowledge.

Reuven Sussman, Robert Gifford, and Wokje Abrahamse. 2016 The Pacic Institute for Climate Solutions: Social Mobilization: How to Encourage Action on Climate Change
http://pics.uvic.ca/sites/default/files/uploads/publications/FINAL%20Soci al%20mobilization-Sussman%20Gifford.pdf

What does Climate Change mean for Stock Markets?
by Tanisha Sheth

John Schwartz, a science writer for the New York Times recently wrote an article concerning the effects of climate change on stock markets around the world. It was found that investors controlling more than $5 trillion in assets have committed themselves to divesting in some or all fossil fuel stocks. This trend emerged from a movement that began on American college campuses in 2011 and since then has expanded into the corporate and institutional world, including insurers, pension funds and religious organizations. Since then, 688 institutions and nearly 60,000 individuals in 76 countries have begun dropping various oil, gas and coal company stocks from their portfolios. The issue of climate change emerged as an ethical concern that quickly matched with financial concerns, and now has eventually become a fiduciary duty. Schwartz comments on the coal industry, saying it is in the midst of a long-term decline. This has been proved with data associated with recent drops of oil and gas prices that have significantly hurt the fortunes of the industries concerned. Although the overall value of funds that have announced their divestment strategy run in the trillions, the actual amount of investment made into these fossil fuel industries is unknown. This is because there is no single industry that predominates in most broad investment funds. However, one cannot ignore the disbelievers of this situation. Some universities have ignored the calls for divestment, citing their fiduciary responsibility to be producing the greatest income from their endowments. One such is Harvard University. Drew Gilpin, the president of the prestigious Ivy League, stated that although Harvard would continue to support research and effort to fight climate change, their endowment is not an instrument they can use to impel any sort of social or political change. Furthermore, under the presidency of Trump, who has globally called climate change a hoax and has pledged to reverse Obama's global warming combat initiatives, activism is key. After carefully analyzing scientific data regarding climate change, it seems that if job growth is the objective, investing in clean forms of energy is the correct path to tread on.

Schwartz, John., 2016. Investment Funds Worth Trillions Are Dropping Fossil Fuel Stocks. The New York Times

Maldives: The Switch from Climate Threat to Mass Tourism
by Tanisha Sheth

Under the presidency of Mohamed Nasheed, Maldives stood as the moral leader in the UN climate talks and helped persuade rich countries to act. However, under new president Abdulla Yameen, Maldives changed its environmental policies saying that mass tourism and mega-developments rather than solar power and carbon neutrality would prepare the island country for climate change. Yameen's ministers outlined plans to geo-engineer artificial islands and relocate populations so as to attract tourism by creating 50 more resorts. Politicians hope to turn the Indian Ocean backwater with green ideals to hopefully a "smart" country with a new capital city, high technology centers, economic free zones and foreign universities to attract the global elite.

Shiham Adam, director of the government's Marine Research center has laid out plans to increase tourism from 1.3 million people a year to more than 10 million within a span of 10 years. He also claimed that fears of immediate sea level rise, which scientists established in a recent IPCC report, and could mean that 75% of the Maldives could be underwater by 2100 were unfounded. The government accepts that its development plans will increase carbon emissions, even without counting the thousands of extra flights that will be needed each year to bring the potential tourists. But it argues that Maldives is responsible for only 0.003% of global emissions and has the right to develop. There have also been plans made to sell the Faafu atoll to the Saudi royal family for $10 billion. This has enraged the political opposition. The Maldives Democratic Party, led by the former president Rasheed who is now in exile in London, said Yameen is acting without consultation. An alleged statement from him says that allowing a foreign power to control one of Maldives' 26 atolls amounts to creeping colonization. However, this has been dismissed by the current regime.

Vidal, John., 2017 'We need development': Maldives switches focus from climate threat to mass tourism. The Guardian

Shell Predicted Climate Change
by Tanisha Sheth

Oil giant Shell foresaw the risks of climate change more than 25 years ago in a 1991 film that has now been rediscovered. The 28-mintue film titled 'Climate of Concern' was made public for viewing, especially in schools and universities. It warned of extreme weather, floods, famines, and climate refugees as fossil fuel burning warmed the world. This warning was "endorsed by a broad consensus of scientists in their report to the United Nations in 1990", the film noted. The predictions made in 1991 film regarding the sea level rises and increase in temperature were remarkably accurate, according to scientists, and Shell was one of the first major oil companies to accept the reality and forthcoming dangers of climate change.

But, despite this clear-eyed view of global warming, Shell invested billions of dollars in highly polluting tar sand operations and oil exploration in the Arctic. It cited fracking as a "future opportunity" in 2016, despite its own 1998 data showing exploitation of unconventional oil and gas was incompatible with climate goals. Furthermore, Shell successfully lobbied to undermine European renewable energy target policies. The company's investments in low-carbon energy have been almost nothing compared to its fossil fuel investments.

Shell has also been a member of industry lobby groups that have fought climate change, including the Global Climate Coalition until 1998; the far-right American Legislative Council (Alec) until 2015; and continues to remain a member of the Business Roundtable and the American Petroleum Institute today.

Patricia Espinosa, the UN's climate change chief, said that until the big oil companies change their policies global warming would be impossible to tackle. The investments oil majors are making in clean energy are too small to have the impact the world needs. Espinosa, who visited Shell's headquarters in the December of 2016 stated that Shell knows that climate change is directly related to the future of Shell, "Not doing anything, will lead to crisis and losses in their business." The irony almost hurts.

Carrington, Damian., 2017 'Shell knew': oil giant's 1991 film warned of climate change danger. The Guardian

Developing Economic Models to Better Understand Climate Change
by Tanisha Sheth

In March of 2014, the Intergovernmental Panel on Climate Change (IPCC) released a report regarding the impact of climate change on humans and ecosystems. When planning for adaptation and mitigation, real risks need to be accounted for. Pricing risks using integrated models of physics and economics lets these costs be compared to those of limiting climate change, and thereby investing in greater resilience.

In 2013, an interagency working for the US government used three leading economic models to estimate that a tonne of carbon dioxide emitted now will cause future damage worth 37 USD in today's dollars. This 'social cost of carbon' represents money saved from avoided damage, owing to policies that reduce emissions of carbon dioxide. Governments and companies use these estimates to approximate how much to invest to reduce emissions. Canada, US, Mexico, the United Kingdom and even the International Monetary Fund have used similar numbers to analyze fossil fuel subsidies.

Economic models have led climate-science and economics experts to reach the conclusion that climate change causes substantial economic harm, justifying the need to take immediate action against climate change. The alternative, assigning no value to reductions in carbon dioxide emissions, would lead to regulation of greenhouse gases that is even more negligent.

The models being discussed aim to integrate estimates of the costs of greenhouse-gas emissions and steps taken to reduce them. They translate scenarios of economic and population growth, and resulting emissions into changes in atmospheric composition and global mean temperature. Then by applying 'damage functions' which are used to approximate global relationships between temperature changes and the economic costs from impacts such as rise in sea level, cyclone frequency, agricultural productivity and functioning of the ecosystem, translate these future damages into present monetary values.

The models show that future costs of climate change could be even higher for four reasons. First, the impacts of historic temperature changes suggest that societies and economies may be more vulnerable than current models predict, and weather variability is more important than average weather for predicting impacts for crop growth and food security. Second, the models omit damages to labor productivity, to growth productivity, and to the value of capital stock, including buildings and infrastructure. Due to lowering of the annual growth rate, these damages could have even deeper and longer-lasting effects on the economy than those predicted by the models. Third, the models assume that the value people attach to the ecosystems will remain constant. However, a basic principle of economics is that as a commodity becomes more scarce, its value increases resulting in greater damage than predicted. Fourth, the US analysis assumes a constant discount rate to translate future harms into today's money. However, economists have said that a discount rate that declines over time should be used.

Although it is possible that future technological developments might better equip society to cope with climate change, the bulk of literature and arguments suggest that social-cost models are underestimating climate-change harms. This is why modelers, scientists and environmental economists must continue to work collaboratively to identify research gaps and modelling limitations. Models should be revised more frequently to accommodate scientific developments and researchers must test model sensitivity to new parameters. The IPCC has committed to help set the research agenda and facilitate efforts to refine estimates of the social cost of carbon.

Revesz, Richard., 2014. Global warming: Improve economic models of climate change. Nature

Costs of Climate Change
by Tanisha Sheth

Despite climate change being an issue of accelerating urgency, global climate negotiations have failed to come to an effective agreement regarding how the burden of climate change mitigation will be shared across countries. Existing bargaining models are not capable of allocating costs to the parties involved. The three general equity principles that are used to determine the allocation of costs are: "ability to pay," "polluter pays," and "beneficiary pays". These translate into capacity, responsibility and vulnerability which in turn shape the country's bargaining stance.

However, because of endogenous relationships among current wealth levels, historical levels of pollutant emissions, and the severity of climate change, a country's stance is further complicated. The authors found that all three of the factors are important determinants of bargaining behavior, and that vulnerability is especially important for understanding bargaining under the uncertainty of future losses. They introduced a new bargaining framework which is a modified version of Rubinstein bargaining. In their variation, players begin the bargaining phase with an initial endowment and must bargain over how to split the cost of climate change mitigation. If they fail to reach an agreement, they lose their endowments, with some probability. The probability has a positive correlation with the number of rejected offers, and the rate of increase is asymmetric.

For the experiment, a sample of 270 subjects were recruited from the general undergraduate population at Stony Brook University and the model was administered over the course of four months. Researchers found that in terms of successful bargaining outcomes, the most success was observed with splitting mitigation costs. Results showed a preference for differentiating burden sharing based on principles of polluter pays and ability to pay. An important observation is that negotiations could be more successful if the media and negotiators highlighted the difference in economic capacity across countries and down-played the differences in vulnerability in climate change. Furthermore, differences in vulnerability caused the less vulnerable to exploit the more vulnerable by lowballing their offers. Consequently, rather than being forced into taking the offer, the more vulnerable parties rejected offers they perceived to be unfair. This could aid permit extrapolations that fairness is relevant in the context of actual international negotiations.

Although the researchers discuss the three equity factors, another factor in terms of distributional equity in climate change mitigation is that of intergenerational responsibility. For example, the causal responsibility for climate change in the world today is "inherited" from previous generations, and the consequences of agreements will affect future generations. The process of bargaining under increasing probability of loss is crucially important, and this study is the first to incorporate the aspect of international climate negotiations into a behavioral model.

Kline, Reuben., 2016 Distributional Equity in Climate Change Policy: Responsibility, Capacity, and Vulnerability

Forest Owners' Response to Climate Change: University Education Trumps Value Profile
by Charlie Thomson

A study conducted by the University of Freiburg in Germany, in conjunction with Lund University in Switzerland, aimed to answer the question of whether or not forest owners' response to climate change had any correlation to their level of education and personal values. The study was conducted to test the cultural cognition thesis (CCT), which has historically cast significant levels of doubt over the frequently-mentioned and criticized "knowledge deficit" model—an assumption that the average person is less concerned about climate change and the effects of climate change due to a lack of scientific literacy and knowledge of the matter. Proponents of the cultural cognition thesis believe that citizens with the highest levels of education and scientific literacy fall under a category of people who are least concerned about climate change, due to a high level of cultural polarization and a difference of cultural values. In addition, those who accept the CCT's hypothesis perceive that individuals with less formal educational backgrounds and a limited scientific literacy are in fact more concerned about climate change and its effects on mankind. This, in contrast to those with higher degrees of knowledge and scientific literacy due in large part to the fact that the CCT predicts that cultural and other values take precedence over a university education with some forest owners. The study was carried out by creating questionnaires designed to evaluate the impact of one's level of education and personal values on their perception of climate change impact. The data collection method assessed an individual forest owner's preferences for a multitude of services and benefits that were offered by that participant's forest. Additionally, the questionnaire gauged participants' perceptions of climate-change risk and the level of education each had received.

At the conclusion of the study, researchers determined that in neither of the two countries where populations were sampled completion of higher education was not a factor in reducing one's perception of human's contributions to climate change. Unsurprisingly, the greater the level of higher education completed, the greater the increased awareness and concern about the risks associated with climate change and human contributions to global warming. The results have proven that the relationship between values, level of education and risk perception as predicted by the cultural cognition thesis are not a factor within the domain that was investigated in this study. While these findings do not refute the claims made by the cultural cognition thesis, the results do not align with what would have been expected had all the mechanisms of the cultural cognition thesis been present. Thus, no evidence was found to solidify the notion that forest owners' personal values possess a greater impact on an individual's climate change perception in comparison to the impact of higher education on one's beliefs.

Blennow, Kristina, Johannes Persson, Erik Persson, and Marc Hanewinkel. "Forest Owners' Response to Climate Change: University Education Trumps Value Profile." Forest Owners' Response to Climate Change: University Education Trumps Value Profile 11 (2016): 1-13. Forest Owners' Response to Climate Change. Public Library of Science, 2 Aug. 2016. Web. 20 Jan. 2017. <http://pub.epsilon.slu.se/13533/>.

Automakers Urge Trump to Undo One of America's Biggest CO_2 Reductions to Date
by Charlie Thomson

Twelve different auto-manufacturers recently urged President Trump to lower fuel-economy regulations, which might have been the single largest CO_2 reduction in human history. On February 21, 2017, U.S. automakers effectively undermined their own long-term viability by pushing for the loosening of critical fuel economy regulations. While the rest of the world is combating climate change, U.S. automakers could reverse the progress made towards reducing the effects of climate change such as local air pollution, dollars saved, and making the auto industry more competitive. Instead, automakers could potentially throw all of this progress out of the window. The motivation behind automakers urges is that more jobs will be created with fewer government regulations. Even if more jobs were created in the short-term, gas-guzzling cars that are uncompetitive have no longevity in the U.S. or abroad. In addition, the U.S. has been in this same situation before, back in 2007, when automakers were bailed out for making inefficient vehicles that nobody seemed to want to buy. Yet it seems that the lessons of that era were not learned by anyone with power, and worse, not by the auto-manufacturers themselves. While the New York Times likes to paint this as a fight between environmentalists and everyone else, is that really the truth? Are environmentalists really the only category of people who think this is a bad idea? Let's not forget that this regulation would save drivers $1.7 trillion in saved fuel costs over the lifetime of most vehicles, and that 1.7 million children die each year from air and water pollution.

The basic argument made by the auto industry is that it is too arduous a task to meet the fuel economy standards of 54.5 MPG by 2025, compared with about 36 MPG today. The automakers claim it is not possible to hit that target which I believe to be false.

Trigg, Tali. "Automakers Urge Trump to Undo One of the U.S.'s Biggest CO2 Reductions to Date." Scientific American Blog Network. Scientific American, 31 Mar. 2017. Web. 02 Apr. 2017.

A Call for Research in Climate Change Economic Policy

by Kelly Watanabe

According to Burke *et al.* (2016), research on the economic impact of climate change is lacking. The authors propose solutions to bridge the gap between science and policy; economic policy can apply scientific research to create a social impact. Economic models of the social cost of carbon (SCC)—which predicts the future monetary loss as a consequence of emitting one ton of carbon—need modification. SCC numbers are derived from studies that are 20+ years outdated. Advancements in physical science research allow for a more accurate prediction on extreme climatic event patterns; economists should analyze current scientific data to generate refined damage estimates and hence improve accuracy of SCC estimates. SCC values should also be modified to account for future nonmarket damage—nonmarket costs arise from human health deterioration, civil conflict, and biodiversity loss. More accurate SCC estimates will serve as the building blocks for effective environmental policy design.

Currently, predictions of climate change policies' economic impact are not matching the actual cost and benefit reactions to the policies. Additionally, research in the natural sciences is needed to reduce the cost of environmentally friendly technology. The authors call attention to finding an optimal combination of emphasis on policy making vs. technological research and development.

Climate change policy is mainly sourced from and implemented by developed nations; this is a problem because developing countries have bigger populations and greater emissions of greenhouse gases than developed countries. Developing countries also have the most potential for economic growth and thus the most opportunity for carbon mitigation. Hence, new policies need to be tailored better to developing countries which have heavily subsidized fossil fuels, higher rates of tax evasion, and lower inclination to adopt costly clean-energy technology. According to the authors, developing countries need quantified empirical data collection—such as census surveys—to create a strong foundation for new economic policies.

Burke, M., Craxton, M., Kolstad, C.D., Onda, C., Allcott, H., Baker, E., Barrage, L., Carson, R., Gillingham, K., Graff-Zivin, J., Greenstone, M., Hallegatte, S., Hanemann, W.M., Heal, G., Hsiang, S., Jones, B., Kelly, D.L., Kopp, R., Kotchen, M., Mendelsohn, R., Meng, K., Metcalf, G., Moreno-Cruz, J., Pindyck, R., Rose, S., Rudik, I., Stock, J., Tol, R.S.J., 2016. Opportunities for advances in climate change economics. Science 352, 292-293.

The Importance of the Nationally Determined Contribution
by Annette Wong

In 2016, Papua New Guinea submitted the final version of their Nationally Determined Contribution (NDC), making it the first country to formally declare its national climate action plan under the Paris Climate Agreement. Eliza Northrop, lawyer and Associate in the International Climate Initiative, explained the importance of the small island country moving on from an "intended" nationally determined contribution (INDC) to the formal NDC.

The Pacific nation's commitment to transitioning to 100% renewable energy by the year 2020 "marks a step forward in the process of implementing" the international climate agreement adopted at Paris' COP21. Before COP21, INDCs were submitted by countries, mapping out the global community's cooperative plan in mitigating climate change. This provides the "legal framework for climate change plans".

Northrop explains that for a country to transform its INDCs into NDCs, it must simply finalize its national climate change plan, then submit a formal version to the United Nations Framework Convention on Climate Change (UNFCCCO). This is preferably to be done as soon as possible after they formally join the Paris Agreement. For the agreement to take effect, at least 55 countries emitting 55% of the global greenhouse gas emissions, must sign and ratify the Paris Climate Agreement treaty. Northrop suggests that countries should increase their climate change plan's transparency and ambition for the global mitigation effort to progress.

Northrop believes that it is important for countries to submit their formal nationally determined contribution because the NDC form framework for the world to achieve the goals of the Paris Agreement. Once official, NDCs will motivate and force countries to achieve their mitigation objectives, by officially reporting their progress every five years. NDCs also help countries to communicate information on climate adaptation. Adaptation components in the NDCs outline activities, goals, and needs for countries to cope with environmental changes like increased drought, storms, and rising sea levels. Countries can thus share information with each other on facing climate change issues. In Northrop's view, only when all countries submit their NDCs will we be able to limit the global temperature rise to 1.5-2 decrees Celsius and "prevent the worst impacts of climate change".

Papua New Guinea's act in formalizing their nationally determined contribution represents the first step to working as a global community to build momentum for a climate-resilient world.

Northrop, Eliza. "Papua New Guinea Is First Country to Finalize National Climate Plan Under Paris Agreement." World Resources Institute. World Resources Institute, 20 Mar. 2016. Web. 07 Feb. 2017. <http://www.wri.org/blog/2016/03/papua-new-guinea-first-country-finalize-national-climate-plan-under-paris-agreement>.

Floating Cities Become a Reality with Climate Change

by Jason Yi

Mike Ives (2017) examines a new proposition to fight climate change. Approved by the French Polynesia government, the aim is to build a city of floating islands in the South Pacific in response to the quickly rising sea levels. According to Ives, the project was first presented by the Seasteading Institute, a nonprofit organization located in California. The institute raised approximately $2.5 million dollars from more than a thousand donors. The company's executive director, Randolph Hencken stated that depending on the economic conditions and "feasibility" of the plan, the project may launch next year.

Ives also reports Mr. Hencken's recent statement that the total cost of these "pilot" islands would amount to $10–50 million with the cost of an average house being similar to that of New York City or London. However, it is a risk that the Seasteading Institute is willing to take, as the completion of such islands would allow the company to demonstrate the possibilities of new breakthroughs in "solar power, sustainable aquaculture, and ocean-based wind farms." Moreover, Mr. Hencken believes that this project could be the blueprint to other artificial islands in the near future.

Contrary to the views of Mr. Hencken, there are critics who believe that the production of such islands will incite harmful environmental side. Furthermore, Ives mentions that experts in climate change doubt that such an expensive project could be scaled up for impoverished countries. There are other technical issues that may stand in the way of a worldwide project. Ives reports that in the previous year, the nation of Kiribati tried to study the practicality of raising its islands to fight rising sea levels, but were ultimately unsuccessful when the United Arab Emirates refused to contribute to the studies of the feasibility of the plan.

Journalist Ives ends the article with a comment from Simon Donner, a geography professor at the University of British Columbia. After hearing the possibility of artificial islands, Mr. Donner stated that such a project will essentially be a "cruise ship" for the rich while leaving the low-class citizens to deal with the effects of climate change.

Ives, M. 2017. As Climate Change Accelerates, Floating Cities Look Like Less of a Pipe Dream. New York Times Jan 27

New Technology May be Needed to Mitigate Global Warming
by Jason Yi

Eduardo Porter (2017) discusses the recent events and possible solutions regarding Climate Change. He reports that over the course of a few months, temperatures in the Arctic soared 35°F above previous records, resulting in low sea-ice levels. Moreover, with President Trump nullifying Mr. Obama's previous efforts on alleviating greenhouse gas emissions, a solution to Climate Change seems more or less likely.

However, many scholars are currently working to resolve this complication as they introduced a new idea to cool the planet. Such a plan would involve loading aerosols into military jets and spraying them into the atmosphere at high altitudes. Another proposal involves spraying clouds above oceans with a saline mist in order to better reflect sunlight back into space. The issue becomes whether the world can afford such technology. Porter adds that because the modern world is producing carbon dioxide at such a fast rate, it is impossible to afford the technology as we could have in the past.

As a result, Porter notes that many people are leaning towards geoengineering as America begins to move away from the 2015 Paris Agreement. Moreover, at a recent gathering in Washington, there was an unanimity to "invest more in research" to help cool the atmosphere. However, there are still many complications regarding geoengineering. Many individuals are concerned with the ethical impacts and the way that the world would govern the use of such technology. Others are concerned with the different impacts on various countries that may arise from geoengineering. One country may experience a drought while another could experience frozen landscapes.

On the bright side, it is estimated that the cost of geoengineering is inexpensive enough that most countries could afford the technology. While there is still much debate regarding geoengineering, it is imperative that the world continues to research new science that can repress the growing climate change issue.

Porter. Eduardo. 2017. To Curb Global Warming, Science Fiction May Become Fact. New York Times April 4

Politics and Climate Change

Donald Trump Launches an Attack on Climate-Change Policy
by Ellen Broaddus

M.S.L.J (2017) covers Donald Trump's recent executive order (called the "Energy Independence" order) regarding climate change policy and the EPA. This policy, signed March 28, told the Environmental Protection Agency (EPA) to "withdraw and replace" the Clean Power Plan, a policy proposed by Obama in 2015 that aimed to reduce power plants' emissions which would cut carbon emissions by 870 million tons by 2030. This initiative, which would have the same effect as taking 80 million cars off the road, was also made to solidify the US role in international climate change measures. However, due to legal backlash from 27 states, the Clean Power Plan was put on hold by the Supreme Court and was never implemented, meaning its "removal" was likely more symbolic than impactful. Despite lack of national policy, more than half of US states already have policies to increase the prevalence of renewable energy. For example, California aims to reduce greenhouse gas emissions by 40% by 2030.

Trumps executive order also requested a reversal of the temporary prohibition on coal leasing on federal lands and discards regulations on curbing methane emissions from oil and gas sites. This request follows Trump's campaign promise to "bring jobs back in the coal industry" by offering large subsidies, although economists think the reason for the decrease of the industry stems from increased efficiency in mining rather than regulation. The possible removal of rules to limit methane (natural gas) emissions could have very negative impacts. Although methane stays in the atmosphere much less time, it is a much more potent greenhouse gas. With proposed budget cuts, the EPA would have much less money to detect and mitigate leaks in the US natural gas supply chain.

While scientists are concerned about this new executive order, many conservatives who think the EPA's efforts have been overreaching are excited by the policies. Luckily, Trump did not follow through authorizing the EPA to reconsider its 2009 "endangerment finding" which allowed it to be "legally responsible for regulating CO_2 emissions" or withdraw from the Paris Agreement, policies that would have disastrous effects.

M.S.L.J. 2017. Donald Trump Launches an Attack on Climate-Change Policy. The Economist.
http://www.economist.com/blogs/democracyinamerica/2017/03/scorched-earth-0

Is China Challenging the United States for Global Leadership?
by Ellen Broaddus

In early April, President Trump met with Xi Jinping, the President of the People's Republic of China. This meeting comes during a time of change in both country's foreign policies, especially regarding climate change, as the US is moving away from global responsibility while China has been stepping up. In the past, China has taken a backseat approach when it comes to foreign policy. In 1992, leaders advised China to "keep a low profile, never take the lead…and make a difference", but more recently, it has shifted towards making a difference "actively". In Mr. Xi's recent speech at the World Economic Forum, he strayed from the conventional topics of domestic economy and instead said that China should "guide economic globalization". China's prime minister, Li Keqiang mentioned *quanqiu* (global) and *quanqiuhua* (globalization) 13 times during his annual "work report", far more than usually mentioned.

The shifting rhetoric towards Chinese presence in foreign policy signifies in growing support for the "China solution", an alternative to the "Washington consensus" that "supports free-market economic policies for developing countries". Although the "China solution" hasn't been explicitly defined, it deals with everything from strengthening global government to addressing and mitigating climate change. China has already had many successes in the international community, investing in and forming ties with many Asian countries as well as creating ambitious foreign policy such as the "Belt and Road Initiative" aimed at investing in the infrastructure along the old Silk Road.

Monetarily, China has also become a big part of the international community, as the third-largest donor to the UN's budget and the second-largest contributor to the UN's peacekeeping, as well as setting up financial institutions. At a recent summit with the world's 20 largest economies (G20), Mr. Xi "made the fight against climate change a priority", saying that despite the Trump administration's plans to dismantle current climate policies, China is prepared to "go it alone", something that could be the first practical application of the "China solution".

Despite their growing presence in the international community, China remains a revisionist power, wanting to "expand influence within the system" rather than overthrowing things. However, as Zhang Jun, a senior Foreign Ministry official said, it is not that "China [is] rushing to the front, but rather the front runners have stepped back, leaving the place to China".

2017. Is China Challenging the United States for Global Leadership? The Economist. http://www.economist.com/news/china/21719828-xi-jinping-talks-china-solution-without-specifying-what-means-china-challenging?zid=313&ah=fe2aac0b11adef572d67aed9273b6e55

Political Orientation and its Effect on Academic Faculties' Beliefs Regarding Climate Change
by Chris Choi

E. Michael Nussbaum et. al (2016) examined the relationship between political orientations with academic discipline on beliefs in anthropogenic climate change among educational faculty. Currently, mass media is one of the only tools for educating people about climate change. Researchers argue that higher educational faculties can also serve as huge sources of information regarding anthropogenic climate change, but their political orientation may affect their views. The overall goal was to see if there was a relationship between political orientations and higher educational faculties' beliefs regarding climate change

Based on past research, it was found that beliefs regarding climate change are generally reliant on political orientation; people tend to view climate change as a political issue rather than a scientific issue. It was found that while the higher academic faculties were still greatly affected by the political aspect of climate change, its affect may be mitigated by the subject they teach. To test this, researchers sent out a survey, consisting of 30 questions, to 324 professors from two state universities from a southwestern state of the United States. Researchers picked professors from different fields of study. Some sections asked the professors about climate change and generally what it was and how concerned they were while other sections asked similar questions except with regard to their students.

After examining the responses, they found that though professors did not believe that climate change was just a political issue; political orientations still had a large influence on their beliefs about anthropogenic climate change. The authors found that even amongst the science professors, political orientation still influenced their views on climate change. Political orientation has less of an influence on liberal arts professors. Researchers theorized that these professors have a wider range of knowledge that gives them a broader view of the world. Overall, Nussbaum et. al found that there are many different dimensions and ways of framing anthropogenic climate change, thus affecting everyone's political views towards climate change.

Nussbaum, E. M., Owens, M. C., & Cordova, J. R. (2016). 'It's Not a Political Issue!'The Interaction of Subject and Politics on Professors' Beliefs in Human-induced Climate Change. Journal of Education for Sustainable Development, 10(1), 101-114.

Does Global Warming Cause War?
by Joshua Dorman

Over the past few years, the world has witnessed an incredible number of violent struggles in relatively poor and ethnically divided countries. But could climate change be a contributing factor? In an article written for *The Guardian*, writer Damien Carrington explores the troubling link between global warming and the frequency of armed conflicts.

According to research published in the Proceedings of the National Academy of Sciences, approximately "a quarter of the violent struggles in ethnically divided countries were preceded by extreme weather." Previously, research has shown a definite correlation between fighting and climate disasters, but the new work demonstrates that these disasters actually occur *before* the violence begins, suggesting a cause-and-effect trend. Incidents such as extreme famine, droughts, floods, and severe heatwaves have been shown to systematically increase the odds of violent clashes between different racial groups in a number of nations. In fact, such data have led John Schellnhuber, a professor and director of the Potsdam Institute for Climate Impact Research in Germany, to declare the combination of ethnic tensions and climate catastrophes an "explosive mixture."

The implications of this information are far-reaching indeed. For instance, new security policies may need to be drafted for countries that are especially prone to the toxic mixture of ethnic issues and global warming-induced disasters, such as nations in central Asia and north and central Africa. Furthermore, the data may make it possible to predict when and where violent clashes will occur by using climate disasters as independent variables and armed conflict as dependent variables. According to Schellnhuber, "you could construct a conflict 'radar' system to anticipate hotspots where the probability of armed conflict is high. Then you could try to diffuse certain things, or say, given the current migration debate, see where the potential sources of emigration are." However, if humanity fails to appropriately tackle and stem the calamity of global warming, in fifty years approximately 80% to 90% of disasters will be directly caused by climate change; the outbreak of violence will be nothing like the world has ever seen.

There appears to be an incredibly meaningful co-benefit to halting global warming: peace.

Carrington, Damian. "Disasters linked to climate can increase risk of armed conflict." The Guardian. July 25, 2016. Accessed March 04, 2017. https://www.theguardian.com/environment/2016/jul/25/disasters-linked-to-climate-can-increase-risk-of-armed-conflict.

Did Climate Change Increase Conflict Among the Ancient Maya?
by Joshua Dorman

Recently, a number of scientific studies have been conducted that show a clear correlation between bellicosity of small, ethnically-divided nations and climate change. Likewise, the Intergovernmental Panel on Climate Change and the U.S. Department of Defense have both classified global warming as a "threat multiplier." However, new research may show that this phenomenon has in fact existed for thousands of years. In an article for online journal Seeker, writer Rossella Lorenzi explores the relationship between temperature increases and clashes among the Classic Maya.

A study, published in the *Quaternary Science Reviews* journal and conducted by Mark Collard of Simon Fraser University, along with Christopher Carleton and David Campbell of Simon Fraser University, elicited some surprising findings.

The team looked at inscriptions on monuments citing periods of violence between 363 and 888 AD. Then, they compared the inscriptions to paleoclimate data from the same period, and the correlation was astounding. According to the paper, "the change in conflict levels between 350 and 900 AD was considerable;" they found that "the number of conflicts increased from 0 to 3 every 25 years in the first two centuries to 24 conflicts every 25 years near the end of the period."

Most importantly, they discovered that the correlation could not be explained by changes in rainfall, but instead by changes in temperature, specifically times of particularly hot weather. Although the group noted that higher temperatures tend to give people shortened tempers, thus making them more prone to violence, they found another explanation to be far more compelling: changes in maize yields. During times when temperatures hovered around 82°F, the maize crop was relatively stable and episodes of violence were relatively few. However, during times when the average temperature rose to 86 86°F—the temperature at which maize becomes unstable— violence increased exponentially. The group theorized that during these periods of heat, large-scale deforestation, urban expansion, and the failure of the crop created a food shortage which resulted in spikes of conflict. It's not hard to see how similar episodes of violence—namely in the Middle East and Africa—can be linked to identical causes. Unless climate change is stemmed, modern full-blown conflicts may make the Mayan wars look like school-yard fights in comparison.

Lorenzi, Rossella. "Climate Change Incited Wars Among the Classic Maya." Seeker. March 31, 2017. Accessed April 12, 2017. https://www.seeker.com/culture/history/climate-change-incited-wars-among-the-classic-maya.

Could Climate Change and Trump's Denial of it be Good for Russia?
by Vikramaditya Jhunjhunwala

In light of President Donald Trump's dismissal of climate change, it is fair to say that the U.S. national policy regarding renewable energy and carbon reduction is set to undergo a monumental shift. If global leaders were to follow in Trump's rhetoric and disregard the climate change phenomenon, the world would have to brace itself for a plethora of changes. While, this would negatively impact most countries, one nation that could gain from this would be Russia.

Oil and gas collectively constitute more than two-thirds of Russia's exports and the two fuels have accounted for nearly 50% of Russia's annual budget over the past decade. Historically, sharp declines in energy prices have sent Russia into deep recessions such as the one in the 1990s.

In the short run, a fossil-fuel friendly policy would hurt Russia as more oil drilling and gas exports around the world would increase competition and lower commodity prices. However, in the long run, Russia's main concern is the renewable energy industry that is simultaneously evolving and becoming more cost effective. Presently, the U.S. government is funding research on battery technology in order to store solar energy and eventually displace oil, gas and coal as energy sources. However, if the United States government ceases to make climate change a priority, it is entirely possible that the money for these grants could be invested elsewhere, thereby keeping Russia's economy secure. Such a decision would have domino effects all around the world as it is highly likely that European countries would follow suit. This could lower carbon restrictions in and around Europe and thus, make these countries even more economically reliant on Russia.

One would perhaps assume that Russia would surely suffer from the natural, physical effects of climate change. However, Russia is rather protected from most dangers of global warming due to its location and could, on the contrary, even benefit from the phenomenon. Much of Russia's landscape is covered in permafrost and tundra, making it unsuitable for agriculture. But rising temperatures, as researchers at Ludwig Maximilians University estimate, could add more than 1.15 million square miles to Russia's arable land. Increased farmland is not the only thing Russia would benefit from: the melting of ice due to global warming could also unearth new fossil-fuel deposits for exploitation and open up key navigation channels around the arctic.

It is true that Russia is not completely impervious to some of the aspects of climate change such as coastal flooding and destruction of infrastructure by melting permafrost. However, Russia would gain more from an economic and geopolitical standpoint than most other countries. Ironically, by treating climate change as a myth, the United States might be helping Russia more than themselves.

Smith, N., Lake, E., & Smith, N. (2016). Russia Wins in a Retreat on Climate Change. Bloomberg View. Retrieved 15 February 2017, from https://www.bloomberg.com/view/articles/2016-12-15/russia-wins-in-a-retreat-on-climate-change

Politics of Climate Change Denial
by Matt Johnson

The underlying causes of climate change denial are found to be much more political than technical, according to an article written by Peter Jacques and Claire Knox (2016). Utilizing social media data, as well as other sources, the article found that the psychology behind climate change denial is a little more complex than what meets the eye.

While acknowledging that the denial of climate change has been well studied, the authors realized that "individual rationales for rejecting climate science remain under-studied", and therefore set out to gather some data on the matter. Jang and Hart (2015), whose study is mentioned, found that Americans tended to think of climate change in a binary fashion: whether it is true or a lie. In comparison to other countries, the underlying causes, implications and solutions are of less importance than the politics surrounding climate change.

Citing a study by Smith and Leiserowitz (2012), the article referenced how about 40% of people think climate change is a conspiracy, 20% deny climate change entirely, 13% doubt the underlying science, and 11% think that climate change is natural. Matthews (2015) found that many people believe that climate change is "politicized for the purposes of Leftist indoctrination".

In introduction to Jacques and Knox's analysis, yet another study is referenced; this one about Twitter. This study found that 50% of retweets came from only 0.37% of users, "indicating concentrated influence by a minority". The Jacques and Knox study includes 9896 twitter messages from 6353 distinct users. The tweets were gathered from the immediate period surrounding Hurricane Sandy in 2012.

The study found that English speaking countries are by far the most skeptical of climate change, dominating the denial-tweets with 88% of the total. Popular themes that arose were opposition to renewable energy policies, opposition to climate-related taxation, and fear of abuse and overreach of government power. The authors concluded that the climate change deniers seemed to believe that the 'hoax' of climate change was an opportunity to profit from renewables, and to increase taxes as well as decrease freedoms. Other deniers claim that renewable energy policies will lead to an inappropriate manipulation of the market; at the same time, they say that supporting green energy is a fantasy, a waste of money, and criminal. The authors found that issues of taxation really get climate change nay-sayers rallied up. Some claimed that climate science is 'a scandal used to try to get people to pay a "carbon tax" that may 'end civilization as we know it'.

The climate change denial countermovement has rallied many against renewable energies and green policies. While the study recognized that climate change denial is becoming less popular, the political power of this movement, backed my many conservatives, creates a powerful barrier to progress in climate science and environmental policy. When discussions turn political and not scientific, many are swayed by the discourse, and may never have the information to form a fact-based opinion for themselves. While we may think the barriers to progress lie in the lack of green technologies, those barriers really lie in ourselves.

Jacques, P.J. and Knox, C.C., 2016. Hurricanes and hegemony: A qualitative analysis of micro-level climate change denial discourses. Environmental Politics, 25(5), pp.831-852.

Republicans and Climate Change... a New Approach?

by Ethan Kurz

Republicans have a clear stereotype of not believing in climate change, and that stereotype exists for good reason. According to Justin Gillis (2017), Republican officeholders used to simply deny the existence of climate change. When that proved too difficult to say without public ridicule, the politicians moved on to the "I'm not a scientist" phase. When that phase grew ridiculous, Republicans began a new approach to climate change. Republicans admit that something is happening, the world is warming up, but according to Republicans we cannot diagnose the main cause of climate change, so humans are off the hook. Trump nominees have tried to avoid saying outright that climate change does not exist, but instead have told their allies that there is not enough evidence or reason to justify creating policies towards emissions and climate change. American climate scientist Raymond T. Pierrehumbert warns the public to not be fooled by the Republican actions. Dr. Pierrehumbert and the majority of scientists stand by the consensus that human activity is the irrefutable cause of climate change. The evidence for this includes physics that cannot be denied, increasing emissions and the corresponding increase in temperature, and the increasing number of extreme weather systems. It is, of course, still possible that natural causes could be at the heart of increase in temperatures, but according to Drew Shindell, ann atmospheric scientist, all possible natural drivers have been investigated and ruled out. What is truly uncertain about climate change is how fast it will grow and affect humans. Timing will become everything with this administration. Republicans are beginning to accept that climate change is happening, but still denying human causation. This proves a problem for creating new policy to help our suffering world. If policy is not created soon, climate change could get exponentially worse in a way no one has thought of. Emissions are going up and Republicans will eventually need to come to terms with this.

Gillis, Justin., 2017. Republicans Try a New Tack on Climate Change. The New York Times. < https://www.nytimes.com/2017/02/02/science/climate-change-republicans.html>.

Who is on Trump's Side with Climate Change...Not Americans
by Ethan Kurz

Donald Trump has a pretty clear stance on climate change, it doesn't exist. Do Americans think that too? There is, in fact, a map that can tell us just that. The "Yale Climate Opinion maps" are a set of maps that answer various questions about American opinions on climate change. The maps were updated in 2016, the first time since 2014 and the results are surprising if your name is Donald Trump. Seven in ten voters believe that the United States should stay in the international agreement to limit climate change. Two thirds of voters believe that the United States should commit to lowering greenhouse gasses, regardless of what other nations do. Around 82% of adults think there should be more government spending going towards climate change research and prevention. This survey was conducted November 8th of 2016.

This new update added new survey questions into the mix including how much people trust scientists, whether people think climate change will affect ecosystems, how often global warming is presented to them in social media, and how often they discuss climate change with family/friends.

The most significant part of this map is that it breaks things down county by county. It is possible to see what towns believe in climate change and what counties don't. For example, 57% of people in Florida are "worried about climate change", whereas in Southern Florida 64% of people are worried. This is very important because we can see how people in Southern Florida care more about climate change because they see the rising sea levels more than the whole of Florida in general. The specificity shows us how different communities respond to climate change. The director of the Yale Program on Climate Change Communication said, "the changes in the maps allow people to get more specific and see estimates of public opinions."

Bolstad, Erika, 2017. Maps Show Where Americans Care About Climate Change. Scientific American. <https://www.scientificamerican.com/article/maps-show-where-americans-care-about-climate-change/>.

James Hansen Agrees with Republicans on Climate Change…Why?
by Ethan Kurz

Donald Trump's executive order from last week could undercut the nation's battle against climate change. It attempts to remove the Clean Power Plan which regulates emissions in the power sector. Renowned climate change scientist James Hansen believes that this road, seemingly opposite of what you might expect, is a better road towards fighting climate change. The solution he believes will work best has been proposed by a group of Republicans: "a carbon fee and dividend". Hansen believes that putting a price on carbon emissions is essential for cutting back on emissions. This price would start somewhere, and over time it would slowly increase, forcing companies to release less and less greenhouse emissions to avoic paying more. Studies have shown that this is a conservative approach in which the market will control the situation. In Hansen's plan, and now the Republican's plan, the money collected from the fee would be given to the public, a dividend to each legal resident. This would stimulate the economy instead of the government just collecting the fee like another tax.

Hansen believes that this fee is the only way to reduce emissions. As long as there are fossil fuels that are still able to be used for cheap energy, few companies will stop using them.

With the Trump presidency, Hansen thinks that with Trump as a president all scientists can do is stay objective. They must stick to science because there is nothing political about science and just explain the science as best as they can. Scientists must fight back against the large fossil fuel companies who have kept them relatively silenced over the past couple of decades. They must come together and provide effective and unbiased advice to the government.

Hansen believes that climate change scientists must communicate with the public on this important matter. The public currently doesn't treat climate change as a high priority issue and that is a problem. We are getting into a situation that's more and more dangerous as emissions continue to rise. Climate change is obvious in the science, now it must become obvious to the public.

Sneed, Annie, 2017. Legendary Climate Scientist Likes a GOP Proposal on Global Warming. Scientific American. <https://www.scientificamerican.com/article/legendary-climate-scientist-likes-a-gop-proposal-on-global-warming/>.

Fossil-fuel Companies Bullying Republicans
by Ethan Lewis

An article from the Washington Post written by Sheldon Whitehouse, a democratic senator from Rhode island, addresses the relationship between Republicans and climate change. Whitehouse starts by describing his conversations with Republicans about climate change saying that it is like "talking to a prisoners about escaping." The truth is that climate change used to not be a partisan issue in Congress. Republicans like John McCain, Lamar Alexander, Susan Collins, and Jeff Flake have introduced climate bills before. It only became an issue in 2010 when five Republican justices were appointed in the Supreme Court. They changed many laws, one of which does not limit corporation spending on political campaigns. According to Whitehouse, unlimited spending lets major fossil-fuel companies direct Republican's say about climate change, disbanding any sort of debate in Congress.

Republicans do recognize the consequences of climate change. They hear the warnings from the military that climate change can cause great conflict. They see countless reports of forest devastation and sea level rise. But they are still trapped. Whitehouse quotes a Republican senator who said "What the hell are you complaining about? They're spending more against us than they are against you!" He then adds that the only solution is from the corporate "good guys." Companies like Walmart, Coca-cola, Bank of America, and Google all signed the American Business Act on Climate Pledge. But these companies never tell Republican senators that they will have their backs if they stand up to the major fossil fuel bullies.

With the election of Donald Trump, Whitehouse says that they need more reinforcements than ever. He says not to believe statements by Rex Tillerson about him recognizing that climate change is real or that Exxon supports a carbon tax. Fossil-fuel companies are moving in to run the show in America. Whitehouse does say though that Republicans will fight and take the side of climate change eventually, it is just very difficult with the corporate pressure that looms over them.

Whitehouse, Sheldon: "Republicans want to fight climate change, but fossil-fuel bullies won't let them." Washington Post, January 10 2017.

Congress Fails to Discuss Climate Change
by Ethan Lewis

Chelsey Harvey, a writer at the Washington Post, wrote on a hearing that was held by several House committees to discuss the social cost of carbon. The social cost of carbon is a way to quantify the effects of carbon dioxide being let into the atmosphere. Unfortunately, the hearing took a hard turn away and instead became a debate on whether man-made climate change exists. Harvey adds that this is not the first time hearing have failed to discuss their intended topics. Just a few weeks ago, the House Science Committee held a hearing to focus on the Environmental Protection Agency and how it can best relay its available scientific evidence of climate change. The hearing ended up being a way for climate change doubters to express the lack of seriousness they had for the issue of human-caused climate change.

Currently, the social cost of carbon is estimated at roughly $36 per ton of carbon dioxide. The number was developed by a federal group founded in 2009. It relied on a set of models which predicted how carbon emissions will affect climate change in the future. It then calculated damages associated with climate change. The hearing was intended to "examine the methods and parameters used to establish the social cost of carbon" by using input from witnesses on how the calculation could be more accurate.

The hearing began with Republicans raising some of the issues that they saw in the calculation. Some of these issues include global costs, compared to domestic ones, as well as assumptions made in the models that the group calculation the cost was using. To combat the issues, a Democratic representative, Michael Greenstone, remarked "The approach has been judged valid, the federal court of appeals rejected a legal challenge to the metric. Furthermore, the Government Accountability Office has said the working group's methods reflected key principles that ensured its credibility."

Harvey, Chelsey. (2017, March 4). Members of Congress met to discuss the costs of climate change. They ended up debating its existence. https://www.washingtonpost.com/news/energy-environment/wp/2017/02/28/members-of-congress-met-to-discuss-the-costs-of-climate-change-they-ended-up-debating-its-existence/?utm_term=.e6498da00444

Trump Boosts Coal While China Leads Climate Change

by Ethan Lewis

Michael Biesecker, a writer for the Washington Post, compares China's and the U.S.'s climate policies. In early April, President Trump hosted President Xi Jinping to discuss their countries' paths for combating climate change. The Chinese government recently cancelled construction of more than 100 new coal-fired power plants and instead plans to invest at least $360 billion in green energy projects by 2020, which are expected to generate 13 million jobs. Trump on the other hand, who claimed climate change is a hoax created by the Chinese, aims to roll back Obama's regulation on carbon emissions. He pledged to reverse decades of decline in coal mining. In contrast, Barbara Finamore, Asia director at the Natural Resources Defense Council says, "clean energy is the next largest global market, and the U.S. risks losing out."

Although China still burns more coal than any other nation, its consumption of coal fell in 2016 for a third consecutive year. An analysis showed an expected corresponding decrease in China's carbon dioxide emissions by 1% in 2017. That puts China on track to meet its 2030 target under the Paris agreement as much as one decade early. China is using the lack the leadership from the Trump administration to craft a stronger role for itself in fighting climate change, and also filling the diplomatic vacuum left by Trump's retrograde position. China's officials are currently filled with a mixture of bemusement and worry about Trump's public statements doubting that human activity is the primary cause of global warming. One Chinese official said that Trumps claim might erode the public's support for taking action to reduce reliance on coal.

Some say that Trump will never recognize the significance of climate change until it is literally at his doorstep. Mar-a-Lago, the site of his meeting with President Xi, is located in one of the regions in the United States most vulnerable to sea level rise. Recent studies say the Trump's prized resort will be underwater by the end of the century.

Watt□|□AP, Michael Biesecker and Louise. "Trump boosts coal as China takes the lead on climate change." The Washington Post. WP Company, 06 Apr. 2017. Web. 08 Apr. 2017.

Chief Executive of CSIRO Withdraws from Climate Change
by Bradley Newton

CSIRO—the Commonwealth Scientific and Industrial Research Organization—has long been at the forefront of climate change, until recently. Larry Marshall, the chief Executive of CSIRO, recently commented that the job of climate change was finished for his organization, and that it was time for it to move on to more relevant matters. His aim is now to update the company with new employees—meaning that many current scientists will lose their jobs—and to move the research agency's focus towards other matters. Matters such as: "titanium ink for 3D printing from Australia's mineral sands, produce cleaner diesel fuel from coal, and breed 'new strains of food and agricultural products that are healthier, [and] more sustainable.'" This redirection cuts 110 jobs form the Oceans and Atmosphere division, which is the bulk of the agency's climate research, and many people fear that such a change to the organization will negatively affect CSIRO's research in the Southern Hemisphere. Marshall believes that the redirection should not be too much of an issue, and that the scientists that will be staying with agency will have no problem "reinvent[ing]" themselves in order to work on areas foreign to them. It is also noted that these cuts will hurt Australia's efforts in reaching a 26–28% decrease in greenhouse gas emissions—as required by the 2015 climate accord—since the country relies on the data collected by CSIRO to meet its goal. Why this dramatic change to the research agency? One possibility is that it is just an adjustment to the cut of more than $15 million to climate and environmental science in the 2014–2015 federal budget. Another possibility is the nature of Marshall's management. Having been previously a venture capitalist from Silicon Valley, Marshall has a mindset for running a business, not a research agency. He has been quoted speaking of how important turnover is in a healthy business, and Nadine Flood—"national secretary of the union in Haymarket that represents CSIRO employees"—has said that Marshall treats the agency as if it is a startup from Silicon Valley.

Dayton, Leigh. "Research Chief Cuts Climate Studies, Sets New Priorities." Science351.6274 (2016): 649. Web. <http://science.sciencemag.org/content/351/6274/649>.

Is Scott Pruitt Qualified to Run the EPA?
by Luis Salazar

Michael Biesecker and Matthew Daley, from The Washington Post, highlight several changes in Scott Pruitt's stance on climate change. The biggest difference being that the President-Elect's nominee for the Environmental Protection Agency (EPA) has finally confirmed that global warming is real. The Republican Attorney General continues to question the ability of scientists to come to a consensus on the relationship between human actions and climate change. He credits his disbelief of fossil fuels as the main cause of climate change to contrasting research results. When asked about rising sea levels, Pruitt avoids the question altogether.

Senator Bernie Sanders pushes for a stricter stance, centering around the Attorney General's beliefs, but Pruitt believes it is not his responsibility to have a personal opinion on the matter in order to best enforce environmental friendly policies.

Both authors cite lawsuits Pruitt has joined, many of which Pruitt is criticized for siding with industries instead of regulations—including lawsuits against the EPA itself. When asked about the impending lawsuits, Pruitt mentions his goal to both regulate and promote economic growth. This stands out as contradictory because Pruitt's records show his relationship with big industries and their contributions to his political campaigns. It is difficult to promote environmentally friendly policies while being controlled by industries who would face the consequences of those regulations.

Both support and frustration were shown at Pruitt's hearing, some with the belief that the EPA would go down the drain if Pruitt is appointed and others with hopes of a creation of coal mining jobs. At the hearing, Pruitt is praised for having strictly enforced environmental laws as Oklahoma Attorney General even though records show the contrary. He is continually criticized for accepting money from energy companies and unknown donors, many who would be negatively affected by restrictions on carbon emissions.

The authors conclude the article by citing another example of Pruitt being criticized, where Pruitt seems to have made an unpopular and environmentally unfriendly decision of not taking action against the earthquakes in Oklahoma for the sake of the economy.

Biesecker, Michael, and Matthew Daly. In Break with Trump, EPA Pick Says Climate Change Isn't Hoax. The Washington Post. WP Company, 18 Jan. 2017

Coming After Trump
by Luis Salazar

President Trump, along with a Congress dominated by Republicans, have issued statements supporting the elimination of the Clean Water Act primarily because it causes an inconvenience to landowners. Lawyers filed a court brief warning Trump and his allies that they are ready to challenge any unconstitutional regulations.

Preparation for this battle comes in the form of advocacy groups. These groups have taken initiative in hiring more lawyers and consulting private firms with interests of volunteering. Donations are encouraged to compensate for the time spent reviewing laws and regulations.

Fear continues to rise for environmentalists as Trump's presidency is underway. After only a week, Trump signed an executive order to continue construction on the Keystone XL and Dakota Access pipelines, which had been previously stopped after weeks of protesting. Similarly, the GOP is trying to work around regulations to control the damage coal mining companies does to rivers.

Jim Burling, a litigator for nonprofits, questions the ability of a new president to affect the law making system because of its profound foundation. He claims that environmental agencies tend to overstate Trump's threats as a form of marketing and urgency. Environmentalists refute this statement by justly addressing the new administration's stance on climate change. Trump's executive order on the continuation of construction of the Dakota Access Pipeline has encouraged the organization Earthjustice to hire more attorneys to speak on behalf of the Standing Rock Sioux tribe. The added attorneys are intended to oversee and file citizen suits pro bono if organizations do not execute proper restrictions on polluters.

Leading up to the inauguration, lawyers showed their support for the 2015 rule that grants the Environmental Protection Agency power to control water. Agencies are being monitored to ensure the proper enforcement of water regulations. Battling Trump is going to require going to the courts and limiting his ability to purge scientific data.

Climate Change & The Humanities

The Associated Press. Environmentalists Preparing to Battle Trump, GOP in Court. The New York Times. The New York Times, 29 Jan. 2017.

Regulating from Within the State
by Luis Salazar

Environmentalists are frustrated with the Trump administration. Trump continually challenges the Paris agreement, which attempts to put a limit on global warming. Along with President Trump, Rex Tillerson, Secretary of State, and Scott Pruitt, the Environmental Protection Agency's next leader, are unwilling to maintain the priority of addressing climate change—most notably, Obama's Clean Power Plan.

States and cities are battling the Trump administration by continuing to acknowledge and implement climate regulations. Companies are doing so with the intention of helping long-term business and health. The author, Jessica Green, cites the C40 Cities enterprise as an example of cities fighting climate change. Over eighty cities, thirteen in the United States, have established a plan to measure and report emissions. Similarly, the Carbon Neutral Cities Alliance has committed to reducing emissions by more than fifty percent in the next decades.

New York anticipates environmental changes, and has subsequently initiated plans to aid disaster. Miami is contributing to battling sea level rise by introducing a plan worth nearly $100 million. States do not require a federal regulation in order to participate in fighting climate change. California, for example, has proven itself by reducing gas emissions and extending state regulations to international affairs.

The California effect is popularly described as federal regulations being changed to meet California state regulations. State laws, similar to those in California, encourage the use of renewable energy; about ten percent of the energy consumption in the U.S. is a result of renewables.

According to author Green, CEOs do not deny climate change because they experience the effects directly, whether it be a drought or flood. Preparation for climate change is imperative, as it helps deal with negative impacts. RE100, a campaign for the U.S. including 32 U.S. companies, has volunteered to switch over to a 100 percent renewable energy.

Energy from coal is becoming more rare. Green argues that even though the administration may be intimidating, Decarbonizing has never seemed more imperative than now that

160

climate change is happening at an alarming rate. Progress will not be shut down by the Trump administration.

Green, Jessica F. The Trump Administration Can't Entirely Roll Back Progress on Climate Change. Here's Why. The Washington Post. WP Company, 10 Feb. 2017.

Rallying for Science
by Luis Salazar

Scientists from all over gather at Copley Square on Sunday to stand in solidarity against the Trump administration, citing the importance of nonpartisan information when creating regulations and acknowledging the severity of climate change. Naomi Oreskes, a Harvard historian, argues that science was politicized by the Trump administration, not scientists themselves. Similarly, Oreskes condemns the attacks on scientists as vengeance for discoveries that have proven to be inconvenient to politicians.

Stand Up for Science, the rally that unfolded in Boston, was organized by many groups—more notably, the Natural History Museum, ClimateTruth.org, and Union of Concerned Scientists—in order to discredit the stereotypical image of scientists, one that pictures the profession as data-spewing engines. The rally flourished with posters, from "Make America Smart Again" to "Objective Reality Exists."

Perry Hatchfield, a PhD candidate at the University of Connecticut, is quoted supporting the vital role of science and education on the future of humans: "Anything less than support for both science and education jeopardizes human activity." According to Anne Rookey, an Information Technology Manager, scientists who attended the rally vary in political views, but have one commonality: science.

The author, Chris Mooney, discusses the importance of rallying against the Trump administration; in addition to challenging human effects on the earth, the administration has proceeded to delete information from government websites. Similarly, immigration restrictions limit the ability of many seeking refuge in the resources and technology of the United States.

The rally served as a preface to the event planned for Earth Day, April 22nd. The march scheduled for earth day has close to a million people registered and has the potential of demanding change from the Trump administration. Everyone is encouraged to march in support of science. If the message gets across loud and clear, there is hope for the movement in supporting scientists and science-based reasoning.

Mooney, Chris. 'We Did Not Start This Fight': In Trump Era's Dawn, Scientists Rally in Boston. The Washington Post. WP Company, 19 Feb. 2017.

Bold Nebraskans

by Alejandro Salvador

The year 2008 marked the commencement of a crucial event in climate change action. The Canadian pipeline construction company TransCanada began to build the Keystone XL pipeline in Nebraska, and with it began a display of community action in the fight against Climate Change. In *Nature Climate Change,* James P. Ordner discusses this event, and how it sets an exemplary model of community action in protection of natural resources.

The Keystone XL pipeline is the perfect example of what contentious politics studies. As defined by Ordner, contentious politics is a way to analyze community mobilizations. They present three elements: claim-makers, collective action, and government intervention. This presents the perfect framework to study social movements arising against energy projects. In Nebraska, TransCanada acted as the claim-maker, looking to intervene in the local agricultural-based community with a project of a large environmental magnitude. The community opposed the project, and multiple organizations emerged in representation of the concerned citizens. Organizations such as Bold Nebraska, the Nebraska Easement Action Team, and the Cowboy Indian Alliance represent the collective action, intertwined from the beginning with the claim-makers, and the constant government intervention present in the episode.

The community at Nebraska fits into the concept of "at-risks communities". When confronted with an energy development project, these communities must decide whether to accept it or not based on the risks at hand. Community action is not always certain; some communities may think that the benefits offset the costs, while others may not. It will depend on the community's risk perception and values. Ultimately, they have only to answers: to accept the project, or to challenge it.

The discussion leads to the question of why did the Bold Nebraska Model succeed, and what drives a community into collective action. In rural Nebraska, natural resources are vital for the functioning of a primarily agricultural society, and the community identifies deeply with them. The Keystone XL pipeline posed a threat to natural resources treasured by Nebraskans. They were worried the pipeline might leak hazardous substances into the Ogallala aquifer, which underlies

80% of the state, or might affect the sensitive Nebraskan Sandhills. Climate Change was another major concern. Nebraskans were worried about future generations of farmers, and the environmental obstacles that the pipeline could impose on them. The Bold Nebraskan model merged this concerns in the public debate. It brought culturally different people together under a common cause.

Bold Nebraska marks a precedent in the development of community action fighting climate change. Collective action is necessary in the fight for climate change, currently framed in market-centered solutions, and we ought to see more of it.

Ordner, James P., 2017 Nature Climate Change 7, 161-163: Community action and climate change
http://www.nature.com/nclimate/journal/v7/n3/pdf/nclimate3236.pdf

Climate Kids Earn Court Case to Demand Climate Stability from Trump Administration
by Kelly Watanabe

The "climate kids"—a group of 21 young American activists between the ages of 9 and 20—are suing the US government for neglecting to provide a stable climate. According to Parker (2017), the lawsuit argues that by ignoring climate change effects, the federal government violates constitutional rights—life, liberty, and property—and the public trust doctrine—a legal law which states that the government must protect public resources such as land and water. Jansen Hansen, a NASA climate scientist, believes that the lawsuit could be the cure to the "suicidal nature" of US climate and energy policy. Parker believes that hard scientific data is the essential driving force for winning the case. The science proves that the federal government's history of fossil fuel promotion and neglect of GHG emissions will create an unsustainable climate system that is unfit for future generations. Mary Wood, a University of Oregon environmental law professor, argues that pure science proves the severity of the court case as a matter of human survival.

The lawsuit was originally proposed against the Obama administration; now that the lawsuit earned a trial, President Donald Trump wants to cancel Judge Anne Aiken's decision to grant a trial. Under Trump, EPA Administrator Scott Pruitt disregarded and attempted to remove scientific records of carbon dioxide emissions and global warming from the EPA's website. Luckily, one week before Trump was sworn into office, lawyers expanded the court file by adding approved scientific evidence of climate change threats. According to Judge Aiken, the court case does not dispute the cause or effects of climate change; rather, the lawsuit aims to determine who—Congress or the Executive Branch—should manage climate change actions. The current lawsuit request asks the federal judge for a recovery plan to reduce carbon emissions from 400 to 350 ppm by 2100.

Parker predicts that the case may move up toward the Supreme Court and possibly be as influential as the 1954 Brown vs Board of Education case—which banned racial segregation in public schools—or the 2015 Obergefell vs. Hodges case—which legalized same-sex marriage. The "climate kids" are working toward creating a constitutional right to a stable climate.

Parker, L., 2017. 'Biggest Case on the Planet' Pits Kids vs. Climate Change. National Geographic Remodeling

Leadership for Climate Change Reform
by Kelly Watanabe

When the world faces a climate crisis, Bateman and Mann (2016) promote the urgent need for strong climate leaders. When bigger organizations fail to take action, smaller groups take up the responsibility. For example, when the US Congress ignored carbon emission policies, West Coast and New England state governors collaborated and took initiative to price carbon themselves. Bateman and Mann use the Paris Agreement as a representation of progressive climate change reform; it effectively outlines the problems and solution initiatives for potential policies, but Bateman and Mann argue that the Paris Agreement consortium lacks climate change leaders to fulfill the outlined responsibilities. To advance the Paris Agreement, leaders should not leave any policy or party behind. In the past, policy makers have often neglected major climate issues because of their complexity. However, the longer policy makers wait to take action, the more difficult and expensive climate action will become. Bateman and Mann present an unconventional approach to studying climate change action: leaders should think about climate change and humans as a "species-level adaptation" to a changing environment. This study involves studying what motivates people to change their environmental behavior. Scientists are trying to create a mathematical model human behavior and environmental factors, but the model is hard to create due to the complexity and great diversity of human populations. With further development,

Bateman and Mann predict that the model will greatly expedite the execution of climate change policies.

Bateman and Mann push for a balance of efforts across all committees to ensure analysis of complex climate issues from all views. Moreover, interdisciplinary meetings are necessary and encouraged for effective leadership. Policy makers should understand scientists, and technologists should understand economists.

Even though the Paris Agreement emphasizes strictly structured climate leadership, Bateman and Mann argue that adaptive leadership—using an open mindset to lead as an interdisciplinary group of leaders—is more effective because the leadership strategy prevents conflict within the leadership hierarchy. Separation of climate change departments—science, economics, psychology, government, etc.—hinders communication and creative collaboration.

Bateman, T., Mann, M., 2016. The supply of climate leaders must grow. Nature Climate Change 6, 1052-1054

The Call for the Teaching of Politics in Climate Science Education
by Annette Wong

In 2016, Data Systems Professor at the Massachusetts Institute of Technology, Noelle E. Selin along with colleague Lawrence Susskind, and University of California Santa Barbra Political Sciences professor Leah C. Stokes published a paper urging for higher education climate science programs to integrate policy literacy into their courses. Selin discusses the need for the public to simultaneously be educated in "science literacy" in hopes of closing the science-society gap in the fight against climate change. In this context, policy literacy is "the knowledge and understanding of societal and decision-making contexts required for conducting and communicating scientific research in ways that contribute to societal well-being" (Selin, 2016).

The benefits of policy literacy "taught alongside and as a complement to climate science concepts" is as follows. Firstly, policy literacy can aid climate scientists in communicating more efficiently with politicians and society. Secondly, policy literacy allows climate scientists to participate more effectively in large climate conferences. Thirdly, scientists who understand climate policy can conduct research that is more useful for society.

Finally, climate scientists will benefit from an increase in policy literacy as it can help them expand their professional careers.

To increase policy literacy in climate science education, Selin, Susskind, and Stokes suggests that students could engage in simulations, mimicking political climate change conferences. Selin and her team developed a role play simulation they coined "The Mercury Game", which simulates environmental treaty-making to improve students' science and policy knowledge. As well as in-class activities, Selin suggests that students should also engage in "hands-on policy experiences" in which they can directly interact with decision-makers and the rest of society. For example, students could participate as observers in COP-21. Another idea Selin has is to require students to utilize social media such as Twitter, to become more aware of mainstream public knowledge and social reactions to new climate change data.

By educating climate science students in the social and political discourse of climate change, Selin, Susskind, and Stokes believe that students will be encouraged to orient their work to alleviate the most critical challenges facing the earth's environment. The professors hope that by communicating more effectively with politicians and society, future climate scientists will be able improve both the public's knowledge of climate change and society's collective ability to mitigate it.

Selin, Noelle E., Leah C. Stokes, and Lawrence E. Susskind. "The Need to Build Policy Literacy into Climate Science Education." Wiley Interdisciplinary Reviews: Climate Change (2016): n. pag. Web.

Donald Trump Refuses to support current Environmental Regulations
by Annette Wong

Steven Overly, Economics and Business Journalism Fellow at Columbia University, and writer for The Washington Post, reported on President Donald Trump's criticism on the United State's "unnecessary" environmental regulations.

In his Washington Post article, Overly highlights the fact that Trump's main argument for the removal of environmental regulations, is that it will encourage the construction of factories, and thus expand jobs in the U.S.. Trump has even scheduled meetings with General Motors, Ford, and Fiat's CEOs in hopes to pressure them into producing more in the U.S., providing Americans with more manufacturing jobs.

Because of the Obama administration's pavement of strict environmental policy, particularly with restrictions in the fuel economy, the cost of producing automobiles has increased. Along with companies all over the U.S. beginning to make the transition to lower production of greenhouse gases, the rising cost of car production is passed onto buyers as higher prices. In addition to job cuts in factories to compensate for higher prices, this leads to high unemployment, particularly in the lower middle-class. Trump noted that "environmental regulations are out of control" and seeks to eliminate those he finds hostile to businesses. Overly points out the irony that despite holding strong grounds against these environmental regulations, Trump still claims he is "to a large extent, an environmentalist."

In response to Trump's statement, Daniel Becker, director of the Safe Climate Campaign, insisted that job creation does not have to come at the expense of environmental regulations. He claims encouraging people to drive less and participate less in the fuel economy will help consumers save money on gas and long-term oil dependence.

Despite strong opposition to reducing climate policy, analysts still expect Trump to ease those regulations, along with a reduction in corporate taxes, and a promise to increase factory jobs.

The question to whether the reboot of manufacturing jobs will remain controversial throughout Trump's presidency. The Trump Administration seems adamant on helping the United States' economy. Therefore, the question that now persists is to what extent is he willing to do so by sacrificing the long-term well-being of both the nation, and the rest of the world?

Overly, Steven, and David Nakamura. "Donald Trump Tells Detroit Auto CEOs That Environmental Regulations Are 'out of Control.'" The Washington Post, WP Company, 24 Jan. 2017, www.washingtonpost.com/news/innovations/wp/2017/01/24/donald-trump-tells-detroit-auto-ceos-environmental-regulations-are-out-of-control/?utm_term=.630ad33a01a9.

China Enters the Climate Change World
by Jason Yi

In early 2017, journalist Edward Wong wrote an article that analyzed China's stance on climate change. Earlier, Donald J. Trump made the statement that climate change is a "hoax" produced by China and expressed his desire to leave the global Paris Agreement which takes the initiative in reducing greenhouse gas emissions. Wong mentions that in previous years under president Obama's term, America pressured China to supply accurate annual coal consumption data. However, with Trump's desire to withdraw from the Paris Agreement, Wong believes that China will quickly lose its current aspiration to provide such accurate information. In the past, China has only submitted two coal consumption estimates for the years 1994 and 2005 while other nations have submitted three or more. Furthermore, on the previous census, China's coal powered energy use was 12–14% higher than the last estimate and in these censuses, it was evident that there existed consistent differences between provincial and national levels.

On a lighter note, Wong reports that it does appear that China has a desire to improve the accuracy of its data. Recently, at a news conference in Beijing, Xie Zhenhua, an "envoy" on climate change stated that because China is still a "developing nation," China's data may not be perfectly accurate when compared to the other countries' estimates. Wong also reports that China receives its "emissions data" from different data sources: the national government, the provincial government, businesses, and a planned cap and trade carbon market. In addition to that, Mr. Xie commented that China has been experimenting with 7 new "cap and trade markets" to prevent climate change. Such experiments are expected to launch by 2017 but will only take full effect in 2019 or 2020. Journalist Edward Wong ends the article on the note that based on the trend of previous years, researchers currently believe China's coal consumption rates are likely either to drop or remain static. It appears that as America backs out, China only now enters the world of Climate Change.

Wang, E. 2017. China Wants to Be a Climate Change Watchdog, but Can It Lead by Example? New York Times Jan 10

Obama's Final Actions on Climate Change
by Jason Yi

In 2016, Journalist Coral Davenport reported President Obama's recent statement to permanently ban offshore oil and gas drilling near the Arctic and Atlantic coast. In order to do so, Mr. Obama called upon a 1953 act known as the Outer Continental Shelf Lands Act which grants him with the jurisdiction to move independently. This action by President Obama essentially bans drilling in 98% of federally owned Arctic waters, along with the Atlantic shore, which estimates to 115, and 38 million acres respectively. Accompanying Mr. Obama's policy, the prime minister of Canada, Justin Trudeau also issued a ban on new drilling in Canadian Arctic waters.

While such actions help prevent further climate change, they also guarantee the safety of endangered species in the region from potential oil spills. Mr. Obama added that should the country continue to drill in those regions, even with "high safety standards," the risks of an oil spill are inevitably high and that the country lacks the capability to clean up a spill in a region with harsh conditions.

Newsperson Davenport additionally reports that it is evident that Mr. Obama's actions are in response to future President Donald J. Trump's assertion that climate change is a "hoax" created by China and that he would make fossil fuel drilling a key feature in his "economic program." In most situations, Trump would have the power to reverse or null most of Mr. Obama's new environmental regulations; however, Mr. Obama's innovative strategy of using the 1953 act may likely be enough to hinder any future actions by Trump. Opponents of the policy such as Andrew Radford, senior policy adviser with the American Petroleum Institute reports that he does not understand how such a policy could be permanent. Mr. Radford further noted that in previous years, President Bill Clinton used the same law as Mr. Obama to prevent oil and gas drilling from 300 million acres of land; however, President George W. Bush later "reinstated" around 50 million acres. Davenport ends on the note that as the legal conflict continues, a possible option for the Republicans is to amend the 1953 law, "explicitly allowing presidents to reverse the drilling bans of their predecessors." It appears that the cloudy situation will only clear up once Donald J. Trump begins his term.

Davenport, C. 2016. Obama Bans Drilling in Parts of the Atlantic and the Arctic New York Times Dec 20

Republicans' New Stance on Climate Change
by Jason Yi

John Schwartz (2017) begins by reporting that a group of Republican statesmen is taking a stance on climate change by calling for a tax on carbon emissions. The leader of this group is a former Secretary of State James A. Baker who stated that a carbon pollution tax is the "conservative climate solution." Although unsure of how the proposal will be met by Congress, Mr. Baker announced that the plan followed "conservative principles of free-market solutions," and therefore is confident that the Republicans will accept the proposal. Moreover, such a carbon tax is currently being met with approval by many Democrats and by major oil companies such as Exxon Mobil.

Mr. Baker's plan would essentially replace the current carbon tax known as the Clean Power Plan set by Obama's administration, which Trump strongly expressed his desire to repeal. The tax would be collected whenever fossil fuels enter the economy and is expected to raise around 200–300 billion dollars a year. Furthermore, the plan would return the money raised to consumers amounting to an estimated 2000 dollars a year.

Mr. Baker's plan is also expected to include "border adjustments." Such adjustments would increase the price of imported goods in order to account for countries that do not have such a system set in place. This will address future "free-rider nations" who will inevitably try gaining a price advantage over domestically taxed goods.

Currently, the plan has not been met with strong disapproval. However, Schwartz reports that the plan will inevitably be met with criticism from all sides. Democrats supporting the Clean Power Plan will likely criticize the plan along with many environmental supporters who would desire for the tax raised money to be used to promote renewable energy.

Schwartz ends on the note that such a plan is only a big issue because it was a widely held belief that many Republicans do not support any actions in response to climate change. However, it seems that the Republicans are now beginning to change their opinions.

Schwartz. J. 2017. 'A Conservative Climate Solution': Republican Group Calls for Carbon Tax. New York Times Feb 7

A Bumblebee Gets New Protection on Obama's Way Out
by Jason Yi

Tatiana Schlossberg and John Schwartz (2017) discuss a recent implementation by the Obama administration which increased protection for the bumblebee. In the past, bumblebees were commonly found in various regions across America. However, since the 1990s, the bumblebee population has been rapidly declining due to several factors, the most serious being climate change. As a result, the Fish and Wildlife Service recently classified bumblebee as endangered species. There was indeed a long delay between the 1990s and the recent classification. However, Federal wildlife officials added that the process of declaring a certain species as endangered generally takes multiple years to get finalized.

Moreover, there are reports that the populations of other species are also rapidly declining. One day before the new protection policy, the Fish and Wildlife Service stated that should the humans continue to ignore climate change, polar bears will soon disappear from Earth. Such results reveal that the world is already beginning to see the effects of climate change as more than 300 species have been listed as endangered during the Obama Administration compared to only 62 species during the George W. Bush administration.

As the populations of different species continue to decline, there will eventually be a chain reaction that causes other species to share the same fate. However, with the recent classification, certain methods of bumblebee protection could benefit other pollinators as well because they share similar habitats.

The article ends on the note that bumblebees are known to be "effective pollinators" because they will pollinate any plant without discrimination. Thus, without pollinators such as bumblebees, "forests, parks, shrubs," and even crops will inevitably be unable to sustain life. In the end, the consequence will only have detrimental effects on our own agriculture.

Schlossberg. T. Schwartz. J. 2017. A Bumblebee Gets New Protection on Obama's Way Out. New York Times Jan. 10

Trump Promoted Energy Efficiency Back in 2012

by Jason Yi

Hiroko Tabuchi (2017) examines the recent climate change dispute between the Obama and the Trump Administration. The Republican faction did not hesitate to ensure that it will uphold and continue to promote the "America First Energy Plan," which vows to discard any "unnecessary policies" regarding climate change.

However, there were reports in 2012 that Mr. Trump once played for the opposite team when he secured approximately one million dollars in "energy efficiency incentives and low interest loans" to remodel the Trump towers. Such new installments included: a new power system for trapping thermal energy, motion sensor hallway lights, and a cover on the rooftop to prevent the swimming pool from evaporating. Tabuchi reports that there are also other records of Mr. Trump actively promoting the idea of conserving energy for the Trump Towers. For instance, in 2011, the Trump Organization participated in several energy-saving projects which sought to rebuild buildings in Manhattan. Ultimately, the Trump Towers managed to reduce its energy use by 21%, saving approximately $300,000 in energy costs. The Trump Towers were at the top of promoting clean energy policies that the managers of other "Trump-branded properties" asked for energy advice. However, Tabuchi states that when asked to elaborate on the reason for Trump's sudden decision to reduce environmental regulations, both the Trump Organization and the White House would not respond.

According to a policy analyst at the Energy and Policy Institute, the most probable reason for Mr. Trump's previous eco-friendly actions was the prospect of gaining profit from upgrading to energy efficient resources. It seems that with Mr. Trump's position as a businessman coming to an end, he believes that he could create even greater profit by taking a different stance on climate change.

Tabuchi. Hiroko. 2017. Trump Got Nearly $1 Million in Energy-Efficiency Subsidies in 2012. New York Times March 3

Trump Discusses His Plans for Climate Change
by Jason Yi

Coral Davenport (2017) reports on President Trump's recent goal to nullify Barack Obama's existing climate change policies. While the exact agenda remains unknown, Mr. Trump has already acted by proposing a budget that would invalidate all existing climate change research and prevention programs while simultaneously cutting 31% of the Environmental Protection Agency's budget. It appears that Mr. Trump is still taking a few environmental precautions as he has yet to explicitly declare America's withdrawal from the 2015 Paris Agreement. However, Davenport reveals that at the current rate of policy reversal, it is impossible to satisfy the emission reduction goals set by the 2015 Paris Agreement. If such a situation were to arise, America would essentially be forced to withdraw from the accordance.

Furthermore, Davenport states that with the help of Scott Pruitt, the E.P.A administrator, Mr. Trump will rewrite Mr. Obama's current environmental regulations known as the Clean Power Plan. This action will even include negating Mr. Obama's previous order which requires federal organizations to bear in mind the consequences of climate change when allowing environmental permits. With such actions taking place, many scientists are quickly expressing their concern, especially because most of Mr. Trump's administration do not believe that climate change is a pressing issue.

Once Mr. Pruitt took the position as the head of E.P.A, many expected Mr. Trump to quickly take action and hold an announcement discussing his future plans to roll back on climate change regulations. However, the briefing was delayed multiple times, to which many believe was due to the legal challenges Mr. Trump's declarations pose along with the many internal strife occurring within the government. It seems that while the desire is strong, rolling back climate change regulations will not be a short and easy process.

Davenport. Coral. 2017. Trump Lays Plans to Reverse Obama's Climate Change Legacy.New York Times March 21

China Takes the Position as a Climate Change Leader
by Jason Yi

Edward Wong (2017) discusses the recent events that occurred in response to America shifting its stance on climate change. During the Obama administration, America took many steps to ensure that China would cut back on their emission of greenhouse gases. However, as President Trump took control of the white house, he immediately signed an executive order that would nullify previous climate change efforts. Such an order may also lead America's decision to leave the 2015 Paris Agreement.

Wong further reports that in the absence of the United States in the agreement, China has indicated its desire to assume America's role as the climate change leader. Chinese officials have already began urging all countries tied to the Paris Agreement to abide by their commitments and added the fact that China will fulfill its responsibilities regardless of the actions of other countries. Moreover, a state-run newspaper known as the Global Times called America's move "irresponsible and very disappointing," further questioning how China, an underdeveloped country can use its resources to better the planet while the rich western countries simply stand by motionless.

Even before Trump's administration, China has made efforts to transition from fossil fuel to energy efficient resources. However, due to Mr. Trump nullifying climate change policies, it is more likely that many of China's pro-coal energy companies will make an even greater effort to resist the limitations on fossil fuel sources. Yet, China continues to promote the Paris Agreement, and recently stated that it will implement a cap-and-trade program which will impose a tax on carbon to limit release of carbon dioxide. It seems that as America takes one step backward, China, on the other hand, is taking the initiative to create a safe environment for its' own citizens.

Wong. Edward. 2017. China Poised to Take Lead on Climate After Trump's Move to Undo Policies. New York Times March 29

China's Smog Issue Worsens with Climate Change
by Jason Yi

Javier C. Hernandez (2017) reports on China's current atmosphere condition. With the 2015 Paris Agreement, China has been actively trying to reduce the level of carbon emissions in order to deal with the severe air pollution. Such efforts were believed to have led to moderate success. However, Hernandez reveals a new report that suggests an issue preventing China from achieving their goal.

Wind usually helps scatter the excess smog, but continually rising temperatures are causing shifts in the weather pattern leading to a decrease of wind throughout northern China. As a result, many cities located in the region are currently suffering from poor atmosphere ventilation. Scientists recount a more severe example that developed in Beijing (2013). The event had brought dangerous levels of "the concentration of PM2.5 particles" which could easily pierce through the bloodstream and harm the individual. Currently, scientists are blaming the event on the "stagnant air conditions" along with the quickly thawing ice in the Arctic.

Hernandez further discusses how such events have lead China to strengthen their climate change policies by further reducing greenhouse emissions during a time when America is taking the opposite role. While China is rapidly and successfully closing down hundreds of coal-fueled power plants, it runs into a problem during the winter when the weather conditions are favorable for smog. As a result, the Ministry of Environmental

Protection has recently issued a statement to reinforce their climate change policies for the winter.

As people closely examine this issue, many are quickly realizing that solving China's air pollution alone will not solve the problem globally. As a result, it is important that the world does more than simply address local emission problems and work together to attain a healthy planet.

Hernandez. Javier. 2017. Climate Change May Be Intensifying China's Smog Crisis. New York Times March 24

Human Displacement and Climate Change

Climate Change Driving Urbanization in Africa
by Bryn Edwards

In this article from the New York Times, the author Nicholas Kristof describes a recent trip to Madagascar. A severe drought in sub-saharan Africa has wrecked havoc among the natives, with an estimated 1.3 million people suffering from starvation and malnutrition. Kristof describes scenes from a horror movie, of zombie-like children so hungry that they are forced to eat ash or boiled chalk. One million people in Madagascar alone need emergency food assistance, according to estimates made by the U.N. These communities are direct victims of climate change. The droughts across southern Africa were originally caused by an extremely warm El Niño which reduced rainfall in the affected parts of Africa, and was exacerbated by climate change. Lack of rain caused crop failure which has lead to the famine today. According to scientists studying the situation, water runoff in southern Africa has been reduced by 48% because of climate change. Kristof argues that the United States is helping with famine relief, it is a disproportionately small amount of aid in light of the fact that the United States alone is the cause of one quarter of carbon emissions in the past 150 years, double any other country's emissions. To Kristof, it seems unfair that the United States is also one of the least affected countries by climate change. Kristof makes a poignant point when he recognizes that Americans lose beach homes to rising waters, while southern Africans are losing their lives on the daily. He suggests increasing food-aid programs in the short-term, and focus on renewable energy and limiting carbon emissions in the long-term.

Kristof, Nicholas. As Donald Trump Denies Climate Change, These Kids Die of It. The New York Times.
https://www.nytimes.com/2017/01/06/opinion/sunday/as- donald-trump-denies-climate-change-these-kids-die-of-it.html

The Effects of Climate Change on Indigenous Alaskans
by Bryn Edwards

As temperatures rise in one of the coldest areas of the planet almost twice as fast as the rest of the planet, the indigenous peoples face drastic lifestyle changes. Thirty-one towns/cities in Alaska are directly threatened by melting ice or coastal erosion. While this season was approximately 3.5° C warmer than a century ago, some areas are up to 20 ° C above the long-term average of the past. Ice coverage has shrunk about 888,000 sq. miles. Such extreme environmental changes have a profound effect on indigenous societies. Even the dialect is changing, as words used to describe sea ice are slowly becoming phased out, since the ice no longer exists. The Yupik people have more than a dozen words to describe ice since much of their livelihood depends on it. Words like "tagneghneq" (thick, dark, weathered ice) no longer serve a purpose. Furthermore, and with a much more direct impact, food sources are becoming harder and harder to find. With basic food staples like milk priced at about $15 a gallon, natives depend on hunting for sustenance. Walruses are the keystone species of their lifestyles, but every year the numbers caught decrease at almost exponential rates. The largest settlement, Gambell, caught about 600 walruses a year in the past. In 2016, they caught 36. Hunters are at a greater risk every year as the sea ice grows thinner, while walruses are forced into crowded patches of safe ice or land; where unnaturally high population densities can lead to walruses being trampled to death. Natives are watching their way of life melt away with the ice as houses sink with no permafrost to hold them up, and as storms hit harder and faster with no ice or coastline to protect the seaside villages.

Milman, Oliver. Climate change is wreaking havoc on indigenous people in Alaska. The Guardian. http://www.businessinsider.com/climate-change-alaska-2016-12.

The Threat of Climate Change to Tibetan Nomads
by Claudia Chandra

In 2016, Jane Qiu, a freelance writer from Beijing travelled across the Tibetan Plateau under the sponsorship of the SciDev.Net Investigative Science Journalism Fellowship for the Global South. She wanted to explore how the rapid changes in Tibetan grasslands threaten the Yellow River and the livelihood of Tibetan nomads. While in Tibet, Qiu observed the climate-and policy-related challenges that befall Tibetan herders who rely on yaks for most of their livelihood—milk, butter, meat, and fuel.

Tibet was annexed by China in 1950. During the 1980s, when China began moving towards a market-based economy, the government privatized pastures in the Tibetan grasslands and gave yaks back to individual households in hopes of boosting productivity. However, starting in the 1990s, the government began implementing policies that forced herders into settlements, limited herd sizes, and drastically reduced grazing space. The problems associated with such policies are understated by the official reports released by the Chinese government, which claim that these policies have instead helped to "restore the grasslands and improve standards of living for the nomads." Qiu and other researchers argue that evidence suggests the opposite; such policies are harmful for both the environment and herders. This is mainly because "the policies are not guided by science, and fail to take account of climate change and regional variations."

In the last two decades, the government has implemented policies to regulate and separate households and villages. As more nomads lead settled lives, it has become easier to control heavily grazing in heavily populated areas. Nevertheless, convenience comes at a price. Fenced pastures degrade more quickly and do not encourage the growth of sedge, the main food for livestock. A 2013 study by Cao *et al.* studied the growth of sedge in enclosed pastures versus larger pastures. Their experiment showed that "despite similar livestock densities in both cases, the sedge grew twice as fast in the larger pastures" because animals were freer to roam and plants had more opportunities to recover.

In the Western part of the country, where altitude is higher and climate is more arid, is the beginning of the Yellow River. Here, Qiu observed that wetlands had dried up and sand dunes had replaced prairies. This indicates that water flowing into the Yellow River is decreasing, leading to recurring water shortages downstream in places where the river has completely dried up "well before it reaches the sea." Such events were not ever recorded before 1970.

As the landscape of the Tibetan plateau and grasslands continue to change, there is growing concern about the changes of vegetation of the area. Sedge species, of the *Kobresia* genus, that previously dominated the Tibetan landscape and fed the livestock, are now being driven away by other vegetation. This creates a threat to the environment as carbon that has been locked up by the sedge may be released and contribute to global warming. Furthermore, a greater variety of poisonous weeds that have only recently been found in the Tibetan grasslands have spread throughout 160,000 square kilometres and killed tens of thousands of animals each year. Changes in vegetation composition poses a significant implication for long-term carbon storage as a shift from sedge to taller grasses will eventually unleash a "carbon sink that has remained buried for thousands of years."

Critics of the new grazing restrictions have complained that the government has blindly imposed these regulations upon them without scientific findings or a proper understanding of their potential consequences. Qiu believes that "having a sweeping grazing policy regardless of geographical variations is a recipe for disasters." Her claim is supported by scientists such as Tsechoe Dorji, who found that the government's way of classifying the health of grasslands is misleading. This is because they only consider the percentage of land covered by vegetation and use this same threshold for all areas, regardless of differing elevations or moisture levels.

Qiu's study points out the need for climate change mitigation and better government policies in the Tibetan plateau. Tibet is a climate change hotspot that experiences a 0.3 – 0.4°C increase in temperature per decade, nearly twice the global average. Furthermore, researchers currently do not have enough information to create models that can accurately predict the extent to which global warming will affect the Tibetan landscape. Science and the government need to undertake studies that can produce policies that work as adaptation strategies. To begin, Qiu suggests a "comprehensive survey of plant cover and vegetation composition at key locations across different climate regimes." The data gathered from such studies provide the basis from which more effective regulations can be created.

Unfortunately, however, Qiu and other scientists do not believe that such actions and reforms will occur soon. This is because as Tibet's resistance to Chinese control continues to rise, the Chinese government is more concerned with maintaining political stability than with scientific research. According to Qiu, this incorrect prioritization could potentially have devastating and irreversible effects onto the Tibetan landscape, which is why it is important to gather support and research to address these issues as quickly as possible.

Qui, Jane., 2016. "Trouble in Tibet." Nature. Vol 529, 142 – 145.

http://www.nature.com/polopoly_fs/1.19139!/menu/main/topColumns/topLeftColum
n/pdf/529142a.pdf

Climate Change and its Effect on Migration Policies

by Chris Choi

Amy Louise Constable (2016) examines the effects of climate change and how they may lead to the migration of people from the Tuvalu and the Marshall Islands. Low-lying coastal areas are most affected by sea level rise (SLR), and SLR rates are increasing. The author notes that if this trend continues, people from Tuvalu and the Marshall Islands may have to migrate to another country. One problem to migration is that it is a politicized issue which may close off potential migration options. Overall, Constable tries to analyze the practicality of certain migration options as well as their legality.

It is challenging to relate migration to the effects of climate change, for people must first distinguish what circumstances would allow climate change-related migration to occur. One media analysis looked at several options for migration and thought to name the people who had to leave as climate change refugees. However, some organizations disapproved of this for they believed that the term 'refugee' has a very narrow meaning. They believe that a refugee is subject to persecution for race, nationality, or religion. Relating this term with climate change was met with criticism. One idea was to allow the gradual migration of Tuvalu and the Marshall Islands to New Zealand. New Zealand agreed to allow seventy-five Tuvaluans migrants per year under the Pacific Access Category, or PAC. However, they were warned not to put in labor schemes as potential migration pathways, for it could limit the number of migrants that would be able to come into New Zealand. These labor schemes are like prerequisites that must be met for these seventy-five migrants to enter New Zealand. Some of the requirements include being proficient in English as well as already being employed before they migrate. These conditions may lower the number of migrants that enter per year. The Marshall Islands made an agreement with the USA in 1986 called the Compact of Free Association (CFA) which allows Marshallese citizens to enter the USA, but for many Marshallese, the cost is too high.

New Zealand and Australia seemed unwilling to allow climate change migrants to their countries. Another plan involves resettling the people, but most of the areas considered are under customary ownership and can neither be bought nor sold, but only given through kinship arrangements. In any case, many Tuvaluans and the Marshallese people wish to stay in their land. They believe their land is the home of their culture and they wish to die there. Others are willing to migrate and are attracted to better job opportunities and services. Constable believes that we need to create a term that describes climate change-related migration. This would help everyone understand under what circumstances migration is acceptable as well as other rights migrants may expect to receive when they migrate. Though climate change and its effects are pressing issues, there is still time for policymakers to determine the most efficient way to migrate and help the people.

Constable, A., 2016. "Climate change and migration in the Pacific: options for Tuvalu and the Marshall Islands". Regional Environmental Change, 1-10. http://link.springer.com/article/10.1007/s10113-016-1004-5

How Climate Change Affects Human Migration in Sub-Saharan Africa
by Chris Choi

Clark Gray and Erika Wise (2016) analyzed how recent climate changes may have affected human migration in Sub-Saharan Africa. They mainly looked at Kenya, Uganda, Nigeria, Burkina Faso, and Senegal when conducting their research. In each of these countries, there is a high dependence on agriculture, and as temperatures have increased, residents have needed to find more resources and adapt to their new environment. Researchers found that past studies have only analyzed one climate data source while ignoring evidence that climate anomalies result from multiple factors. They analyzed both temperature and precipitation rates.

The researchers derived their data from the African Migration and Remittances Surveys (AMRS) which gathered data on international and internal migration for approximately 2000 households in each country. People told AMRS the reasons for their migration as well as where they were migrating to. Approximately 9,800 households were surveyed over a six-year period. Researchers then defined migration as the number of migrants who are ten years or older and left their homes in a certain year. They then analyzed temperature and precipitation anomalies relative to a base time period (1981 – 2010). Based on these two factors, temperature seems to have a negative effect on agricultural output across Sub-Saharan Africa while precipitation tends to have positive effects, but the latter effect is not consistent.

The only country whose migration rates increased as temperature increased was Uganda. The other countries were relatively unaffected or showed decreased levels of migration. The researchers then combined their results with the second climate data set: precipitation rates. They conducted a test to see which combination of climate conditions would lead to the highest levels of migration in each country, finding that in Kenya, cool and rainy seasons would lead to the most human migration while in Uganda and Nigeria it was warm and rainy weather that caused higher levels of migration. In summary, Clark Gray and Erika found that the variability of temperature had a larger effect on internal than on international migration, and that found variations in precipitation do not have a consistent positive or negative effect on migration.

Gray, C., & Wise, E. (2016). Country-specific effects of climate variability on human migration. Climatic change, 135(3-4), 555-568.

Climate Change and Refugees
by Ethan Kurz

When thinking about climate change, the usual thought process leads to comments about changing weather patterns and how the world is heating up. However; according to Carment, Betrand, and Yiagadeesen; climate change shouldn't be looked at from a scientific method, it should be looked at from a humanities perspective, and that is where the connection between Refugees and climate change emerges. Climate change has a large impact on developing countries, specifically countries with high fragility ratings. Climate change affects the development, security, and legitimacy of a state in addition to changing just the environment. The development or infrastructure of a country can be affected adversely though worsening weather conditions due to climate change. The security of a country can also be affected through extreme weather events, which are getting more common because of climate change. The legitimacy of a state may be brought into question as climate change causes bad conditions and the relocation of people. The effects of climate change on development, security, and legitimacy affect the poorest of the poor the most and cause these people to become displaced or refugees.

As a result of climate change, institutions must be put in place to help protect the people. These institutions must have authority, capacity, and legitimacy. The problem is that the already fragile nations may not have the ability to create institutions to protect their people. With the current negative state of institutions in fragile countries, climate change will have a great toll and cause the amount of refugees we see in the coming years to increase greatly. If climate change related relocation movements or refugee movements are to be avoided, larger countries with the economy and ability to help fragile countries must put their resources to use and help. Even though refugees stem from many things, climate change is significant in the relocation of people.

Carment, David; Langlois-Betrand, Simon; and Samy, Yiagadeesen. "Assessing State Fragility, With a Focus on Climate Change and Refugees: A 2016 Country Indicators for Foreign Policy Report." Country Indicators for Foreign Policy (2016): n. pag. Web. 21 Jan. 2017. <http://reliefweb.int/report/world/assessing-state-fragility-focus-climate-change-and-refugees-2016-country-indicators>.

The Impacts of Climate Change on Children
by Ethan Kurz

When thinking about climate change, usually children do not come to mind. However, according to Rema Hanna and Paulina Oliva (2016), children in developing countries are an important aspect to remember when discussing climate change. Climate change is more dangerous to children in developing countries than in developed countries because of the developing countries' limited social safety nets, extreme poverty, poor or no health care systems, and weak governments unable to help the poorest of the poor adapt to climate change. Children in developing countries already start off at a disadvantage, and climate change just increases the difficulty in raising a healthy and thriving child. Most of the population in developing countries relies on agriculture for income. With climate change and the resulting new extreme weather patterns, agriculture becomes even less reliable as an income source. A drought could cut off the chances of a child getting medical attention because the family cannot afford it. Children in developing countries also face greater risks of interaction with air or water pollutants. Because of the lack of a strong central government or regulation, children in developing countries have fewer things protecting them from airborne and waterborne contaminants. They also face threats from more parasitic diseases, plagues, and anything that can be contributed to changes in weather pattern or climate change.

According to Hanna and Oliva, the international community must come together to help shield children from threats due to climate change. But, the international community must also respect each nation's sovereign rights. Some policies that should be developed include funding of research, creating more weather resistant crops creating better access to clean water, and help developing countries create safety net programs for all of their citizens. If we come together as a globe, we have a chance of helping the most in need.

Hanna, R. & Oliva, P., 2016. Implications of Climate Change for Children in Developing Countries. The Future of Children, vol. 26 no. 1, pp. 115-132. <https://muse.jhu.edu/article/641237/pdf>.

Alaskans and Climate Change
by Ethan Kurz

The Inupiat people have hunted and fished on Alaska's western coast for centuries, but a new danger is appearing which threatens their lifestyle. Flooding, by fall storms, is the imminent threat created by climate change. Alaska is warming at twice the rate of any other state in the United States. The villages most in danger are the smallest ones with not enough people and infrastructure to get funding to move from the government. It costs upwards of 200 million dollars to move a small village. That leaves small villages with a difficult choice: move or stay. Moving would be nearly impossible due to a lack of funding from government, but staying would mean greater danger each year.

Villages that are in this sticky situation have to come up with their own solutions. A village called Shaktoolik has constructed a berm to serve as a barrier between them and the ever encroaching ocean. They built the berm themselves because the state engineers ran out of money designing it. This berm gives this village some hope, but the village mayor, Eugene Asicksik, says it is only a temporary solution and the government needs to step in. The flood related erosion is threatening all of the village's key resources: water supply, airport, and fuel tanks. Another huge problem this village is beginning to face is how to keep village residents safe in a storm. No current plan exists and is good enough to prevent loss of life. Shatoolik, as a village, has a wish list: evacuation road, better water supply and fuel storage, a new hospital, and some sort of shelter in case of emergencies. The problem with this wish list is that it costs over 100 million dollars.

The Obama administration's proposed 2017 budget included 400 million dollars to be sent to Alaska for relocating villages, but with the new administration that may not happen. Without any federal help, these villages will continue to be in danger, with no real solution.

Goode, Erica., 2016. A Wrenching Choice for Alaska Towns in the Path of Climate Change. The New York Times. <https://nyti.ms/2jWRdxJ >.

Climate Change and Mass Migration
by Ethan Lewis

An African Independent writer from the Washington Post investigated the large scale issue of mass human migration stemmed from climate change. The writer met with ANM Muniruzaman, a Bangladesh Politician, who recently attended an international migration policy meeting and said "The international system is in a state of denial." He then continued to say "If we want an orderly management of the coming crisis, we need to sit down now." Displacement of humans due to climate change is already ongoing with natural disasters like droughts, floods, and storms. Saying exactly how many people will have to migrate in the future is difficult, but statistics from previous years can help form an estimate. Roughly 203 million people were displaced between 2008 and 2015 due to natural disasters.

The rate of this migration is increasing and the repercussions will revolve around various countries efforts to plan in the future and take action in the present day. The African Independent continues the article with examples of migration that has happened. Desertification in Africa is causing major agriculture issues in tribes and cities causing thousands to find work elsewhere. Similarly, the Island nation of Kiribati which is at risk of being enveloped by rising sea levels will eventually have to migrate 100,000 citizens. The writer also addresses the vulnerability of South Asia because out of the 203 million people internationally displaced, 36% came from South Asia.

The African Independent also points out that a pattern is arising worldwide. Countries are addressing climate change but fail to bring any attention to migration policies and plans. Large numbers of migrants in countries could raise unemployment levels and crime rates around the world. Also, as islands disappear under rising seas, conflicts between countries could arise as they race to claim maritime territory. Unless migration is addressed, the world not only has a large humanitarian problem, but a security problem as well.

African Independent (2017, Jan 27)
Climate Change Mass Migration Threat:
    http://www.pressreader.com/search?query=climate%20change&languages=e
    n&hideSimilar=0

Climate Change and Migration
by Ethan Lewis

Kelly M. McFarland, a writer for the Washington Post, addresses the issue of how the detrimental effects of climate change force human migration. In 2015, the U.N. Refugee Agency counted 65.3 million people around the world as "forcibly displaced," including about 40 million within their home countries. Wars, ethnic conflicts, economic stresses, famines and disasters are among the reasons people leave their homes.

Less understood is how climate-induced environmental changes such as increased flooding, salinization, droughts or desertification, amplify these drivers of migration. Questions such as, what are the policy options to help people stay in place or minimize the security concerns related to migration are becoming more and more relevant. The Institute for the Study of Diplomacy at Georgetown University convened a working group on human migration and climate change. Bringing together experts on climate change, resource management, migration, foreign policy and national security. The group reported a number of guiding principles for policymakers and issues to keep an eye on.

First and foremost, tensions over water problems are very likely to rise according to the NIC. This could pose national security problems for many countries that undergo extreme droughts. Similarly, extreme weather events such as cyclones, storm surges, and hurricanes that hit unprepared communities will trigger people to evacuate areas. Another major problem involving migration is many displaced people heading to nearby cities. Many of these cities do have have the jobs, and capacity to keep up with these new residents.

Another observation that came up in the groups discussion is adequately defining environmental migrants. Those who relocate within their own nations rely on the protections and assistance of their government. But how do we identify and protect those who cross national borders in search of safety from environmental harm?

Lastly, planned relocations will be much more frequent. Countries are already developing land to cope with the migration crops and livestock coming inland from the coast. None of these challenges are easy to fix but many government organizations are looking for ways to reduce the risk of necessary migration.

McFarland, Kelly M., and Vanessa Lide. "Analysis | The effects of climate change will force millions to migrate. Here's what this means for human security." The Washington Post. WP Company, 23 Apr. 2017. Web. 23 Apr. 2017.

Human Health and Climate Change

The Largely Unacknowledged Impact of Climate Change on Mental Health
by Ellen Broaddus

Eva and Robert Gifford (2016) assess the relationship between climate change and mental health, looking at the environmental causes, effects, and social factors, the individuals and communities that are most vulnerable, and possible solutions. This largely untouched field of climate change research traces many of today's physical and mental diseases to the environmental uncertainty and fear-driven anger caused by both drastic and incremental weather pattern changes.

The most ubiquitous link emphasized the increase in climate-connected psychological responses: citing floods and droughts accompanying "anxiety, shock, depression, sleep disruptions", and heat waves being linked to increases in "homicide, suicide, and spousal abuse". In addition to these short-term reactions, environmental insecurity has led to long-term consequences, especially in children. Recently there has been a rise of respiratory conditions and asthma as a result of air pollution, causing anxiety for children and their families. The link between natural disasters and prevalence of social withdrawal and PTSD has been shown to alter the stress responses of adolescents, putting them at "higher risk for later health challenges".

Seniors and Americans of lower socioeconomic status are also disproportionately affected because they have fewer physical and economic resources available, making it difficult to develop effective coping mechanisms. Arguably most affected are those already struggling with mental illness. In addition to disasters exacerbating "preexisting limitations to access to mental health care", weather changes increase the symptoms of "mood disorders, substance abuse, [and] reactive psychoses", while medications used for treatment often "impair the body's heat regulation ability" and lead to more trauma and hospitalizations.

While certain individuals are affected most, Gifford and Gifford stress that this is a universal issue. It is estimated that climate change will cause emotional distress in 200 million Americans, threatening increased social vulnerability, societal incoherence, inequality, anger, and distrust. This is seen on both a personal and diplomatic level, as politicians predict climate change to become the "primary cause of conflict globally". Other effects are subtler, such as the decreased nutritional value of many foods due to increased CO_2 levels. This magnifies the already monumental issue of malnutrition and leads to widespread fatigue and depression.

Despite the seemingly negative rhetoric, the authors suggest positive steps can be made using the media, education and health care systems, and increased research on the issue. They advocate distribution of positive and encouraging, yet consistent and accurate, information about climate change, as well as increased funding of mental health structures and research on coping mechanisms. Mostly, the authors express the need for individual and community empowerment and promoting trust and social collaboration.

Gifford, E; Gifford, R. 2016. The largely unacknowledged impact of climate change on mental health. Bulletin of the Atomic Scientists, 72, 292-297. http://www.tandfonline.com/doi/abs/10.1080/00963402.2016.1216505

Climate Change and the Spread of Tropical Pathogens
by Claudia Chandra

In an article for Nature, Emily Sohn explores the relationship between climate change and the spread of tropical pathogens into the Northern hemisphere. She studied an occurrence from 2009 when a dog in Scotland was diagnosed with *Angiostrongylus vasorum*, a disease also known as lungworm and French heartworm. This infection comes from eating parasite-carrying snails and slugs, which were previously limited to warmer tropical regions. This case became evidence that the parasite was travelling northwards, especially to places such as Scotland where average temperatures "have risen by more than 1°C over the previous four decades." A study found the same parasite in 11% of slugs and snails in a park near the home of the aforementioned infected dog. Currently, scientists still cannot calculate the rate of *vasorum* infection among dogs, but cases of the disease have also been reported in Sweden, Germany, and the United States.

Like *vasorum,* many other types of parasites are benefiting from global warming through expanding into new territory. Other rampant pet diseases include "mosquitoes, ticks, and flies, such as heartworm, lungworm, Lyme disease and leishmaniosis. Sohn claims that understanding how diseases are changing among pets could help predict where pathogens might spread in the future. It may also help us to "better prevent, recognize, and treat outbreaks." As well as pet health, human health may also benefit from this research. As humans and animals are affected by numerous identical vector-borne diseases, animals can "act as sentinels" for threats to human health.

Sohn notes that in humans, diseases including malaria, cholera, and dengue have spread to areas where average temperatures are on the rise. For pets, heartworm (*Dirofilaria immitis)* is the largest cause for concern as this parasite, historically, could only be found in the South. As of the 1980s, heartworm has begun to infiltrate Northern countries including Hungary, Switzerland, and Poland.

Sohn cites Eric Morgan, a veterinary parasitologist at the University of Bristol, who claims that "climate is undoubtedly a factor" of the spreading of parasites. Nevertheless, this implication of climate change is also caused by other environmental influences. Sohn uses a study conducted by Donato Traversa at the University of Teramo in Italy to exemplify this point. Teramo studied the diseases in pets rescued after Hurricane Katrina in 2005. After the disaster, mosquitoes "flourished in flooded areas" and many pets lost their homes. They were forced to spend more time outdoors and became more vulnerable to the growing mosquito population. As these animals were put in shelters, Traversa found that among the 414 dogs and 56 cats rescued, more than 50% of them "had been infected with at least one disease, and many had signs of multiple illnesses." Even though many of these infections existed before Katrina, the dispersal of these rescue pets into other parts of the United States where vets may not think to test for them posed a significant health threat. Thus, even though climate may create the perfect conditions for the spread of a parasite, it is often other situations that allow the disease to emerge in the first place.

To get a better understanding of climate change's role in transmitting diseases, scientists try to create maps and models of conditions that allow certain parasites to multiply. They also use them to make predictions about where particular parasites may spread next. Some relationships are straightforward; warmer water means more mosquitoes as larvae develop more rapidly and adults feed more to produce more eggs. If temperatures are warm enough, mosquitoes can also be infectious year-round. Sohn states that "there is fairly good evidence for a role for climate change, but it would be unfortunate if that were the only emphasized environmental change in a deeper story." She demonstrates this through deforestation, which is driving many predators of rodents, hosts for ticks, into extinction. The decreasing number of predators allow more rodents, and therefore ticks, to breed.

Unfortunately, it is impossible to conduct controlled climate experiments for every type of parasite. Furthermore, there is a huge potential for wide variation as different species do not respond to climate change identically. Therefore, as quoted by Sohn, "warmer climate doesn't universally translate into more disease." Each pathogen has its unique ideal temperature range, and all have limits. For instance, extremely warm temperatures can make mosquitoes less active. The relationships between pathogens and their hosts may also change with climate. Thus, Sohn concludes that "not all host-parasite interactions are going to experience the same sort of effects of climate change." Nonetheless, understanding these interactions are valuable as then "perhaps we can do something about it."

Sohn, Emily., 2017. "Hothouse of Disease." Nature. Vol 543, 45–46

Failure to Address Global Warming Will Cost Many Lives
by Bryn Edwards

Climate change has wide-spread, sweeping and deadly-serious impacts on more than just the environment. In 2005, the death toll associated with climate change was an estimated 150,000 people, and just ten years later in 2005 it was estimated at 400,000. Tago and Thomas (2015) attributed the deaths to three main categories: extreme weather (direct), environmental/ecosystem changes (indirect), and societal systems. Extreme weather is becoming more and more common as temperatures increase. Heat waves, flooding, hurricanes and tsunamis are occurring at higher frequencies. Warmer weather also increases biodiversity, by allowing disease-carrying organisms to spread to more northern regions. Societal effects make up the highest percentage of the climate change-related deaths. When crops die, a lack of food leads to population stress and conflict over limited resources, and eventually causes malnutrition which then in turn puts stress on the health care systems as well. Overall, climate change will put more pressure on unstable areas. For example, it is estimated that in 2030, over 98% of "deaths related to climate change will occur in developing countries." Already, limited resources lead to conflict across the world. Even scarcer resources with simply exacerbate existing situations and go on to create new ones. The refugee crisis that President Trump is failing to handle will only be multiplied in the coming years, with an exponentially increasing number of people displaced by climate change needing a new home. A lack of action on climate change by the United States, a world leader, will only make matters worse.

Tago, D. and Thomas, A., 2015. Failure to address global warming will cost many lives. The
Economist.http://www.economist.com/blogs/freeexchange/2015/12/climate-change.

Global Warming's Effects on West Nile Virus Infections
by Matt Johnson

A study lead by Sara H. Paull and A. Marm. Kilipatrick (2017) analyzed the effects of climate change on West Nile Virus epidemics in the United States. The study specifically targeted mosquitoes, but as the authors note, the findings are applicable to many other vectors and viruses.

Global warming is already providing evidence of how changes in climate temperature affect precipitation. Depending on the region, global warming's effect on precipitation levels can be in either direction.

Increased precipitation levels affect the replication rates of mosquitos. In already wet regions, like the eastern United States, increased precipitation flushes out mosquito nests, whereas decreased precipitation increases the quality of those same breeding grounds. In drier climates, increased precipitation increases the abundance and replication of mosquitos. In both scenarios, drought increases contact between virus vectors and hosts, "due to host movement to mosquito habitats".

On the temperature side, global warming is likely to increase the risk of disease in colder regions: specifically, those where virus transmission is limited by low temperatures. The study doesn't mention whether the direct effects of increasing temperatures decrease infection prevalence in already warm regions.

This study analyzed mosquito data across the U.S., but specifically focused on Colorado. The authors found that drought "was correlated with elevated infection prevalence in the two most important mosquito vectors in the state...", however the infection prevalence was "uncorrelated with mosquito abundance". The direct relationship between drought levels and infection prevalence implies that other factors are involved with infection rates, as droughts tended to decrease vector abundance. The authors suggested that droughts may lead to fewer predators, or increase vector-host contact frequency.

The authors also found that the prevalence of infections was highly dependent upon immunity rates within a population. This being considered, the authors predicted that increases in drought could double West Nile virus infections nationally, with even more infections in regions of low immunity; like Virginia. The authors' model predicted an eight-fold increase in the number of West Nile infections in this state, due to the low immunization rate. States with high immigration levels or different demographics could also be at increased risk. While precipitation patterns change in more temperate climates, warming at higher latitudes will widen the season for vector reproduction, and therefore increase the prevalence of infections. Because of the increasing drought prevalence throughout the US, vector-borne disease transmission rates in general are going to change. These variations must be studied on a case-by-case basis if we are to stay ahead of the problem.

Paull, S.H., Horton, D.E., Ashfaq, M., Rastogi, D., Kramer, L.D., Diffenbaugh, N.S. and Kilpatrick, A.M., 2017, February. Drought and immunity determine the intensity of West Nile virus epidemics and climate change impacts. In Proc. R. Soc. B (Vol. 284, No. 1848, p. 20162078). The Royal Society.

Climate Change's Effects on Allergies
by Matt Johnson

The prevalence of allergies has seemingly spiked in the last few decades. Some of this may be due to more advanced processes by which we are able to identify allergies, but an article lead by Kathrin Reinmuth-Selzle and Christopher Kampf (2017) states that such prevalence "has genuinely increased with industrialization and the adoption of a "Western" lifestyle". But why is that so?

Since pre-industrial times, we have seen a strong increase of carbon dioxide, ozone, nitrogen oxides, and numerous types of particulate matter in the atmosphere. The combination of these has been shown to have induced chemical modifications in many allergens. This is only one of the problems. The risk factors for allergic diseases are dependent upon one's genes, childhood exposure to pathogens and parasites, diet, stress, and pollution levels in one's environment. The increases in pollutants and particles in the air, combined with global warming, have changed everything from vegetation cover to pollination patterns. The authors note that these changes have skewed biological processes toward the development of allergies. The most major causes for this development have been increased oxidative stress and inflammation. "The imbalance between oxidants and antioxidants in favor of oxidants can lead to irreversible damage of cellular lipids, proteins, nucleic acids, and carbohydrates, eventually resulting in cell death".

As anyone who has allergies knows, high winds tend to be unfriendly. Unfortunately, the frequency of high winds and dust storms is predicted to increase in the following years. Dust particles, consisting of both organic and inorganic particles, are known to travel with pathogens and allergens attached. These allergens can also travel on many other types of airborne particles including soot and diesel exhaust particles. Since many of these host particles are tiny, less than 2 microns in size, they are classified as PM2.5. PM2.5 can travel deep into one's respiratory system. A result of this is that respiratory allergies are directly linked to traffic-related air pollution exposure. Localized airborne particles near highways, for instance, include road dust, tire and break dust, soot, diesel exhaust particles, hydrocarbons, and nitrogen oxides, to name a few.

Allergen's effects on us are highly dependent on our microbiome. This biome is now considered to be threatened by the environmental changes listed above. Increased pollution is increasing oxidative stress as well as inflammation. Particulate matter, when ingested with food, can alter the biome in one's gastrointestinal track, inducing inflammatory disease. The multitude of threats present, or soon to become present as our climate changes, tells us of the immediate challenges present if we are to maintain public health. Now, the next steps lie in identifying exactly which biological mechanisms are effected, so we can better care for ourselves today and in the future. Let's hope that scientists are up to the challenge.

Reinmuth-Selzle, K., Kampf, C.J., Lucas, K., Lang-Yona, N., Fröhlich-Nowoisky, J., Shiraiwa, M., Lakey, P.S.J., Lai, S., Liu, F., Kunert, A.T. and Ziegler, K., 2017. Air Pollution and Climate Change Effects on Allergies in the Anthropocene: Abundance, Interaction, and Modification of Allergens and Adjuvants. Environmental Science & Technology

Olympic Games Feel the Heat
by Rachel Ashton Lim

What effect is climate change going to have on the fate of the Olympics? A 2016 study published in *The Lancet* examined the effect of future temperature, humidity, wind and radiation projections on the viability of hosts for future Olympic events. Limiting the cities under consideration to those with populations upwards of 600,000 and below 1 mile elevation, the study claims that by 2085, only 32 countries worldwide will be viable hosts for future games, a mere 8 of which are located outside western Europe. This leaves 535 of the remaining cities considered in the study out of the running for Olympic hosts in the next 70 years.

This estimate measures "the ability to run an Olympic Game" using the "low risk" temperature of 26°C and below, the temperature under which marathons may be run safely. The study argues that since the marathon is the most demanding endurance event, this is likely a fair indicator of whether climate conditions will be suitable for sports across the board. However, even when the temperature is raised to the "medium risk" category of 26–28°C, the number of cities which may host the Olympic Games safely only rises by a meager 33 countries.

Athletic events worldwide are already feeling the heat. In 2007, the Chicago Marathon was cancelled mid-race, as hundreds of runners dropped out to seek medical attention. More recently, at peak temperatures of 25.6°C, only 70% of US elite athletes were able to complete the Olympic Team Trials Marathon in Los Angeles.

In the face of high investment, long periods of planning and risks to a country's reputation, it is crucial that the Olympic council is aware of climate challenges to the games. If not, the study warns, the Games may have to be run either entirely indoors, during the winter, or risk abolishing marathon and other heat-sensitive endurance events completely.

Smith, K., Woodward, A., Lemke, B., Otto, M., Chang, C.J., Mance, A.A, Balmes, J., Kjellstrom, T. 2016. The last Summer Olympics? Climate change, health, and work outdoors. The Lancet, 388, 642–648.

Exploring the Health Effects of Climate Change in Alaska

by Alex McKenna

In 2010, David Driscoll and three colleagues from the Institute for Circumpolar Health Studies conducted research across Alaska in order to study the health effects of climate change. Focusing on the villages of Point Hope, Nenana, and Klawock, each located in an ecologically distinct region of the state, the team used a participatory, community-based system composed of surveys and community interviews to collect data on environmental conditions and syndromic health outcomes. What they discovered is fascinating. The presence of unseasonable environmental conditions, undoubtedly linked to climate change, not only increases the rate of unintentional injuries during winter months, but also doubles the incidence of summer respiratory issues.

Perhaps the most salient effect of climate change on health is the increase of injuries sustained over winter months. Because natives rely on ice and snow when traveling, the rise in temperature and influx of intense rain storms forces them to travel over more circuitous land-based routes – ice is simply too dangerous to navigate when thawing. Not only do these storms make navigation perilous, but the longer and often unfamiliar routes also increase the likelihood of getting hypothermia and frostbite. In the data collected, communities were 4.5 times as likely to report an injury resulting from unseasonable environmental conditions if they also reported changes in travel plans. Moreover, 72.9% of the communities surveyed stated that they experience unseasonable conditions. If this number increases and climate change intensifies, the terrain may become extremely dangerous to traverse, resulting in even more injuries and mortalities.

Driscoll also found that unusual weather patterns are linked to a variety of respiratory problems. For example, communities that experience unseasonable conditions are more than 1.5 times more likely to report pollen and allergic symptoms. But what causes this reaction? In the summer months, warm and dry conditions associated with wildfire smoke, dust from riverbeds, and automobile pollution make communities up to 20 times more likely to experience pollen allergy symptoms and up to 7 times more likely to report asthma symptoms. Although there is little data detailing the exact number of respiratory issues experienced, 39.5% of participants reported dust as a serious contributor to air pollution, with 40.5% and 39.2% reporting smoke and trash burning, respectively. These are startling statistics. If people continue to pollute the air, and climate change leaves the terrain dry and dusty, respiratory issues may become so widespread that the land is uninhabitable.

Can we do anything to combat these effects of climate change? While the Institute for Circumpolar Health Studies is optimistic about helping Alaskans adapt, the answer may be that there is very little we can do. After analyzing the data, Driscoll and his team concluded that there is a strong association between the changing environment and health syndromes. So, with no sign of climate change slowing down and their health at risk, people may decide to start migrating sooner rather than later.

Driscoll, D., Mitchell, E., Barker, R., Johnston, J., Renes, S., 2016. Assessing the health effects of climate change in Alaska with community-based surveillance. Springer Science, 455-465.
http://link.springer.com/article/10.1007/s10584-016-1687-0

Implanting Solar Panels in our Bodies to Power Medical Devices
by Alex McKenna

In 2017, scientists in Switzerland developed a prototype for an implantable solar panel that powers cardiac pacemakers. Potentially saving millions from the bills, anxiety, and hassle of replacing battery-dependent devices, these panels could drastically alter the future of medical implants.

Before being used on humans, the solar-powered pacemakers were tested on pigs, whose skin has qualities comparable to humans, and later on coated glass that emulates the light-transmitting properties of the epidermis. Getting very promising results, the team selected 32 human volunteers to wear the new technology. Participants wore the panels around their biceps all day long in summer, autumn, and winter months. In addition, they were required to keep logs of their daily activities and record weather conditions, covering the device anytime their neck would be covered—scientists believe that the neck is the best place to implant them. What the team discovered is fascinating. Daily life produced more than enough energy to power pacemakers, even when indoors! Furthermore, participants aged 65 and older, the group most likely in need of pacemakers, generated the most power.

The results of this study are very promising. Implantable devices, including cardiac pacemakers, don't require much energy to function. Andreas Haeberlin, PhD student at University of Bern, says that most implants require just 10 microwatts of energy, an amount that a solar small panel could produce on artificial light alone. Although this technology is not on the market yet, researchers are hoping to include an "accumulator"— a small battery pack or capacitor— to power the device during darkness and a function that issues alarms during a malfunction. Moreover, these solar panels would be very well concealed, nearly as thin as a dime and flexible enough to be barely noticeable.

Scientists hope that this new technology will not only reduce the number of pacemaker procedures and complications, but also provide a way to power these devices through clean and efficient methods. It may not be long before solar is powering these implants indefinitely!

Akst, D., 2017. A solar panel implanted inside your body? The Wall Street Journal, 1-3. https://www.wsj.com/articles/a-solar-panel-implanted-inside-your-body-1483654391

Vitamin B: a Weapon Against Air Pollution
by Alex McKenna

According to a new study, taking vitamin B supplements may help control the effects of air pollution on our health. Researching PM2.5, an air pollutant known to cause severe damage to the lungs and throat, the team of international scientists found that taking a daily dose of vitamin B can drastically reduce the impact of air pollution on the human body. With nearly 92% of the United States population living in regions classified as having an unhealthy level of PM2.5 in the air, this discovery has potential to make a significant impact on the future of our health.

Particulate matter, the type of pollution researched in this study, consists of both tiny molecular clusters and pollen. Chak Chan, professor of Atmospheric Environment at Hong Kong's City University, stated that the particles are so small that they can go into our respiratory system and get trapped in our lungs. Once inhaled, they can cause inflammation and stress. In addition, the scientists believe that PM2.5 can create epigenetic changes to our cells, mutations that damage health.

Despite these adverse effects however, the researchers in this study believe that vitamin B supplements can prevent further damage. To test their hypothesis, they gathered 10 volunteers, exposed them to clean air, and gave them a placebo to record their baseline responses. The group then took a placebo for four weeks while being exposed to heavily polluted air in the downtown Toronto area, where 1,000 cars pass by every hour. The experiment was then repeated, with each participant taking a daily vitamin B supplement made up of 2.5 mg of folic acid, 50 mg of vitamin B6, and 1 mg of vitamin B12. What the researchers discovered is fascinating. After taking the supplements for four weeks, the damage of PM2.5 exposure was reduced by 28 to 76%.

The results of this study are very promising for the future of PM2.5 damage prevention. Andrea Baccarelli, professor of environmental health studies at Columbia University, thinks that this discovery is the first step to completely containing the health effects of air pollution. Next, the researchers plan to conduct more thorough studies in order to validate their findings and to fully understand how we can use vitamin B to combat the effects of air pollution.

Perry, J., 2017. Vitamin B an unlikely weapon in the war against pollution. CNN News team, 1-5. http://www.cnn.com/2017/03/14/health/vitamin-b-pollution/

Medical Professionals Raise Alarm about Climate Change
by Alex McKenna

In 2017, more than half of the U.S. medical professionals united to discuss the effects of climate change on our health. As part of a newly formed consortium with over 434,000 practitioners and a dozen top medical associations, the nonprofit coalition aims to lobby Fortune 500 executives, governors, mayors, and the Trump administration to invest in renewable energy and cut back on greenhouse gas emissions. They argue that these emissions, undoubtedly linked to global warming, are causing an increased risk for asthma, Lyme disease, lung illnesses, and anxiety in patients across America, especially among children and the elderly. One of the practitioners in the consortium, Samantha Ahdoot, states that climate change is not only about our grandchildren or great-grandchildren, but also about people and their health today in 2017.

Despite their rising concerns, however, the group faces an uphill battle against President Donald Trump. Since his first day in office, the President has made eliminating environmental regulations a priority, already proposing Environmental

Protection Agency budget cuts and lifting regulations that protect against toxins. While his administration believes that these actions will boost the economy, the vast majority of Americans disagree. According to survey data from the Yale program on Climate Change Communication, nearly 70% of Americans believe in global warming, and 53% understand that humans are to blame. Furthermore, 97% of climate scientists who regularly publish in peer-reviewed journals agree that greenhouse gases are warming the planet.

Now, both climate scientist and physicians are raising alarms about climate change. Mona Sarfaty, professor at George Mason University, believes that the new consortium will be able to communicate with Americans more closely than scientists were ever able to. These medical professionals have a closer relationship with the public, and they feel a responsibility to speak directly to them. Among their top concerns are rising temperatures, air quality, wildfires, mental health, and mosquitos, all of which put our health at risk. More specifically, the consortium outlines three types of maladies associated with global warming: injuries and death due to violent weather, including wildfires caused by rising temperatures, diseases spread through insects that thrive in warmer climates, and mental health issues such as depression and anxiety. Examples include the spike in lung disease during the 2008 Evans Road wildfire in North Carolina and the increase in Lyme disease during Novembers in Chicago, a month when the city is typically too cold for ticks to survive.

For the past decade, 97% of climatologists have stated that rising greenhouse gases are warming our planet. Now that the effects have intensified, medical professionals from across the country are voicing their concerns as well. It is clearly time to step up and make a change.

Kaufman, A., 2017. More than half of U.S. medical professionals unite to raise alarm about climate change. The Huffington Post, 1-8. https://tinyurl.com/hwl67fd

Climate Change is a matter of Public Health
by Charlie Thomson

Published in U.S. News, an opinion written by Hugh Sealy asserts that climate change is no longer just an environmental crisis, but a world health crisis as well. It was recently confirmed by NASA scientists that the hottest month in recorded history was experienced last august — a statistic that meteorologists are connecting to the recent increase in severe flooding across the globe. In addition to the widespread increase in flooding, higher temperatures are upsetting global ecosystems and food production, which is leading to more sporadic and extreme weather conditions and wildfires. The increase in temperature threatens coastal communities with a rising sea level and setting up the perfect conditions that allow for deadly diseases to spread. This increase in temperature causes a higher level of ground-level ozone, the key ingredient in smog. Ozone irritates eyes and worsens lung function in humans — especially within the young and elderly. In addition to these adverse health risks due to climate change, the increase in temperature is increasing the population of animals that carry disease—animals such as fleas, ticks, mosquitos and other creatures that thrive in hotter temperatures. The increase in heat allows for such insects as the mosquito to live longer, incubate faster and spread faster and in greater numbers than ever before seen. Not only is climate change increasing the prevalence of disease transmission factors but it is increasing human's susceptibility to contracting disease as well. Rising temperatures in the world's water supplies is putting humans at increased risk of bacterial infection. Bacteria and parasites thrive in these warmer conditions.

Luckily, there are organizations and world leaders tackling the worsening problem of climate change. Last year, 196 countries signed the landmark Paris Agreement, which aims to limit the rise in global temperatures to 1.5 to 2°C above pre-industrial levels. All participating countries have agreed to publish yearly reports on their progress as a method of holding each other accountable for our goals, which in turn will benefit the world and mankind's health in the generations to come.

Sealy, Hugh. "The Coming Public Health Disaster." U.S. News. U.S. News, 5 Oct. 2016. Web. 29 Jan. 2017. <http://www.usnews.com/opinion/articles/2016-10-05/climate-change-is-a-matter-of-public-health>.

Doctors Warn Climate Change Threatens Public Health

by Charlie Thomson

Growing up in southwestern Pennsylvania, Patrice Tomcik had never heard of Lyme disease—a highly infectious, flu-like illness that is transmitted by ticks.

Yet in the last couple of years, five of her friends there have caught the disease. As a result of this she's had to have her dog vaccinated and now regularly finds herself pulling ticks off her family members. It can be disconcerting, she said, having to worry about an illness which had never been of concern to her in the past. "It's getting warmer, so the season for ticks is lasting longer," said Tomcik, a Moms Clean Air Force field consultant. "There are so many more of them, and they just don't die off. It's a big issue here in Pennsylvania, because we have so much wood. Our family has 29 acres of land out in the woods, and I'm picking ticks off my dog and my kids like I've never seen before."

Lyme disease isn't the only contagious illness that is spreading into new regions due to a shifting climate. All across the country, physicians have noticed an influx of patients whose ailments, they say, are directly or indirectly related to climate change. Now, 11 medical associations—representing about half of all the doctors and physicians in the country—are building a group that aims to confront the links between climate change and health risks.

"I view this as one of the largest environmental health crises of our time because of the many pathways in which climate affects us—be it from direct heat effects and heat waves in urban centers, ground-level smog, ozone red alert days, stagnant air masses and warmer temperatures, to some infectious diseases," said Jonathan Patz, director of the Global Health Institute at the University of Wisconsin, Madison.

The Medical Society Consortium on Climate and Health, which the group is named, intends to advocate for health and climate awareness among the public and policymakers. Director of the consortium, Mona Sarfaty, said its message is urgent: "that climate change is harming the health of Americans and that we have to act now."

"We wish to start that conversation and are eager to talk to everybody about it. We will be speaking to people in environmental organizations, we'll be speaking to members of Congress, we'll be sending reports and having conversations with other policymakers throughout the country," she added.

Balaraman, Kavya, and E&E News. "Doctors Warn Climate Change Threatens Public Health." Scientific American. Scientific American, 17 Mar. 2017. Web. 20 Mar. 2017. <https://www.scientificamerican.com/article/doctors-warn-climate-change-threatens-public-health/>.

Creating Funding for Interdisciplinary Climate-Health Research in Australia

by Kelly Watanabe

According to Green *et al.* (2017), Australia needs development in interdisciplinary climate-health research—computational, evaluative, and comparative analysis of climate change's impact on human health. A recent IPCC report recognized a research gap in climate-health, especially in low-income countries. Indirect health impacts from natural disasters include diminished water quality and damaged crops which affect nutritional health. During an El Niño in Australia, a heatwave with high temperatures and high humidity caused the direct health impact of high morbidity. Because Australia is affected by the El Niño and has a diverse range of climate zones, Australia is an optimal location for climate research. Australia's climate change models can serve as a proxy for the whole Asia-Pacific region.

Despite a recent Australian government report that supported investment for research on climate change's impact on human health, climate-health research receives less than 0.1% of Australian's health funding. In the United States, the National Institutes of Health (NIH) developed a specific classification of climate-health research which focusses on air quality impacts, waterborne illness, and the effect of climate change on mental health. Unlike the US which has major philanthropic sectors such as Bill & Melinda Gates Foundation, Australia receives funding primarily from the government with little money from philanthropic sectors. Australia has two major government funding organizations: the National Health and Medical Research Council (NHMRC) and the Australian Research Council (ARC). Green suggests that climate-health project proposals have a low success rate of receiving funding because the NHMRC lacks expertise in climate research and the ARC lacks expertise in health research. In 2016, 0 out of 256 NHMRC-funded project grants were focused on climate change. Moreover, the success rate for research grants decreased from 30% to 15% over the past decade. According to Green, higher competition causes organizations to favor safe research over risky research such as climate-health interdisciplinary projects.

To promote climate-health research, Green suggests a solution through collaboration between NHMRC and ARC. Additionally, Australia needs mathematical models to predict the effect of severe climatic events on public health, political science to create climate-health policy, and economic analysis to properly allocate limited research funding.

Ecology and Climate Change

Is Climate Change Causing Seagulls to Become...Cannibals?
by Joshua Dorman

Climate change has been proven to wreak innumerable damages to the habitats of a variety of sea animals. Now, the members of these oceanic ecosystems are being forced to turn to new—and sometimes unorthodox—methods to survive the onslaught. In an article published in The Washington Times, Tristan Baurick explores an unusual side effect of climate change for seagulls: cannibalism.

Jim Hayward, a seabird biologist based in the Strait of Juan de Fuca, has been monitoring the largest gull nesting colony in the Puget Sound area since 1987. However, he's recently noticed a rather disturbing trend: over the past ten years or so, the gulls have developed an appetite for their companions' chicks and eggs. As Hayward has frequently observed, the typical chick-snatching scene is "hard to watch." A stray youngling is quickly grasped in the beak of another bird as its mother tries vigorously—but unsuccessfully—to fend off the attackers. Another gull swoops in for a bite at the legs, and the feeding frenzy begins. However, the trend appears to be inextricably linked to global warming. According to Hayward, "a one-tenth of a degree change in seawater temperature correlates to a 10 percent increase in (the odds of) cannibalism." His data taken over a decades-long period, combined with the statistical modeling employed by his wife, a mathematician, has unearthed some troubling findings. In fact, they found that "over the last eight years, there's a 100 percent correlation between hot years and high cannibalism." Additionally, they discovered that gulls have begun to synchronize their egg-laying, most likely in response to the threat of cannibalism. Upon close analysis of the situation, it's easy to see why these feathered animals are altering their eating habits. During a gull's nesting period, it cannot venture far in search of nourishment, so its diet consists of whatever food lies in its general vicinity. Typically, seagulls forage small ocean-side organisms, such as sand lice and herring. However, due to high sea temperatures, these creatures are slowly beginning to disappear, leaving the gulls to result to cannibalism in order to **survive**.

The implications of such a trend are troublesome to say the least. In general, cannibalism can be employed to help a single species make it through a particularly rough year or two. However, when carried on for an extended period of time, it poses a serious threat to the population, with the potential to literally wipe out an entire species. The effects of climate change on seagulls, it seems, are much more **extreme than previously** thought.

"Climate change may be turning gulls into cannibals." The Washington Times. July 31, 2016. Accessed March 11, 2017.
http://www.washingtontimes.com/news/2016/jul/31/climate-change-may-be-turning-gulls-into-cannibals/.

Are Plants Slowing Climate Change?
by Joshua Dorman

Perhaps one of the most overlooked effects of climate change, the growth of vegetation on Earth over the last few decades, has been staggering. As the planet becomes hotter and hotter, places that were previously inhospitable for greenery are now perfect places for growth. In fact, between 1982 and 2009, approximately eighteen *million* square kilometers—roughly double the size of the United States—of vegetation had appeared on Earth's surface. A group of researchers led by Trevor Keenan of the Lawrence Berkeley National Laboratory have an unearthed some surprising findings related to this incredible appearance of greenery; it may be helping to slow climate change.

As is commonly known, plants actively use water and energy from the sun to engage in photosynthesis, converting CO_2 from the air into sugars. In 2014, about 37.5 billion tons of CO_2 were pushed into the atmosphere by humans. Unsurprisingly, that figure has been steeply climbing since around 1950, when roughly 6 billion tons were pumped into the air each year. However, since 2002, the rate of increase of CO_2 levels in the atmosphere has barely budged. Keenan's team believes that the photosynthesis employed by the millions of acres of new greenery has, in a way, helped counteract the influx of CO_2 into the atmosphere. In other words, although we are continually pumping more CO_2 than ever into the atmosphere, less of it is lingering than would be expected.

While this may sound like good news, the reality is that the effect is too small to reverse climate change as a whole. And, according to Dr. Keenan, it won't last for much longer. In fact, some researchers believe that the positive effects of this process, known in the scientific community as "global greening," are already beginning to come to an end. Corinne Le Quéré, a climate researcher at the University of East Anglia in Britain, points to the particularly strong El Niño in 2015–2016 as a sign that the world's plants may be sucking up less CO_2 than during the period of time that Dr. Keenan focused on. Global greening, it seems, offers little relief; a full assault on fossil fuels remains our only option for preventing catastrophe.

"Earth's plants are countering some of the effects of climate change." The Economist. November 12, 2016. Accessed March 29, 2017. http://www.economist.com/news/science-and-technology/21709947-more-photosynthesis-means-slower-rise-carbon-dioxide-levelsfor-now-earths.

Overfishing and Shark-Finning Could Increase the Pace of Climate Change
by Bryn Edwards

In this article, written by Rick Stafford, a marine biologist from the U.K., explains how removing predators from the top of the oceanic food chains can expedite the process of climate change. Practices such as shark-finning, where fins are cut off live sharks which are thrown back into the ocean to die, can destroy ecosystems by removing key predators that help maintain balance within the food chain. Extremely popular in Asian countries, the fins are considered a delicacy and it can cost up to $100 for a bowl of shark fin soup. Such high prices ensure a strong incentive for fishermen to continue these practices, legal or not. Removing these larger species leads to more carbon dioxide being produced by oceans. Stafford explains this with a basic biological rule. Every time one organism consumes another, only 10% of its energy passes up to the next level; 90% of the energy is lost. By removing top predators, the species at the bottom of the food chain like small fish and zooplankton have fewer species preying on them. Thus up to 90% more can survive, which leads to much more respiration and thus much more carbon dioxide being produced. Furthermore, large marine species are crucial in providing nutrients to phytoplankton. Phytoplankton absorb a majority of the ocean's carbon dioxide, making them a part of the process of slowing down climate change. Species such as whales are big enough to move across layers of the ocean, thus spreading the nutrients from different layers around, and push them up to provide food for the phytoplankton. Reducing pelagic species such as whales and sharks, may be thus increasing the pace of global warming.

Rick, Stafford. How overfishing and shark-finning could increase the pace of climate change. The Conversation. http://theconversation.com/how-overfishing-and-shark- finning-could-increase-the-pace-of-climate-change-67664

Moving Forward with Climate Change: Protecting Biological Diversity
by Matt Johnson

A popular solution to extinction is to identify a narrow set of species, and somehow interfere with the environment in which those species live to directly counter or subdue the negative effects of climate change on that species. The problem with this approach is that it is very narrow: normally targeting only one or at most a handful of species. A paper headed by Michael S. Webster (2017) points out that focusing on specific species, both the winners and the losers, neglects the value of diversity in our biological environment.

There is a "growing recognition" of the need to manage specific ecosystems. As climate change data continue to roll in, our understanding of the fragility of our environment only continues to broaden. The authors of this paper argue that more attention needs to be shifted towards biological diversity in the future: how are the current species going to adapt? They argue that the current methods of "predict-and-prescribe" are insufficient. While one may identify a species in threat of extinction, and then act towards protecting that species, one may, at the same, totally neglect other species under the same threats. This method of predict-and-prescribe normally relies on countless predictions. Inherently, when acting on predictions, there is a chance that one may be wrong. While acting in favor of just one species isn't bad, it just may not be the best use of time and resources.

The authors suggest an ecological adaption method that favors adaptive processes. "By prioritizing portfolios of biological and ecological combinations, management could increase the probability that winning combinations can arise, persist, and spread during periods of environmental change". The main method by which this is done is reducing local anthropogenic stressors; and in this case with consideration for a diverse group of species, not just one. Especially in environments with high gene flow, rapid adaption is likely to occur, as the article mentions: "genetic adaption is most likely to occur via selection on pre-existing genetic variation rather than new mutations". One of the problems that this same concept entails is that 'winning' genes may be swamped by others. However, the authors note that species are going to have to adapt so quickly in many environments that advantageous genes are likely to be greatly favored. By supporting large portfolios of species, communities and environments, we protect diversity while leaving ourselves less prone to false predictions and unexpected events. Let evolution do its thing.

Webster, M.S., Colton, M.A., Darling, E.S., Armstrong, J., Pinsky, M.L., Knowlton, N. and Schindler, D.E., 2017. Who Should Pick the Winners of Climate Change?. Trends in Ecology & Evolution.

Seagrass
by Ethan Kurz

Seagrass is something that few people have heard of, but it is as important as rain forests when it comes to climate change. All continents are surrounded by prairies of seagrass. Seagrass "meadows" are the most endangered ecosystems on this planet. They are very important when talking about the health of the ocean because they house fish species, extract pollutants from the ocean water, and retain large amounts of carbon. Scientists believe that one acre of seagrass provides more than 11 thousand dollars of filtering. In addition to all those values, scientists have recently discovered that seagrass absorbs pathogens from the ocean that affect humans and corals. The only problem with seagrass is that it is disappearing at the rate of a football field every 30 minutes.

When seagrass first came into existence, by a land grass evolving into a seagrass, it spread across the ocean building up soil and creating room for new ecosystems to exist. Manatees, which only eat seagrass, came into existence, and young fish had a safe area to hide and grow. Humans depend on these seagrass meadows because the fish we eat are born and raised in seagrass meadows. Seagrass is considered the most economically valuable systems on our planet.

Since the 19th century, a third of seagrass has already died off, and now is disappearing faster and faster. The two main reasons that seagrass dies are changing currents kick up soil and the soil in the water blocks the sunlight from the plants and the adverse effects of climate change. With warmer waters, the plants don't retain as much oxygen and as a result are poisoned by toxic sediments that would have been oxidized. All the seagrass in the world right now holds around 9 billion tons of carbon. As the meadows die off, this carbon goes straight to the atmosphere, accelerating climate change, which in turn accelerates meadow die-off. There is a little bit of hope, however. Dr. Robert J. Orth, a seagrass expert, has successfully grown seagrass meadows off the coast of Virginia. Will his activities be enough and in time? Only time will tell.

Zimmer, Carl, 2017. Disappearing Seagrass Protects Against Pathogens, Even Climate Change, Scientists Find. The New York Times. <https://nyti.ms/2lc5Yyb>.

Deforestation Never Left
by Ethan Kurz

The "Save the Rainforest Movement" initially did its job, dramatically slowing down rainforest deforestation in the Amazon region, but a decade later and things aren't looking too good. Deforestation is happening at alarming rates in some of the largest forests around the world, especially in Brazil. In the Brazilian Rainforest, deforestation jumped from 1.2 million acres per year to 1.5 million acres per year last year. Bolivia also is facing major deforestation problems, with an average of 865 thousand acres of land deforested per year.

The advocacy group, Mighty Earth, has found out exactly what is fueling the accelerating deforestation in Brazilian and Bolivian forests; soybean farms. Two large American companies, Cargill and Bunge, are moving into Brazil and Bolivia to buy all the soybeans the farmers can produce. Mighty Earth used satellite imaging of the areas where Cargill and Bunge were active and found alarming results. Between 2011 and 2015, there was more than 321 thousand acres of deforestation where Cargill operates. Bunge, on the other hand, has been linked to 1.4 million acres of deforestation between 2011 and 2015.

Both these companies, however, deny deforestation and claim to do everything they can to prevent it. Cargill is "committed" to ending all deforestation by 2030. According to Mighty Earth, 2030 would be too late, "we would have no forests left". Bunge claims deforestation isn't its fault alone, and instead calls upon more companies to adopt zero deforestation commitments. This is ridiculous because right now Bunge doesn't have a zero deforestation policy and that comment just proves that they won't do anything unless a worldwide law is passed against all of them.

Deforestation is the number one cause of climate change. The burning of the wood after clearing generates 1/10th of all carbon emissions. There are only around 15% of the Earth's forests left. The rise in deforestation can all be pointed back to the rise in agricultural production due to large international agricultural companies. As deforestation laws are enforced one place, companies go to more and more remote areas where the anti-deforestation laws don't exist. These global agricultural giants need to be stopped soon if we want to have forests on this planet.

Tabuchi, Hiroko and Rigby, Claire and White, Jeremy, 2017. Amazon Deforestation, Once Tamed, Comes Roaring Back. The New York Times, < https://nyti.ms/2mfLlEq>.

Should Dams be demolished or not? New Update

by Ethan Kurz

Over 4,000 dams in the United States are rated unsafe because of structural or other deficiencies. To bring the network of 90,000 dams across the United States up to code, the cost would exceed 79 billion dollars. As a country which is almost 20 trillion dollars in debt, most dams that are under code are demolished. The over 700 dams that have been demolished over the past decade have theoretically helped open up old habitats and restore fish ecosystems.

A new study in the *Biological Conservation* highlights dam demolition and calls into question whether it is truly the correct thing to do for fish. The South African and Australian scientists admit that reopening rivers usually leads to "increased species richness, abundance and biomass" they have found that some threatened fish species actually benefit from dams. South Africa and Australia are experiencing record breaking dry periods. Most native fish species have been driven back by non-native fishes from rivers into reservoirs created by dams. These reservoirs are crucial and often the only habitat these fish have to live in. Other native fishes have developed hibernation habits, hibernating in mud leftover when rivers dry up. Because of the increasing dry season, even these endemic fishes aren't surviving and the only places they have left now are reservoirs created by dams. Therefore, demolishing dams for purely economic reasons hurts these fish. The removed dams would allow non-native fish species to continue to eliminate native species and would also hurt the endemic fishes.

The article continued with a warning of a trade-off; isolating native species with dams may prevent them from taking old migratory routes, preventing gene flow from one population to another thus increasing risk of extinction.

The conclusion is that the debate about dams has always come down to ideological or exclusively economic arguments. The challenge now is to actually step back and look at each dam individually and do what is best for each location.

Conniff, Richard, 2017. Climate Change Complicates the Whole Dam Debate. < https://www.scientificamerican.com/article/climate-change-complicates-the-whole-dam-debate/>.

Climate Change's Relationship with Coral Reefs Has Not Changed
by Ethan Kurz

Large swaths of the Great Barrier Reef, located in Australia, have recently been found dead. Hundreds of miles of corals, previously thought by scientists to be very alive, along the most pristine north sector have been killed by warm seawater. Now southerly sections that barely escaped are now getting bleached at record paces. According to Terry P. Hughes, director of a center for coral reefs at James Cook University in Australia, "We didn't expect to see this level of destruction to the Great Barrier Reef for another 30 years."

The health state of coral reefs is a strong indicator of the health of the ocean. The stress and death that faces the coral reefs is a telling sign that global climate change is affecting our oceans. If most of the coral reefs in the world die, which is what scientists are assuming will happen soon, tourism would die and economies would collapse. However, in poorer countries, the stakes are higher because many people in poorer countries rely on protein from reef fish. The loss of that food supply could lead to a humanitarian crisis.

Reef scientists have no doubt when it comes to identifying the responsible party. They warned everyone decades ago that continued fossil fuel use is releasing greenhouse gasses into the atmosphere, thus warming the oceans. Emissions have continued to rise since then and the temperature of the ocean has done the same. When the water close to a reef is too hot, the algae growing on the reefs begin to produce toxins. To defend themselves from that, corals expel the algae and turn white or "bleached". If water temperature drops soon after the coral have expelled the algae, the coral can acquire new algae and survive, but if not, the coral may starve. Even if the coral die, some reefs may eventually recover by recolonization. If water temperatures stay moderate for a long enough time, 10-15 years, damaged sections of the Great Barrier Reef may be covered with new corals. The problem is that the ocean temperature is becoming too warm for that to ever happen and global bleaching events are on the rise.

With the international effort to fight climate change losing speed with the election of a conservative government in the United States and in Australia, the hopes of stopping emissions is not looking promising. This means that the ocean temperatures will continue to rise and we will never have the amazing corals we had 10 years ago.

Cave, Damien; Gillis, Justin; 2017. Large Sections of Australia's Great Reef Are Now Dead, Scientists Find.
<https://www.nytimes.com/2017/03/15/science/great-barrier-reef-coral-climate-change-dieoff.html>.

Hot Chicks, Cool Dudes
by Ethan Kurz

Biologist Jeanette Wyneken has a saying that goes, "hot chicks, cool dudes," when discussing predicting the gender of sea turtles. Unlike humans, chromosomes don't determine the sex of a sea turtle. Instead, there are a lot of external environmental factors that determine sex, one of which is temperature. Warmer conditions hatch more females and cooler conditions produce more males. Recently, scientists are noticing an overwhelming amount of the hatchlings are females on Florida beaches. It is something to take note of because a highly skewed sex ratio could affect the species as a whole.

Florida's beaches are laying ground for around 50,000 sea turtles. In the last 12 years, there has been a strong female bias in the hatchlings. In the last 5 years, the bias has been skewed even more, with some beaches reaching 95% female. The increasing temperatures in the region are the direct reason for this abundance.

The way scientists test for gender is interesting. The hatchling can't be looked at to determine sex because the sex organs haven't developed yet. Instead, scientists stain the eggs with a gender specific protein, female eggs get stained and male eggs don't. This technique was first tested on loggerhead turtles and now is used on all turtles including leatherbacks.

There is now a direct link between global warming and sea turtle survival. Warmer incubation temperatures mean more females, and there are concerns now that some beaches are producing all or almost all females. From a conservation standpoint, this has significant ramifications. A word of caution must be taken before using this information to start manipulating sex ratios. Climate change is leading to more female hatchlings, but scientists don't know enough to say that is "bad" for the turtle species. Continuing on that, scientists don't know that a 50:50 male to female ratio is ideal. Having a greater percentage of females may be beneficial because of the increase in amount of egg layers. That is where the study needs to continue in the future.

Balaraman, Kavya, 2017. Is Climate Change Producing Too Many Female Sea Turtles? <https://www.scientificamerican.com/article/is-climate-change-producing-too-many-female-sea-turtles/>.

Whales are Reducing the Impact of Climate Change
by Ethan Kurz

Scientists now believe that whales may have been reducing carbon emissions in the Pacific Island area, and as the number of whales dwindle, there may be an increase in the release of greenhouse gasses in the atmosphere. According to Angela Martin, a project lead with Blue Climate Solutions, "whales eat carbon not fish." Whales facilitate carbon absorption in two critical ways. Their movements, including dying, push nutrients from the deep ocean to the surface. The minerals and other materials moved upwards by whales in turn feed phytoplankton, other marine flora, fish, and some small animals. Their second way of facilitating carbon absorption is less glamorous; fecal movements. By pooing, whales introduce nutrients that are critical for marine plant growth and survival. By facilitating marine flora and plants, whales are contributing to the reduction of carbon in the atmosphere.

As water in the Pacific Islands region gets warmer and warmer, scientists don't know how much longer whales can comfortably exist there. Temperature change directly influences where whales travel, but beyond that, climate change is also affecting the acidity of ocean water which affects whales' prey. As all marine species move away from high temperature and acidic water, there will be increased competition. Increased competition will make life more difficult for whales, furthering their decrease in numbers.

There have been several studies that have pinpointed whales' significance to helping our atmosphere. One study suggests that each year sperm whales sequester as much carbon as a 694 acre forest in North America. Another study in Hawaii suggests that the movement of 80 whales can absorb the same amount of carbon as a 208 acre North American forest.

The survival of whales has both impacts on cultures of islands and their economies. The whale watching business alone is worth 21 million dollars and that can change quickly if whales become rarer or harder to find. Long story short, whales are essential to life on earth.

Balaraman, Kavya, 2017. Whales Keep Carbon out of the Atmosphere. Scientific American. <https://www.scientificamerican.com/article/whales-keep-carbon-out-of-the-atmosphere/>.

Who's to Blame for Biodiversity Loss?
by Rachel Ashton Lim

What needs to be done to protect biodiversity? A study in *Nature* (Maxwell *et al.* 2016) sets out to answer this question, as the issue of climate change continues to dominate both the media and policy discussions in addressing biodiversity loss mitigation efforts. The authors of the study examine the number of species affected by various threats such as pollution and urban development, and have found that issues of overexploitation and agricultural activity pose the biggest danger to species worldwide. By focusing on climate change (which comes 7th on the list of "big killers") and not on these more pressing issues, the authors warn that we may fail to act to truly protect the flora and fauna that remain on the Earth today.

The study draws on the IUCN Red List of Threatened Species to make its calculations, including a total sample size of 82,845 species and their population projections across three generations (or a ten-year period, whichever is longer). Of this list, 6,241 species are affected by overexploitation, an umbrella term encompassing human logging, hunting, fishing and plant gathering activities. To put these numbers into context, 72% of these overexploited species are already of threatened or near-threatened status including the Sumatran rhinoceros, Western gorilla and Chinese pangolin. Similarly, 5,407 species are threatened by the agricultural expansion and intensification of crops, livestock, timber and aquaculture, and 62% of these species are listed as threatened or near-threatened including the Africa's cheetah, hairy-nosed otters, and huemul deer.

Comparatively, the effects of climate change such as flooding, habitat modification and droughts currently place 1,688 species under threat. While this figure must not be taken lightly, 19% of the species in this number is classified as threatened or near-threatened—a considerably lower statistic than that due to overexploitation and agriculture.

Although the paper acknowledges limitations to the way these threats have been treated as discrete, to taxonomic records, and to population projections, it emphasizes that the results do not change drastically; no matter how they are viewed, and, as a result, we must act swiftly and decisively against the most dangerous threats to biodiversity: mitigating overexploitation of species and agricultural expansion must take precedence over climate change action if we are to save the Earth's species, and we must not let newer problems overshadow massive and long-standing ones. Therefore, the paper makes recommendations for policy makers to develop sustainable harvest regimes, curb the use of pesticides and fertilizers, establish key biodiversity areas and enforce regulations to protect these areas.

Maxwell, S.L., Fuller, R.A., Brooks, T.M., Watson, J.E.M. 2016. Biodiversity: The ravages of guns, nets and bulldozers. Nature, 536, 143-145.

The Need for Legal Reform in Conservation Objectives
by Rachel Ashton Lim

In order to improve the climate adaptability of current conservation policy, a group of researchers has consulted various stakeholders in governmental, planning, and public advocacy organizations on the limitations of legal objectives in Tasmania's environmental law, proposing improvements to the system through reform. The importance of legal objectives was attributed by these researchers to their ability to guide the development, funding, implementation, and assessment of conservation action in the region. Their discussions have uncovered three main limitations in the legislation: firstly, that ecosystems are viewed as static in their statuses and locations, failing to recognize the shifting nature of ecosystems accelerated by climate change; secondly, that individual species classified as "native" and "rare" are overvalued, compromising the protection of both less charismatic and more functional (but perhaps common) species; and thirdly, that there is an overemphasis on reserves within spatial boundaries, creating an artificial concept of what is not, and by extension, what *is* acceptable for human exploitation, and restricting the restoration of degraded land. While acknowledging and naming a range of barriers to legal reform, the paper published by the researches concludes by suggesting tangible methods for reforming these legal objectives.

The paper states that Tasmania provides an interesting case study because its conservation policy is shaped not only by its own state laws, but also by national (ie. Australian) and international law through conventions such as the Convention of Biological Diversity (CBD). It is also cooler than mainland Australia, and thus provides a refuge for the migration of mainland species as the climate warms.

However, the paper aptly points out that endemic species from Tasmania do not have a place to find refuge. Current Tasmanian law cites the importance of "protecting" and "maintaining" nature, but the stakeholders criticize the limited definitions of these two terms, because it does not elucidate whether the metric for analyzing them relates to species richness, evenness, or abundance, and does not state if the objective seeks to simply prevent extinction, or stabilize current population sizes. However the definition of these terms are clarified, the paper emphasizes that because evolutionary processes are continuously affecting change, environments are not static, and phrases such as the "natural state" of a habitat suggest a baseline that is unhelpful for effective conservation policy. Areas outside of current nature reserves must be made available for future conservation efforts, and the latitudinal and altitudinal connectivity between habitats must be enhanced to support the migration of non-human species. Therefore, the legislation must avoid prescriptions about how wilderness and nature should be (i.e. "untouched" and pristine), and the words used in framing conservation objectives must be chosen carefully to include how they really are or *can* be.

The key barriers to legal reform cited in the paper include underfunding, the influence of popular views about what our laws should do, the lack of political will, the difficulty of transitioning to climate adaptive conservation when current biodiversity conservation projects already do not receive enough support, inflexible international agreements (for example, the CPB), which emphasizes in situ conservation, and fears of legal objectives becoming diluted rather than enhanced.

The paper keeps a positive outlook by stating clauses in the legislation where change can still be effected, such as areas in international law that value habitat connectivity. In order to respond more quickly and effectively to on the ground shocks, such as disasters or changes to funding, whilst maintaining accountability standards, the paper suggests state level, site-specific management, monitored at the national and international level.

The researchers state that they are not proposing a wholesale upheaval of the current legal system, recognizing the social and cultural importance of iconic species. What they *do* propose is a shift in legal objectives and definitions, to recognize explicitly the dynamism of ecosystems, aim for landscape rather than species-level policies (thus allowing common but extremely functional species to flourish), and be open to ex situ conservation programs. The reform of legal objectives is the first step to better conservation policy. However, the fight must continue for the effective implementation guided by these objectives, and, the paper concludes, there must be a deeper engagement with the indigenous people of Tasmania in conserving these ecosystems.

McDonald, J., McCormack, P.C., Fleming, A.J, Harris, R.M.B., Lockwood, M. 2016. Rethinking legal objectives for climate-adaptive conservation. Ecology and Society, 21(2): 25.

Is Climate Change to Blame for the Rise in Shark Attacks?
by Alex McKenna

After the release of *Jaws* in 1975, people started thinking twice before getting in the water. Decades later, they still remember the stories, newspaper articles, and photographs of swimmers collapsed on the shore, covered in shark bites. But do they have reason to be concerned? Recent trends in climate change suggest that they actually do. Over the past 30 years, the frequency of unprovoked shark attacks has drastically increased, with the majority of bites being recorded in Florida, South Africa, Australia, and the Bahamas. While researchers argue that there are many reasons behind this influx, Dr. Blake Chapman, professor at Bond University in Australia, points to climate change as one of the principle explanations. He believes that rising temperatures, heavy rains, and anomalous weather patterns, all results of climate change, fundamentally alter marine ecosystems and are ultimately to blame for the recent spike in shark attacks.

The number of unprovoked attacks in the United States is rising by nearly 1.07 bites per year. While this may seem insignificant, it is actually quite an alarming statistic, especially considering that during the peak year of 2001, when 50 bites were recorded, all attacks occurred in the spring and summer months. This raises an important question. Do warmer temperatures correlate with shark attacks? Chapman argues that abnormally high sea surface temperatures can shrink the habitats of prey, forcing sharks to look closer to shore when feeding. If temperatures continue to rise, which is inevitable at this point, who knows how close they will get? Warmer waters are already drawing some species into shallower areas, and the predators will certainly follow, even if it means encountering a human.

Rising temperatures have also brought along heavy rains, especially in Volusia County, a shark attack "hotspot" in Florida that is highly susceptible to runoff. Nearly 75% of the bites between 1957 and 2008 occurred in turbid, muddy, or murky waters, a direct result of these heavy rains. In addition, runoff of pesticides and fertilizers can be lethal for fish, altering the trophic structure and forcing sharks to explore new habitats that may be occupied by humans.

An increase in anomalous and extreme weather patterns is also linked to the recent influx of bites. In South Africa, although the rate of unprovoked attacks has remained relatively stable at 4.4 per year, there were a record 16 in 1998. Unsurprisingly, this spike was attributed to an erratic climatic event that caused shifts in the current patterns, ultimately disrupting natural upwellings of nutrients. This altered biological productivity in the ecosystem, threatened prey availability, and forced sharks towards the shore, where there were more fish to feed on- and humans. Similar events have occurred in Australia, where in 2009 they experienced seven tropical cyclones and the highest annual bite record in history. Although this data was recorded nearly a decade ago, it can still be applied to attacks today. Climate change is producing stronger and more widespread storms, and because these storms naturally bring nutrients into shore, they draw in predators as well. Maybe in a few years they will be swimming by our feet.

So, what can we do to prevent future attacks? This question will become harder and harder to answer as the repercussions of climate change intensify. If temperatures continue to rise and storms persist, sharks will slowly begin inhabiting areas dangerously close to shore. Even worse, with diminishing habitats and toxic runoffs, these creatures must search for new prey, and at the moment, it may just as well be us.

Chapman, B., McPhee, D., 2016. Global shark attack hotspots: identifying underlying factors behind increased unprovoked shark bite incidence. Elsevier, 72-84. http://www.sciencedirect.com/science/article/pii/S0964569116302058

Using Satellites to Assess the Effects of Climate Change on Animals

by Alex McKenna

Terrestrial and marine habitats across the world are rapidly deteriorating. But how exactly is this affecting wildlife? In 2016, the American Geophysical Union answered this question at a conference by analyzing satellite images of the earth's surface. What they presented is fascinating. From their unique vantage point, satellites are able to observe habitat transformations and help forecast the impacts of climate change on the distribution and migration of animals, specifically for polar bears, mountain lions, and wild reindeer. Thus, using this technology, scientists have been able to conclude that habitat degradation, undoubtedly sparked by climate change, is inextricably linked to the recent decline and shift in these wildlife populations.

Perhaps the most salient effect of climate change is the melting of sea ice around the Arctic Circle, an area that polar bears inhabit to hunt, travel, and breed. Satellites from NASA have actually been tracking these changes over the past three decades, and not surprisingly, have found that the ice shrinks by an average of 20,500 square miles per year. This is a very worrisome statistic, as polar bears are dependent on this sea ice for survival and forecasts only predict further losses as climate change accelerates. Using satellite images, scientists predict that at the current rate of ice loss, over 30% of the global population of polar bears will disappear in the next three to four decades. In certain areas, including the Hudson Bay, studies already show that the survival and reproduction of these creatures is seriously in danger, as the number of bears is directly proportional to the amount of sea ice present.

Scientists also use satellite images in the southwestern region of the United States to study the populations of mule deer and mountain lions. As this area becomes more and more prone to drought and loss of vegetation, the number of herbivores, including mule deer and their main predator, mountain lions, may drastically decrease. So, using imagery from NASA's Terra and Aqua satellites, David Stoner, wildlife ecologist at Utah State University, was able to draw a strong correlation between plant productivity and both deer and mountain lion densities. He then created a model that links a 30% decrease in vegetation to a 22% and 43% decrease in deer and mountain lion density, respectively. In addition, as droughts make human landscapes more attractive to these creatures, we will see a rise in vehicle collisions, damage to gardens, and even an increase in recreational hunting, all of which will further threaten their livelihood.

Finally, scientists were able to use satellite images to explain the 40% decline in the Taimyr reindeer population, the world's largest herd in Russia. Andrey Petrov, associate professor at the University of Northern Iowa, examined data going back to 1969 and discovered ongoing changes in the distribution and migration of these reindeer due to climate change. Traveling farther and farther north each year to avoid rising temperatures and mosquitos, these herds are experiencing spikes in calf mortality. However, using satellite images to examine the plant biomass, Petrov determined that overgrazing is not to blame for the recent decline, as previously thought by researchers. Rather, it is strictly climate change and the longer distances that they must migrate because of it.

So, is there any way we can use this new technology to combat the effects of climate change? While satellites can certainly help us identify the repercussions, and even link them to the decline in certain animal populations, they unfortunately cannot do anything to stop it. In other words, they have opened our eyes to the real problem that we are facing, but it is still up to us to find a solution.

Viñas, M., 2016. What satellites can tell us about how animals will fare in a changing climate. NASA Earth and Science News Team, 1-5. https://tinyurl.com/zp8x7lo

Effects of Rising Temperatures on Desert Songbirds
by Alex McKenna

According to a new study by NASA, the acceleration of climate change, specifically the increase in duration and magnitude of heat waves, is beginning to threaten the livelihood of desert songbirds in the southwestern United States. Using hourly temperature maps and data from the North American Land Data Assimilation System, researchers investigated the rates of evaporative water loss in response to higher temperatures among five songbird species: the lesser goldfinch, house finch, cactus wren, Abert's towhee, and curve-billed thrasher. After analyzing these data, they were not only able to forecast the effects of future heat waves on desert songbirds, but also investigate how quickly dehydration can occur among these species.

By the end of the century, most scientists predict that summer temperatures in the United States will rise by as much as 4°C. While this may not seem significant, the rise actually puts all five species studied at a greater risk of lethal dehydration. Blair Wolf, professor of biology at the University of New Mexico, states that birds are susceptible to heat in two ways. When temperatures are extremely high, their bodies cannot evaporate enough water to cool themselves down, causing them to die from heat stroke. In less extreme cases, the high rate of evaporation depletes so much water from their reserves that they die from dehydration. According to a study by Alexander Gerson at the University of Massachusetts, these songbirds start panting at around 40°C, and can only tolerate water losses of approximately 15 to 20% of their body mass before they die.

In NASA's study, the scientists found that smaller songbird species, such as the lesser goldfinch, lose water at a proportionately higher rate than do larger birds. For example, in 50°C, the lesser goldfinch loses 8 to 9% of its body mass to evaporative water per hour—enough to die from dehydration in less than 110 minutes. While larger birds such as the curve-billed thrasher only lose about 5% of their mass per hour in the same temperatures, researchers forecast that by the end of the century, the number of days that these songbirds will be susceptible to lethal dehydration will rise annually from 7 to 25.

As climate change continues to accelerate, the livelihood of desert songbird species will undoubtedly be at risk. But is there anything we can do to save them? Scientists from NASA think that climate refugia, microclimates such as trees, washes, and mountaintops will be essential to ensuring their survival. Using data collected from this study, they will also be able to identify refugia that best match the temperature profiles of these songbirds. While these five species are certainly in danger, researchers are very eager to learn more, and plan to conduct studies in South African and Australia to better understand their physiological responses to more powerful heat waves.

Reiny, S., 2017. U.S. desert songbirds at risk in a warming climate. NASA Earth Science News Team, 1-4. https://tinyurl.com/jumkqga

3-D Printing Could Save Coral Reefs
by Kele Mkpado

It is a modern day travesty that due to climate change and the rising of temperatures in our oceans we are at risk of losing

90% of our coral reefs. Luckily for us, there's a group of scientists who say that innovative 3-D printing might be the solution to our problems. An article by Jeremy Deaton in Popular Science explains just how to do it.

Coral colonies comprise of very small polyps that attach to rocks on the seafloor. From there, they constantly release a calcium compound at their base that builds up over time. These coral structures create a habitat for algae and plankton that are then eaten by fish and larger predators living in the reef. The algae are also what gives the coral its vivid color and beauty. When temperatures get too hot, the polyps in the coral reject the algae and die, causing the whole ecosystem to collapse. On top of rising temperatures, increased carbon pollution is making the ocean more acidic and the polyps cannot produce their calcium deposit as well.

Humans have been creating artificial reefs for a while, sinking ships and placing artificial objects under water. With 3-D printing we can accurately mimic the environment these corals create, and attract polyps and algae to them with bright colors of healthy coral. The artificial coral will be made of sandstone with a porcelain coating to closely mimic the texture of actual coral. In another model, a designer created an artificial coral placement that would slowly dissolve and neutralize the pH in the water around it, creating a more hospitable environment for the surrounding organisms.

Coral is vital to the health of our oceans, and this could be the invention that saves them. As 3-D printing becomes more reliable and cost effective, it is easy to imagine governments investing in a corral saving strategies. Half a billion people rely on coral reefs to sustain their way of life, so it is not something we can readily ignore. If the temperature of the water increases by 1.5°C, we could lose 90% of our coral reefs. If this method proves effective, we could restore most of our coral reefs to their former glory.

http://www.easybib.com/cite/view
Deaton, Jeremy. "3D Printing Could Save Coral Reefs." Popular Science. N.p., n.d. Web. 10 Apr. 2017.

Preserving Biodiversity
by Luis Salazar

A member of the Wildlife Conservation Society, James Watson, saw an image circulating online that detailed rare and common deaths in Australia. The deaths ranged from war and pregnancy to cancer and heart disease, most rare to common respectively. James Watson then questioned the possibility of replicating this relationship with all of nature.

Nijhuis (2016) explains the complexity of why we have not been able to replicate common death threats to all of nature, noticing in particular the lack of data that has existed in the past decades. Threats have been investigated on a specific basis rather than investigating collective threats. Recently, more investigations have been open with the purpose of finding a threat to many species.

Nijhuis then cites Watson and Sean Maxwell, a doctoral student, working together to analyze and create a list of threats that would affect close to nine thousand species. According to an article they published in the journal *Nature,* a majority of the species studied are threatened by human activity. A large majority of species is affected by a change in natural environment. Surprisingly, only a small percent of the species from the study are threatened by climate change.

Writers have been hesitant to cover climate change because it is unpredictable. Nijhuis argues that because there are multiple contributing factors to climate change, there is a difficulty in narrowing down the timeline of the effects. The threat of climate change is being pushed with a short term goal of maintaining average global temperatures below the threshold of 2°C.

Other threats that have been around for decades get less media attention and are only brought up when the threat has followed through with its course. It is imperative to not only focus on climate change, but to also dedicate some time to immediate threats so that we can still have a diverse species when we battle climate change.

Nijhuis, Michelle. Are Conservationists Worrying Too Much About Climate Change? The New Yorker. The New Yorker, 10 Aug. 2016.

Preserving Biodiversity in Hotspots
by Luis Salazar

Climate change and commercial fishing are damaging ocean hot spots of life. According to an international team, it is important to use marine biodiversity as a resource to finding the hotspots in oceans. It is not a coincidence that these hotspots are collocated with warmer temperatures and higher rates of fishing.

According to Andre Chiardia, a penguin-focused scientist, the hotspots are at a higher risk than other ocean regions because they experience change faster. With the support of other climate scientists, Chiardia argues that fishing should be reduced in these areas for the sake of preventing the accelerated effects of global warming. An outside observer and marine ecologist, Maria Vernet, describes the human legacy as the preservation of marine diversity.

New biodiversity research has uncovered interesting connections to Darwin's research of evolution. The connection is made by the most active hotspot, near the South American coast. Charles Darwin was continually astonished by the Galapagos Islands and pursued the theory of evolution in this region.

The discovery of more hotspots have uncovered similar results. According to Chiardia, biodiversity exists in excess near the Pacific ocean and southern hemisphere. Chiardia argues that biodiversity is a result of isolation: "On land, we have kangaroos and weird animals like the platypus. And in the ocean it's not different." Commercial fishing in hotspots near the Pacific negatively affect marine biodiversity. Biodiversity, such as Australian sea dragons, must be preserved; the uniqueness of marine biology is being damaged enough by global warming—humans can relieve the effects of global warming on marine biodiversity by discontinuing fishing and in areas populated with thousands of species. As cited by the Associated Press, penguins are being directly affected by the change in water temperatures. Similarly, Chiardia illustrates that warm water has, "decimated Galapagos penguins and the population of southern African penguins has dropped by 90 percent in just 20 years." This is an issue that must be addressed sooner rather than later. If humans can control the effects of climate change, it would be beneficial to still have biodiversity.

The Associated Press 2017. In Hot Water: Climate Change Harms Hot Spots of Ocean Life. The New York Times. The New York Times, 22 Feb. 2017.

The Drawbacks of an Early Spring
by Tanisha Sheth

The U.S. Geological Survey's National Phenology Network, which tracks seasonal changes in plants and animals, noted that this year biological spring arrived three weeks earlier. Jack Weltzin, the executive director of the National Phenology Network then explained what was happening; Mr. Weltzin's team uses a model that combines weather data with historical data on the leafing and flowering of lilacs and honeysuckles, early indicators of spring, to create a biological map of the onset of spring. There have been no previous trends in weather patterns to indicate such behavior. Mr. Weltzin noted that this year was an anomaly. Due to the recent heat, the biological spring has been pushed forward. The early spring moved up the United States from the South till it stalled New York City.

A model used by the network earlier found that spring-times at 75% of 300 national parks over a span of 100 years provided evidence that the climate is changing. He then spoke about the downsides of an early spring stating several disadvantages to this phenomenon instigated by climate change. An early spring implies that when a hard frost follows a period of early flowering, plants can be damaged and crops will be lost. The mosquito season and tick season will start earlier, and possibly spread more disease. Furthermore, the pollen season will tend to last longer and we will experience an increase in its intensity. Migratory species, like birds, will arrive sooner due to the notion of this 'false spring' and will have trouble finding food.

This observation when extrapolated to current scientific data suggests its potential to disrupt the entire food chain. These gradual climate shifts have started occurring throughout the world. This highlights that just the onset of an early spring should not be deemed irrelevant, and climate change has become a pressing issue.

Vidal, John., 2017 'We need development': Maldives switches focus from climate threat to mass tourism. The Guardian

African Countries Mobilize to Battle Invasive Caterpillars
by Charlie Thomson

In a 2017 article published in Scientific American by Sarah Wild of Nature Magazine, the issue and prevalence of invasive crop pests in Africa was discussed and attributed to global climate change. The crop pest in question is the fall armyworm, a caterpillar. Beginning in Africa, this species of caterpillar has wreaked havoc on staple crops such as maize, millet, and sorghum — experts on the issue have warned that Europe and Asia could be next if the ravenous caterpillars are not stopped. In an emergency meeting organized by the regional Africa office of the Food and Agriculture Organization (FAO) of the United Nations in Harare, Zimbabwe, government officials met to coordinate their response to the problem. As a result of this meeting, sixteen African countries agreed to actionable measures that would increase their capacities to manage crop pests more effectively and efficiently. According to Joyce Mulila-Mitti, the FAO's crop officer for southern Africa, "The meeting in Harare was basically aimed largely at strengthening preparedness for the countries." The pest is the larval form of the fall armyworm moth, which possesses a voracious and indiscriminate appetite — devouring its way through over 100 different plant species that include the aforementioned crops. In a report given at the Harare meeting, it was estimated that at least 290,000 hectares of cropland across 4 countries have already been destroyed by these pests. Even more alarming than this statistic is the fact that experts cautioned the figure to be an underestimate and that the exact figure is likely much higher. The pest originated in Central and South America, and was first identified in West Africa in January of 2016. Since the caterpillar was identified in West Africa, it has spread to at least 12 countries on the continent having reached 7 of those in the last two months alone. The fall armyworm is a serious problem in the countries where it is endemic. According to the FAO, it is estimated that Brazil alone spends US$600 million each year to control infestations and prevent further crop destruction. Although no one knows exactly how the insect made its way into Africa, experts say it is likely due to increased trade and climate change. As stated by Ken Wilson, an ecologist at Lancaster University in the United Kingdom, "With global climate change, we can probably expect more of these fluctuations in temperature and rainfall. In addition, with increased global trade and travel, we can expect greater movement of pests within and between continents." This could be exacerbated by food shortages that necessitate an increase in movement of agricultural produce. This caterpillar endemic is just one of many problems our world faces as a result of global climate change — and the problems are only multiplying and getting worse.

Wild, Sarah, and Nature Magazine. "African Countries Mobilize to Battle Invasive Caterpillars." Scientific American. Scientific American, 23 Feb. 2017. Web. 26 Feb. 2017. <https://www.scientificamerican.com/article/african-countries-mobilize-to-battle-invasive-caterpillars/>.

Cherry Blossoms May Bloom Earlier Than Ever This Year
by Charlie Thomson

In a 2017 article by Brittany Patterson, in Scientific American, the earliest blooming of Washington D.C's cherry blossoms were discussed. The National Park Service predicted that peak cherry blossom bloom in 2017 will occur sometime between March 14th and 17th, the earliest on record. The earlier bloom of the blossoms this season is likely due to a milder winter and unusually warm temperatures throughout the year, said Mike Litterst, chief of communications for the National Mall. "Our scientists and any meteorologist will tell you the same thing: Blossoming depends first and foremost on the weather," he said. "We had a mild winter, the warmest February on record and basically no snow. All of that goes into the mix." Many plants and trees, such as cherry trees, rely on temperatures to regulate their biological clocks. Climate change is not only altering when the spring season begins, but is altering many phenological phenomena like flowers blooming and leaf color changes in the fall as well. Weather station measurements across Washington have shown the area experiencing a 1.6°C per century since 1946—double the global rate. The average date of peak blossoms is April 4, although since record-keeping began in 1921, that date has shifted up five days, Litterst said. The colder temperatures of winter tell cherry trees to go dormant, but warmer temperatures are causing them to bloom progressively earlier. "In flowering trees, heat breaks winter dormancy, so earlier cherry blooming is consistent with heating caused by climate change," said Patrick Gonzalez, a National Park Service climate change scientist. The earlier blossoming of cherry trees is just one example of many as to how global warming and climate change is altering our planet, begging question of when is enough, enough? At what point will all these record breaking changes in natural phenomena stir enough reaction from our planet's population to get everyone on the same page with regards to climate change and it's harmful side-effects?

Patterson, Brittany. "Cherry Blossoms May Bloom Earlier Than Ever This Year." Scientific American. Scientific American, 02 Mar. 2017. Web. 05 Mar. 2017. <https://www.scientificamerican.com/article/cherry-blossoms-may-bloom-earlier-than-ever-this-year/>.

Effect of Climate Change on National Parks
by Kelly Watanabe

National parks are areas of undeveloped land which preserve natural resources for the public to enjoy. However, Hansen (2016) suggests that these parks—especially their trees—are threatened by climate change. Unlike animals in the park, trees suffer more due to their limited mobility; trees cannot migrate as quickly as animals can. Climate change projects have developed projection models to help park managers figure out which trees should have priority in being saved.

According to Hansen, increase in temperature, increase in atmospheric CO_2 concentrations, and decrease in annual rainfall could destroy just as many forests as humans did through cutting down trees. In eastern North America, the Landscape Climate Change Vulnerability Project uses scientific modeling to compile a database that projects climate change effects on specific park locations and individual tree species. Because majority of the forests in the eastern US are frequently cleared due to natural disasters and human deforestation, the database is most useful for answering the question, What species of tree to should park managers plant in which area? Hansen emphasizes the need for a diverse spread of tree species; the majority of eastern forests are homogenized due to replanting of a few species. Patrick Jantz and Brendan Rogers of the Woods Hole Research Center predict that the Appalachia will have fewer frost days and thus a longer growing season. This gives trees the potential to thrive more, but Rogers suggest that trees may not reach their maturity due to climate change happening too quickly. Due to climate change, less precipitation with higher maximum temperatures and a longer growing season yields potential for more droughts. Jantz and Rogers suggest that the maple and eastern hemlock will suffer while the blackjack oak and black hickory will thrive in warmer climates.

In the western parks of North America, Andy Hansen of the Great Northern Landscape Climate Cooperative recognizes that the West has more extreme elevations and more frequent droughts than the East. NASA's Terrestrial Observation and Prediction System (TOPS) is the computer model specialized for western areas. TOPS predicts forest growth rates so that park managers can preserve the existing trees instead of replanting new species. Due to increasing temperatures, Hansen predicts that the whitebark pine—the iconic tree of the west which provides food for grizzly bears—will migrate to higher and higher elevations in search of a cooler habitat. However, Hansen worries that the whitebark pine will eventually be "pushed off the mountaintops."

Hansen, K., 2016. Natural Beauty at Risk: Preparing for Climate Change in National Parks. NASA Earth Observatory.
http://earthobservatory.nasa.gov/Features/NationalParksClimate/printall.php

Climate Change Caused the Extinction of Ancient Megafauna in Australia
by Kelly Watanabe

Long ago, Australia was inhabited by bizarre animals such as a 500 lb kangaroo, giant lizards, and flightless birds. A scientific study conducted by DeSantis *et al.* (2016) provides evidence of climate change as the cause of extinction for 88 megafauna species in Australia. Between 400,000 and 450,000 years ago, megafauna—abnormally large mammals, birds, and reptiles—experienced slow weather shifts which caused an increase in aridity. The decrease in water availability caused a decrease in megafauna food supply, which led to megafauna extinction via competition and lack of resources.

To study the relationship between climate and megafauna diet, DeSantis *et al.* used fossilized marsupial teeth found in Cuddie Springs, Australia. Analysis of the chemical composition of modern kangaroo teeth proved to be a good proxy for humidity levels and diet. Thus, analysis of oxygen and carbon isotopes in ancient marsupial teeth created predictive models for climate and diet levels during the era of megafauna. The changes in relative concentrations of stable oxygen isotopes indicated shifts in temperature, humidity, and precipitation. Change of carbon stable isotope ratios indicated seasonal differences in diet and eventual lack of food source for the marsupials. As the climate became more arid, marsupials shifted away from their original food source: the saltbush plant. Saltbush had a high concentration of salt, which required marsupials to have a high water intake to combat the salt. Saltbush is a type of C4 vegetation. Fossilized teeth showed a shift from C4 vegetation to C3 vegetation. Moreover, DeSantis *et al.* used dental texture analysis of megafauna teeth to determine changes in diet. By examining the scratch patterns on the teeth, DeSantis *et al.* concluded that the drier climate caused megafauna to shift to other plant resources. However, the decrease in precipitation caused the water content in plants to decrease, which caused a lack of nutrition for megafauna.

Because many megafauna could not migrate due to a lack of cool climate areas in Australia, megafauna went extinct.

DeSantis *et al.* provides evidence against the theory of human hunting as the cause for megafauna extinction. While there is no existing empirical evidence of human hunting, carbon analysis of Genyornis—a large flightless bird similar to the modern emu—teeth proves that C4 vegetation decreased during a time of unfavorable climate change. Genyornis teeth date back to 50,000 years ago when there was a low human population density. DeSantis concludes that Genyornis extinction is unlikely to be correlated to human interaction, but rather due to a drier climate.

DeSantis, L. R. G., Field, J. H., Wroe, S., Dodson, J. R., 2016. Dietary responses of Sahul (Pleistocene Australia-New Guinea) megafauna to climate and environmental change. Paleobiology 1-15.

Tourism Amplifies the Effects of Climate Change on Maldvies Islands
by Kelly Watanabe

Maldives—an archipelago in the Indian Ocean—introduces geographical problems as it introduces tourists. According to Schultz (2017), rising sea levels and erosion along the shore are effects of both climate change and human modification of the environment. Before 2008, the Maldives government designated islands to be privately owned resort islands. These separate islands had expensive villas for tourists to rent. In the 2008 election, Maldives shifted from autocracy to democracy. To boost Maldives economy and create more jobs, the president passed a law allowing residents to open guesthouses on local islands. Affordable guesthouses catered toward frugal travelers while villas catered toward rich vacationers.

Schultz argues that Guraidhoo—a Maldives island home to local residents—suffered from the tourism industry. Holiday Inn Resort on Kandooma—a neighboring tourist island which used to be a coral rock island—dredged sand from Guraidhoo to fill Kandooma's beaches. The beach modification caused erosion and destruction to the coastal reefs. Because reefs are a natural barrier against higher waves from rising sea levels, the effects of climate change coupled with invasive construction caused a spike in damage from sea level rise. Residents are now using leftover concrete from old buildings to create sea walls around their homes. Moreover, coastal erosion forced residents to modify their harbors.

Guraidhoo has a domestic population of 1,900 and a tourist population of 1,000. Some Guraidhoo local residents want to stop the opening of guesthouses because they fear that tourism is overpowering their government and their religion. Maldives is 100% Sunni Muslim. Because revealing swim suits are not acceptable in Sunni Muslim religion, "bikini beaches" were formed as designated beach areas for tourists.

In 2015, Maldives government implemented a green tax which charged tourists $6 extra a night for villas and $3 extra a night for guesthouses. Green tax revenue was supposed to fund a conservation project to hire marine biologists and build sea walls, but Maldives's recent 2017 budget proposal did not reveal the allocation of the green tax revenue. According to Schultz, local Maldives residents are concerned that the government is prioritizing the economic advantage of tourism over the islands' protection.

Schultz, K., 2017. As the Maldives Gains Tourists, It's Losing Its Beaches. New York Times.

Is It Possible Climate Change Could Help Plants?
by Jason Yi

Chelsea Harvey (2017) begins the article with the fact that there are many consequences of climate change. However, the most urgent problem is the future impact on agriculture. As the world continues to grow, the population will soon exceed nine billion people and the safety of food has become a pressing issue for many. Previous studies suggested that as the temperatures reach 86 degrees, the growth of many plants quickly declines. Moreover, Harvey cites a recent study done by Schauberger, a PhD student and researcher at Potsdam Institute for Climate Impact Research which acknowledged that high temperatures are indeed harmful for most crops.

However, such research is inevitably limited because plants react differently to temperatures depending on the crop and region. In naturally cold locations, the rising temperatures are, in fact, beneficial for plant life and experience the "greening effect." Nonetheless, the problem lies in fact that most places around the world have moderately warm climates. As the temperatures continue to rise, there will be a detrimental effect on the plants.

Harvey further adds that there are others who support the idea that climate change could possibly help the plants' growth due to increased carbon dioxide levels. More carbon dioxide essentially means more energy for the plants. However, new studies reveal otherwise. The study utilized three crops: maize, soybean and wheat. The researchers then subjected them to changes in temperature and recorded the results. Once again, the results were that under high temperatures, 97 degrees specifically, the plants' growth rates declined up to 49%. It was also found that more water could potentially help lessen some of these detrimental effects. Moreover, when plants are suffering from a lack of water, they enter a series of steps to help them survive. One step is to close stomates on the leaves to prevent any further water loss. This step forces plants to take in less carbon dioxide. As a result, increased carbon dioxide levels ultimately would not benefit the plants. Harvey concludes with a statement from Schauberger that the best method to combat climate change is to simply cause less of it.

Harvey, C. 2017. Climate Change Will Hurt Crops More Than It Helps Them, Study Suggests. Washington Post Jan 19

Food and Water Supplies and Climate Change

Is Climate Change Making Wine Better?
by Joshua Dorman

A 2016 study conducted by Cornelis van Deeuwen and Philippe Darriet and published in the *Journal of Wine Economics* aimed to gauge the impact of climate change on the world of viticulture and wine quality. Considering elements such as temperature, water deficit, wine acidity, and wine typicity, the two researchers found some surprising trends. As the Earth's temperature has increased, wine quality appears to be improving along with it.

First, the two researchers decided to look at how temperature itself affects phenology, the seasonal growth states of grapes relative to climate factors. They found that an increase in temperature causes a clear advance in the natural process, leading growers to pick their grapes significantly earlier than usual. In fact, "since the 1980s, harvest dates have advanced by two weeks in Alsace and Bordeaux, France" and similar increases have been noted in wine countries throughout the world.

However, wine vintages are also getting drier. Dryness of a vintage, it seems, is inversely related to the amount of rainfall a specific region receives during the growing period. As is commonly known throughout the scientific community, overall rainfall in many agricultural regions of the world has been steadily decreasing as a result of climate change. Leeuwen and Darriet analyzed the data and found that the water balance—a measure of the amount of water held in soil—of the Saint-Emilion region in France has been steadily decreasing over the past sixty years. Correspondingly, "among the 20 driest vintages in 61 years, 10 occurred in the period 2000–2012." Most importantly, however, they charted water balance against vintage quality and found a surprising correlation: the drier the soil, the higher the wine was rated. Their conclusion; higher temperatures caused by climate seem to enhance the dryness of vintages, a quality that so many connoisseurs look for. Yet unfortunately the news was not all good.

In another batch of data related to climate change, the researchers found the potential alcohol in grapes in the Languedoc region in France to have increased from about 11% in 1984 to about 14% by volume in 2013. In the 1980s the alcohol level was deemed "too low" for many, so grapes benefited from an increase. However, now grapes are often being picked with alcohol levels above 14%, an amount deemed "too high for optimum quality." Moreover, higher temperatures are predicted to increase evapotranspiration, the process which increases soil dryness by letting soil water evaporate into the air at an increased rate. While it does indeed increase vintage dryness, such a phenomenon will surely lead to decreased grape yields in wine countries across the world, a significant trend that is already being observed. Furthermore, climate change has been known to allow increased levels of UV-B radiation to escape through the atmosphere, an effect that can cause sunburn on grapes and severely impair the quality of white wine.

Although climate change has appeared to improve wine up till now, Leeuwen and Darriet recommend that growers adapt quickly to the changing viticulture landscape before global warming begins to severely harm wine quality. For the past few decades, the wine industry has flourished. But if growers refuse to alter their practices, they'll have a lot less to toast to.

Leeuwen, Cornelis Van, and Philippe Darriet. "The Impact of Climate Change on Viticulture and Wine Quality." Journal of Wine Economics 11, no. 01 (2016): 150-67. doi:10.1017/jwe.2015.21.

Will Sushi Become Climate Change's Next Victim?
by Joshua Dorman

In 2050, the average trip to a local sushi restaurant will likely be absent of the multitude of colors and flavors that currently fill a plate of chef's-choice sashimi. Rather, a pile of overpriced indistinguishable sea creature will occupy your platter. In an article written for the news organization Vice, staff writer Mike Pearl explores the impact climate change is wreaking on the sushi industry and how both consumers and producers must adapt their expectations to fit a bleak culinary landscape.

Scientists and researchers alike are quickly coming to the conclusion that the fish which will appear on a sushi table in

2050 are likely to look a lot different than the ones we're seeing today. Warmer water, combined with higher concentrations of ocean acidity, will make life hard or even impossible for many fish we routinely purchase off the menu. William Cheung, a researcher and associate professor at the University of British Columbia, compiled data on climate change and the fishing industry and published a report which forecasts an outlook for as far as 2055. Not only did he conclude that sushi itself will look completely different in forty years' time, but he predicted that "some [average] fish may not be so easy to get in the future, as they become really premium fish." Unfortunately, evidence of this phenomenon is already coming to pass; a single bluefin tuna recently sold for $600,000. In other words, those fatty *toro* rolls that you enjoy so often at your local joint may not stick around for much longer, or they'll become so expensive as to be virtually unaffordable.

Nevertheless, any hope for the future of sushi seems to lie in culinary creativity. As Cheung suggested, "there may be new inventions of new sushi using new fish that may become available." In fact, some innovative chefs are already moving beyond the commonality of spicy tuna rolls to find more sustainable and environmentally friendly options. For instance, Bun Lai, owner of Miya's restaurant in New Haven, Connecticut, gathers regional invasive crabs, insects, Asian carp, and woodland plants to add to his rolls. Unfortunately, if sushi joints refuse to go Lai's route and adapt to the changing demands of the industry, in forty years jellyfish might become the new California roll, and sushi will die a cold and salty death as we know it.

Pearl, Mike. "Sushi as We Know It Will Be Wiped Out by 2050." Vice. February 2, 2017. Accessed February 14, 2017. https://www.vice.com/en_us/article/sushi-as-we-know-it-will-be-wiped-out-by-2050.

Lower Quality Tea Thanks to Climate Change
by Bryn Edwards

Major tea-producing areas across Asia such as Japan, China's Yunnan province, and Assam and Darjeeling in India are being affected by increased rainfall caused by rising global temperatures. This is detrimental to tea production in that compounds valued by tea drinkers—flavor, antioxidant properties, and caffeine levels—are being diluted as the ideal threshold of rainfall for tea plants is surpassed. So, global warming takes its toll across the globe, tea production will be one of the many casualties. For every 1° F that the Earth's surface temperature rises, the atmosphere's water-holding limit increases by about 4%. Areas such as those mentioned above that are already prone to flooding during monsoon season will be even more at risk. Farmers are changing processing methods to hide tea imperfections and diluted flavors. Green tea is minimally processed, and thus harder to hide imperfections in; so farmers are switching to black or oolong tea instead since the longer fermentation process disguises flavor imperfections. Aside from rainfall, producers also face increased temperature variability. High temperatures encourage early blooms, followed by aggressive frosts damages and even kill the plants. Selena Ahmed, an assistant professor of sustainable food systems at Montana State University has a few ideas for saving the tea industry. She suggests growing tea in more diverse ecosystems as opposed to in monocultures, growing the plants from seed instead of propagating them from cuttings to encourage stronger root systems and to diversify the genepool and organic farming. She also discussed the importance of tea as an indicator species of the changing ecosystem. As there are many factors that affect the flavors of tea, minute changes in the ecosystem that might not otherwise be apparent are easy to trace simply through flavor. Looking to the future, she encourages emphasis on quality over quantity of tea.

Wei, Clarissa. The Future of Tea Looks Bleak, Thanks to Climate Change: Warmer Weather is Stripping Flavor From Your Cup. Eater. http://www.eater.com/drinks /2016/7/8/12111038/climate-change-tea-leaves-flavor.

How Food Consumption and Nutrition React to Climate Change
by Claudia Chandra

According to the Food and Agriculture Organization of the United Nations, 805 million people suffered from hunger and undernourishment in 2014. With this, 2 billion people experienced a micronutrient deficiency (iron, vitamin A, zinc etc.) These problems are now paired and compounded by obesity and other diet-related non-communicable diseases (NCDs). With the world's population predicted to be 9 billion by 2050, this matter is bound to affect our food system's ecological footprint.

In 2016, researchers Michelle Holdsworth and Nicolas Bricas published "Climate Change and Agriculture Worldwide," a journal which examines the connection between climate change and nutrition. The journal begins by going through global nutritional problems, their determinants, and the ways in which dietary changes caused by food sector industrialization and urbanization contribute to increasing malnutrition and climate change. Subsequently, the study also investigates the impact that climate change has on food and nutrition. The study concludes by suggesting what future research should focus on to resolve growing global food scarcity and malnutrition.

Holdsworth and Bricas found that climate change and diet-related NCDs share many of the same determinants. The increasing demand for food has led to the use of more non-renewable energy sources that in turn has stimulated rapid industrialization in agriculture, which has outstripped population growth. More costly plastic and metal packaging is needed with higher food production — due to this, "agriculture and the agrifood sector (processing, distribution, catering) have become heavy GHG producers" (Griffiths *et al.* 2008). Food overproduction also contributes to an increase in waste and global warming because not only is some of the energy that goes into its production wasted as some of the food is unconsumed, but also because the detrimental impact on the environment increases as more waste is processed. In this way, increasing demand and overproduction create a vicious cycle that negatively affects global climate change.

The researchers use meat over-consumption to exemplify rising GHG emissions in the food system. The average global meat consumption is 100g/day/person. However, this figure masks the disparities that exist because of socioeconomic differences. In low and middle-income countries, the figure is 47g/day/person, while in high income countries the figure are five times higher at 224g/day/person. Not only does overconsuming meat increase the risk of heart disease, the inefficiency of its production is also cause for concern. As "livestock must, on average, consume 7 kcal of plant fodder to produce 1 kcal of meat," meat's growing demand translates into rapid increases of grain production, which has obvious implications in terms of GHG emissions and accelerating climate change.

The impact of climate change on undernutrition and communities dependent on agriculture is also discussed. Holdsworth and Bricas noticed that climate change is worsening existing undernutrition as it undermines antipoverty initiatives. For instance, droughts in sub-Saharan Africa have caused food scarcity and even famines (i.e. in Somalia). Elevated food prices, one of the most obvious consequences of increasing climate variability, will also give rise to food insecurity and civil unrest especially in poorer areas where a large percentage of income is spent on food. Data gathered in Congo between 1986 and 1991 show that during a food crisis, "food prices can increase the incidence of overweightness (including obesity) among urban women and also increase the number of underweight people." For communities dependent on agriculture, long-term climate change will influence households' access to resources, leading to unstable food supplies. Extreme climate events will have a profound effect on all aspects of food, including "security, access, availability, utilization, and stability." Climate changes that affect ecosystems will lead to changes in livelihoods, diets, water availability, and eventually nutritional status.

Due to the concerning nature of the influence of climate change on the food system, the study suggests future research that should be undertaken. Different research approaches need to be considered in developing countries because of the complexity of nutritional problems. The study asserts that research should "focus on both over- and under-nutrition," and also the connection between the two. Since food scarcity and health issues will likely intensify in the future, food research should focus on preventing all forms of malnutrition. Furthermore, researchers should focus on the role of women in mitigating GHG emissions because more women have jobs related to gathering firewood and supplying food for the household. And finally, because there is currently not enough reliable knowledge on the changes in agricultural production zones and food availability due too changing climates, Holdsworth and Bricas assert the need for extensive research on the organization of food systems in response to climate. This is especially significant as each country's share of local production and imports is expected to change, but the consequences of such changes on the population's diet and nutrition is yet to be assessed.

Holdsworth, M., Bricas, N., 2016. "Impact of Climate Change on Food Consumption and Nutrition." Climate Change and Agriculture Worldwide. Springer Netherlands., pp 227–238.
http://link.springer.com/chapter/10.1007/978-94-017-7462-8_17

The Impact of Climate Change on Wine
by Claudia Chandra

In 2016, scientists Benjamin Cook and Elizabeth Wolkovich researched the influence of climate change on grape phenology, harvest dates, and wine quality.

To do this, they analyzed grape phenology and climate data in France and Switzerland for a period of 400 years between 1600 and 2007, including years without anthropogenic interference in the climate system. Historically, early grape maturation and harvest were enabled by warmer summer temperatures, generated by droughts, and hindered by wet conditions in the spring and summer. Cook and Wolkovich's study found that the relationship between drought and temperatures has weakened in recent decades (1981–2007) due to increasing anthropogenic climate change. Warming caused by anthropogenic greenhouse gasses (GHGs) can mimic the warmer temperatures traditionally brought about by drought conditions, leading to more frequent early harvests. Thus, the study found that climate change has "fundamentally altered" temperatures and growing conditions, the climatic determinants of wine grape harvests. These alterations could affect viticulture management and wine quality in the future.

Cook and Wolkovich examined wine ratings and other metrics of wine quality and observed that "high quality wines are typically associated with early harvest dates" and are also "favored by warm summers with above-average early-season rainfall and late season drought." This is because, as temperature is the most influential factor on wine grape phenology, the grape's full cycle of development (budburst, flowering, and maturity) is accelerated in warmer temperatures and delayed where there is increased precipitation.

Through statistical analyses, the study established an overall trend towards earlier harvest dates in the past 3 decades, and that there have been changes in the strength of the relationship between grape phenology and the climate determinants of moisture and temperature. More specifically, Cook and Wolkovich noted that the significance of the relationship shared between grape growth and moisture (from precipitation) has declined in recent years. However, the relationship between grape growth and temperatures has remained relatively stationary. This means that although the temperature sensitivity of harvest dates has remained the same over time, the importance of precipitation for wine grape phenology has diminished.

The scientists predict that there are two factors that have allowed moisture to have a smaller influence on grape growth. The first is the "apparent weakening of the soil moisture-temperature relationship over Western Europe," wherein the moisture variability of the region no longer has a significant impact on its temperature changes. The second is that with the strengthening of anthropogenic climate change, added artificial heating has "made it easier for summers to reach critical heat thresholds needed for early harvest dates." This was previously impossible as drought conditions were necessary to reach such temperature extremes. Cook and Wolkovich's findings suggest a large-scale shift in the way climate contributes to early harvests in the wine growing regions of France and Switzerland. Fortunately, grape records and wine quality data show that warmer temperatures have consistently led to earlier harvests and higher-quality wines.

The study acknowledges that its results do not confirm an inevitable future where wine quality is influenced completely by environmental and climate changes. This is because grape harvest dates depend on factors beyond climate including grape varieties, soils, and winemaker practices. What the results do show, however, is that the large-scale climatic drivers that influence factors such as soils and winemaker practices, have fundamentally changed due to anthropogenic climate change. This information has broad applicability as global warming is predicted to intensify in all wine-growing regions.

Cook, Benjamin. I., Wolkovich, Elizabeth. M., 2016. "Climate change decouples drought from early wine grape harvests in France." Nature Climate Change. Vol 6, 715 – 719.
http://www.nature.com/nclimate/journal/v6/n7/pdf/nclimate2960.pdf

Future Predictions Regarding Climate Change's Effects on Water Scarcity.
by Chris Choi

Simon Gosling and Nigel Arnell (2016) analyze how climate change can have an impact on water scarcity in the future. Water scarcity is a large global issue and is becoming a more prevalent problem. Climate change as well as an increase in human population will reduce the availability of water in many watershed areas including East and South Asia. The authors created several global climate models (GCMs) to emulate different scenarios in which emissions and populations vary and how these factors relate to water scarcity.

To test the GCMs, the authors used hydrological models to predict the future annual runoff. Some models were made to measure the number of people exposed to water scarcity in watershed areas over thirty year periods (climate change is absent for these models), and others emulated increased temperatures. They were used to calculate two measures of water scarcity. The first is the Water Crowding Index (WCI), a measure of annual water resources per capita in watershed areas. The second is the Water Stress Index (WSI), the ratio of water withdrawals to resources. These two measures together indicate levels of exposure to water scarcity. From these measures, the authors tried to figure out whether climate change would lead to the reduction, or the increase in water scarcity.

The authors first examined the time models. Though the simulations showed that the global population increases over time, they also demonstrate that water scarcity in both WCI and WSI increase over time. The models also show that the annual runoff in areas such as East and South Asia increases. Researchers then examined models with increasing temperatures and how they could affect water scarcity. Based on the results, water scarcity rises non-linearly with the global mean temperature. As the temperature initially increases, water scarcity goes up very steeply. Later, however, it begins to stabilize again.

After conducting these simulations, the authors found it hard to make direct comparisons between changes in exposure to water scarcity due to the differences in which the GCM's were applied. Variables such as emission rates and population differed in each model. However, based on all the models that they created, they found that climate change patterns tend to lead to an increase in water scarcity rather than a decrease, and these projections are more sensitive to climate change than emissions scenarios.

Gosling, S., Arnell, N., 2016. "A global assessment of the impact of climate change on water scarcity". Climactic Change, 134, 371-385
http://link.springer.com/article/10.1007/s10584-013-0853-x

Climate Change's Effects on Alaskan Subsistence Resources
by Chris Choi

Todd Brinkman and other professors (2016) researched both Interior Alaska and the coast of Northern Alaska on how climate change is affecting the subsistence resources available to the indigenous people. The researchers attempted to asses the effectiveness of Traditional Ecological Knowledge (TEK) to help maintain a stable level of resources. However, those outside the indigenous population do not believe in TEK and instead try to implement their own methods to keep these resources available. The main objective of this study was to identify how climate change affects the availability of local resources as well as to figure out how the amount of subsistence resources will change in the future.

To determine how each of the populations lived, researchers cooperated with local organizations to design and implement a research approach. The local organizations were either tribal councils or village corporations, and they picked people and resources that best represented their harvest system. Harvesters participated in three interviews. The first interview focused on each of the populations' subsistence resources and the effects of environment on their availability. The second interview examined how climate-related environmental variables have changed since the 1960s. The final interview looked at how relationships between subsistence resources and environmental trends have affected the availability of each resource.

After conducting the interviews, researchers found that the populations of Interior Alaska experienced climate-driven changes in temperature. Average temperature has increased, thus leading to an increase in wildfire frequencies. As for the coastal communities, they saw decreased amounts of sea ice. All populations saw that their land was becoming more dry and believed that the supposed increased precipitation rates were false. Current climate trends indicate that the subsistence resource availability will remain the same or decrease within the next 30 years.

Though researchers gained a better idea of how climate change affects subsistence resources, they were only able to examine a small subset of climate-related changes. For future research, Brinkman believes that models of temporal and spatial interactions among environmental variables may allow researchers to better understand climate-related impacts on subsistence resource availability. Overall, the study conducted by Brinkman and other researchers sets the stage for future studies to find the specific consequences of climate impacts on maintaining subsistence resources.

Brinkman, Todd J., et al. "Arctic communities perceive climate impacts on access as a critical challenge to availability of subsistence resources." Climatic Change 139.3-4 (2016): 413-427.

Climate Change and its Effect on Shorter Snow Cover Durations

by Chris Choi

Geoffrey Klein *et al.* (2016) examined how average snow cover has decreased over the past decades in the Swiss Alps and other lowland areas and mountainous areas. Researchers believe that this is caused by the increasing global temperatures which could accelerate snowmelt and reduce snowfall during the winter. To see if this trend was true, they examined how snowpack in the Swiss Alps and how it has changed from 1970-2015. This would allow researchers to determine if the decrease in snow cover is due to earlier snowmelt or later snow onset or a combination of both.

Researchers selected stations in different areas of the Swiss Alps. They picked stations that had continuous snow cover for 90% of the years. At each station, they analyzed different snow parameters related to the maximum snow depth. At each station, they analyzed the parameters from September 1st to August 31st of the following year. This period would capture the first day of continuous snow cover and the first snow-free day. Out of all the stations they looked at, only three of the stations showed continuous snow cover less than forty days. After analyzing all the parameters, researchers found that stations experienced a much earlier snowmelt than usual, leading to a shorter snow cover duration. They also found that the maximum snow experienced a significant drop every decade during the study, thus demonstrating a correlation between snow depth levels and snowmelt.

Based on the results, researchers believe that the shorter snow cover duration as well as the decreasing snow depth are caused by increasing mean temperatures. They found that temperatures at all elevations in the Swiss Alps during the Spring increased as the years passed. They also found that the reduction of snow cover duration is a result of earlier snowmelt rather than later snow onset, the former cause being twice as important as the later. Overall, Klein *et al.* found that there is a clear reduction of the snow pack from 1970-2015 in the Swiss Alps. They found that the snow season today starts 12 days later and ends 26 days earlier than in 1970.

Klein, Geoffrey, et al. "Shorter snow cover duration since 1970 in the Swiss Alps due to earlier snowmelt more than to later snow onset." Climatic Change 139.3-4 (2016): 637-649.

Climate Change and Its Effect on Vietnam's Rice Harvests and Market

by Chris Choi

Trang T. H. Le (2016) analyzed the effects that climate change has on Vietnam's rice market. Climate change poses a major threat to Vietnam's agricultural sector, for paddy rice plays a major role in its economy. It provides food security and helps create rural employment opportunities as well as creates revenue in exports. Overall, Vietnam accounts for 20% of the world's total rice trade. Due to its economic significance and its high climactic vulnerability, research was necessary to determine how yield could be further impacted in the future.

After researching how temperature affects rice yield, Le found that increased nighttime temperatures led to smaller yields. It was also found that while the increase in daytime temperatures led to an increase in rice yield, thus counteracting the effects of the higher nighttime temperatures. However, higher daytime temperatures could impede rice growth as they do in the Philippines and Malaysia. Le then analyzed when rice was harvested. Generally, farmers harvest three times a year (spring, autumn, and winter). Le studied yield data that was recorded from 1975 to 2014 by the General Statistics Office of Vietnam; yields have greatly increased since 1975 with the spring crop being more productive than the other two harvest periods. The spring harvest season saw the lowest maximum/minimum temperatures and precipitation. Once Le recorded all the data, he ran a series of cointegration tests to test the effects of increases in temperature on rice yield. If there was a 1% increase in maximum temperatures, the spring crop yield would decrease by 29% and the autumn crop yield by 44%.

Overall, if temperature were to increase by 1°C, than the average amount of rice harvested would decrease. Researchers argued that this would lead to a 0.94% increase in farm and wholesale prices of rice while increasing FOB prices by 3.51%. The effects of climate change on the export market are greater than on the domestic market, thus demonstrating the higher export demand of rice than the domestic demand. To conclude, researchers believed that if Vietnam does not implement new cropping advancements, there is going to be a 18% decrease in total milled rice in Vietnam by 2030. The amount of rice exports would decrease by 55% and farmers would suffer a sales loss.

Le, Trang TH. "Effects Of Climate Change On Rice Yield And Rice Market In Vietnam." Journal of Agricultural and Applied Economics 48.4 (2016): 366-382.

Climate Change and its Effect on Global Food Security
by Chris Choi

Terence P. Dawson *et al.* (2016) analyzed how climate change could potentially have an effect on the amount of food resources throughout the world. Approximately 13% of the world's population is considered chronically undernourished, and the increasing population size is not helping this issue. This as well as decreasing crop production are putting a strain on Earth's resources, and food security is becoming a more prevalent issue. Food security was defined as the 'availability at all times of adequate world supplies of basic food-stuffs'. It was based on factors such as availability to food and the access to supplies to produce the food. The goal of the research was to determine the effects that climate change could have on food security based on a model created by the researchers.

The model they developed was called FEEDME. The two big factors driving this model are climate change and socio-economic drivers, each of which leads to different scenarios in the model. It analyzes food deprivation based on how much of the population is considered undernourished. The researchers also created an energy requirement to say which populations were considered underfed. To see if climate change does play a role in decreasing food security, they examined how the production of each food type changed. While they took into account the carbon dioxide fertilization effect, they did not account for air pollution such as ozone in their models.

After running the simulations and examining future climate change projections, researchers found that climate change will have a negative effect on the production of wheat, maize, and soybeans. They were expected to have up to 50% reduction in production in South America, Africa, Australia and central Asia. This as well as the expected increase in population would cause 50% or more of their population being at risk of undernourishment. Just considering the effects of climate change, the model found that an additional 1.7 billion people would be at risk of undernourishment by 2050.

Overall, the researchers believe that the FEEDME model is a very good predictor of the future. It takes into account food balance sheets which can manipulate food production, international trade, and the amount of land used for food production in each country. If no agricultural advancements are made and no changes in agricultural trade occur, a higher percent of the global population could be at risk of undernourishment by 2050 if this model holds true.

Institute, Climate Change, Food Security, Undernourishment, FEEDME Model
Dawson, T. P., Perryman, A. H., & Osborne, T. M. (2016). Modelling impacts of climate change on global food security. Climatic Change, 134(3), 429-440.

Can Drones Replace Bees?
by Joshua Dorman

To say bees are in trouble is a blatant understatement. Last year, the United States lost over 44% of its honeybee colonies. Some bee species, such as the Hawaiian yellow-faced bee and the rusty-patched bumblebee, are perilously close to extinction. A world without bees is a frightening prospect indeed. In fact, about 75% of our major crops reproduce only with the pollination help of these indispensable orange and yellow flying insects; without bees, our very food supply could fail. With this in mind, several scientists have been racing to find a solution, and they may have discovered one in the form of an unlikely savior: drones.

Eijiro Myiako, a researcher at Japan's National Institute of Advanced Industrial Science and Technology, had the revelation. He attached a number of horsehairs to the bottom of a kiwi-sized drone and coated them with a sticky gel he had previously developed. Then, his team maneuvered the tiny drone onto a lily. When the hairs on the bottom of the quad-copter touched the "male" region of the flower, it picked up pollen and then transferred it to the "female" part of another lily, thereby pollenating it. Myiako is hopeful that someday a similar process—albeit on a much larger scale—will allow swarms of micro-drones to assist in the pollination of crops across the country.

However, some scientists aren't as confident about the idea. Christina Grozinger, director of the Center for Pollinator Research at Penn State University, draws attention to the numerous technical challenges facing the project. For instance, there are over 20,000 species of bee in the world that each specialize in pollinating specific crops, and the entire drone pollination process would have to be automated in order for the solution to be viable. "The idea that we can mechanize [this] is not really likely," Grozinger says. Moreover, the implications of such an endeavor are troublesome to say the least. "If we really do get rid of the pollinators then that means that our whole ecosystem is probably in trouble," she added. In essence, the possible extinction of bees poses a terrifying threat, not only to our food supply, but to the world's entire natural environment as a whole. For the time being, at least, it seems that drones may be the most promising alternative.

Hall, Shannon. "Scientists have some wild ideas for solving our big bee problem." NBCNews.com. March 23, 2017. Accessed March 25, 2017. http://www.nbcnews.com/mach/environment/scientists-have-some-wild-ideas-solving-our-big-bee-problem-n737796.

Predicting Drought in the Middle East
by Bryn Edwards

Recent decreases in rainfall in the Middle East have prompted scientists to peer into history; by drilling 1,500 feet below the Dead Sea, creating the first timeline for regional climate history of the area. Scientists have found thick layers of crystalline salt from 120,000 and 10,000 years ago indicating times of severe drought. Layers of salt indicated times when the water in the Dead Sea evaporated leaving only salt, layered upon mud from times of heavier rainfall, telling the stories of thousands of years of precipitation. Salt accumulates at a rate of about half an inch per year. In the two prominent areas mentioned above, layers of salt were 300 feet thick. This period was between two ice ages, when Earth's surface temperature was about 4 degrees warmer than our current time periods, which also happens to be the predicted average temperature from climate change models at the end of the 21st century. By measuring small fluid bubbles embedded in the salt, researchers determined that runoff decrease ranged from 50–80% from what is today, lasting from tens to hundreds of years. This is alarming news for the future of the area. The water level in the Dead Sea is already too low because of human water usage. Rising surface temperatures on top of that could reduce the water and runoff levels to almost nothing. While considering the implications this has on natives of the area, one must recall that the current civil war in Syria can be directly linked to the severe drought from 1998–2012 and oil reservoirs being depleted faster than ever. This creates many questions about the long-term survival and health of the area's natives, where current inflammatory issues and conflicts will only be furthered by dwindling resources.

Ayre, James. Middle East Rainfall Fell To 1/5 Modern Levels 120,000 Years Ago (& 10,000 Years Ago As Well) — Implications For Anthropogenic Climate Change. Clean Technica. https://cleantechnica.com/2017/04/04/middle-east-rainfall-fell-15-modern -levels-120000-years-ago-10000-years-ago-well-implications-anthropogenic-climate-change/

Impact of Climate Change on Food Crops

by Vikramaditya Jhunjhunwala

Global demand for food has never been higher and with ever-increasing global population growth, it is certain that food demand will keep rising in the near future. However, the way in which we source our food and the nutritional value that we derive from it is set to undergo a massive change due to climate change.

Initially, the consensus in the scientific community was that rising carbon dioxide levels might increase crop yield by acting as a fertilizer. However, recent findings indicate that increased carbon dioxide, coupled with rising temperatures and precipitation changes, is likely to lower global yields for staple crops such as corn and wheat. Moreover, most food crops are grown in tropical regions where pests are ubiquitous. In addition to the decreased yield in these regions, rising temperatures are likely to increase the population of organisms that pose a serious threat to agricultural produce. It is expected that the expanded presence of pests is likely to result in a crop loss of over 40% in the coming years.

In recent times, farmers in the tropics have relied on predators of crop pests, like birds, to keep their produce secure; however, global warming is causing birds to delay their migrations, leaving crops unprotected during the agricultural season. The fishing industry in and around the tropics is bearing the brunt of animal migration as well with warmer waters in the tropics causing fish to migrate towards polar regions.

Decreased production of crops is not the only crisis that will impact people. According to a study by Dr. Sam Myers at the Harvard T.H. Chan School of Public Health, crops grown in the carbon dioxide levels estimated to occur 50 years from now also lack essential nutrients for human health. The study showed that wheat and corn grown in CO_2 levels mimicking those in 2057 had lower levels of protein, zinc, and iron than those produced in the current atmospheric state. With over 1 billion people suffering from iron and zinc deficiencies, such changes present grave dangers to human lives.

Although regions closer to the poles are likely to experience warmer weathers that are more conducive to agricultural growth, it is highly improbable that this growth can make up for the immense loss of food production in the tropics. Given that almost all of human population growth is predicted to take place in the tropical regions, the decreasing food production near the equator is likely to harm a significant section of global population.

Miller, G. S. (2017). Climate Change Is Transforming the World's Food Supply. Live Science. Retrieved 27 February 2017, from http://www.livescience.com/57921-climate-change-is-transforming-global-food-supply.html

Evolving Comparative Advantage and the Impact of Climate Change in Agricultural Markets

by Kele Mkpado

In early 2016 Arnaud Costinot, an MIT professor and member of the National bureau of Economic Research, and his team of Dave Donaldson and Cory Smith, looked into the impact of climate change on a global scale. They attempted to discuss the macro level consequences of thousands upon thousands of micro level events in small farms. With the rising global temperatures, the crops that could no longer be grown in countries previous to climate change drastically affects their imports and exports. In some cases, the country would have to completely change the crops they grow in order to have successful yields and import the crops they can no longer grow. Authors determined that global reduction in GDP would amount to 26%, which is close to about 1/6 of total crop value globally.

They began asking a few questions: How do rising temperatures affect crop growth, and what are the global implications? Even for high-ranking economists, it is very difficult to predict how certain changes will affect a market, so they simplified their model to control the changes they input into their market structure. They determined that the main factors that would quantify a shift in the market were trade, technology, and culture. The bases of these claims were that there are cultural staple foods that were once part of a diet in some parts of the world, where that food might be used less due to barriers of trade between countries, and just other countries refusing to grow a certain crop. Take China, for example, if they could no longer grow rice, and the lands now suitable to grow it due to climate change now reside in Russia, Russia might refuse to grow rice due to low profit margin due to travel costs. The price of rice might rise if they choose to grow it, but now much of the Chinese market cannot pay for it.

In the end, the researchers concluded that farmers must ready themselves for the seemingly inevitable change in the climate, but also prepare for loss of some crops because the global market likely will not be able to shift fast enough to prevent losses.

Arnaud Costinot, Dave Donaldson, and Cory Smith, "Evolving Comparative Advantage and the Impact of Climate Change in Agricultural Markets: Evidence from 1.7 Million Fields around the World," Journal of Political Economy124, no. 1 (February 2016): 205-248.

Ethiopian Farmers' Adaptation to Climate Change
by Bradley Newton

The agricultural sector in Ethiopia is consistent with the past, where farming persists as the main source of livelihoods for those in rural communities. However, due to climate change farmers have had to employ different techniques to try to keep their crops alive and well. The study surveyed smallholder farmers from the Arsi Negelle district of West Arsi Zone, Oromia Regional State of Ethiopia which is 250 km south of the national capital, Addis Ababa. Of the farmers they interacted with, 90% were aware of climate change and 85% had taken action in response to it. Some of the practices that were observed to be in use were crop diversification, planting date adjustment, soil and water conservation and management, increasing the intensity of input use (shortening the rest period for the soil between harvests), integrating crop with livestock, and tree planting. The researchers also narrowed down certain factors that affected whether or not farmers would change their ways in response to climate change, and if they did react, what adaptation practices they ended up using. These factors consisted of: education, family size, gender, age, livestock ownership, farming experience, frequency of contact with extension agents, farm size, access to market, access to climate information, and income. Climate change is a pressing problem, and it is often out of reach for smallholders to adapt by their own means. The researchers concluded that external influence is needed in addition to the indigenous practices being employed in order to help sustain the livelihood of these people. The external influence is composed of institutional, policy, and technology support. The article also noted that it would be helpful to introduce the farmers to other non-farming endeavors to help create another source of income that is not affected by climate change.

Belay, Abrham, John W. Recha, Teshale Woldeamanuel, and John F. Morton. "Smallholder Farmersâ Adaptation to Climate Change and Determinants of

Their Adaptation Decisions in the Central Rift Valley of Ethiopia." Agriculture & Food Security 6.1 (2017): n. pag. BioMed Central. Web.
https://agricultureandfoodsecurity.biomedcentral.com/articles/10.1186/s40066-017-0100-1#Abs1

Global Markets, Climate Change, and How They Affect the Food Supply

by Bradley Newton

Global trade has swiftly grown in the past three decades, helping lift millions of people out of poverty. However, its quick expansion has caused manufacturing wages to decrease in some high-income countries which has led to the atrophy of competition in some communities. This economic change has led to some nationalist ideas of decreasing or stopping trade expansion in the United States and Europe. The effects of anti-trade policies have been exacerbated by the increasing petitions from lower income countries to try to participate in the global economy. Brown *et al.* (2017) seek to clarify exactly what the consequences might be of a changed trade policy. The authors describe the situation as a "double exposure", where both the population and the current frameworks in place for food are shaken by strain from changing political views toward trade and extreme weather events cause by climate change. If trade restrictions increase in prevalence, then the combination of restricted trade markets and rapid changes in climate could threaten the food security of millions. Food security has been defined as, "all people at all times have physical, social, and economic access to sufficient, safe, and nutritious food to meet their dietary needs and food preferences for an active and healthy life." The changing climate will force food industries to adapt and will affect the access and utilization of currently present food supplies. It is possible, however, for trade to be manipulated such that it could fill gaps in food supplies left by the inability of current farming techniques. In order for it to work, trade would need to be managed so that it would be introduced to new markets and kept away from international competition to prevent market volatility. As long as any anti-trade notions are quelled and trade is regulated as stated above, it is reasonable to believe that we can maintain the food security of many people who would otherwise be threatened.

Brown, Molly E., Edward R. Carr, Kathryn L. Grace, Keith Wiebe, Christopher C. Funk, Witsanu Attavanich, Peter Backlund, and Lawrence Buja. "Do Markets and Trade Help or Hurt the Global Food System Adapt to Climate Change?" Food Policy 68 (2017): 154-59. Web.
http://www.sciencedirect.com/science/article/pii/S030691921630481X

The Future of the Colorado River
by Luis Salazar

After being in a drought, the Colorado River Basin is being aided by both snow and rain. Recent winter storms have helped decrease water shortages—as described by federal water managers. These storms, however, are only helping in the short term.

Long-term effects of the fifteen year drought are sustained. According to Water Resources Research, global warming is projected to decline the river flow by 35% within the century.

Global warming has already begun impacting the river flow. The drought in particular has contributed to flow reduction. Similarly, as argued by Brad Udall, "the major difference today is that the region is hotter than it used to be."

The study conducted supports the argument. In a little over a decade, the Colorado River has seen decrease of as much as 19%. Nearly half of this river flow change is credited to the 1.6 degree temperature increase.

Scientists Udall and Jonathan Overpeck are interested in seeing how the river flow might change in the next couple of decades. In particular, they are interested in the impact of higher temperatures. Weather is uncertain, but there is one certain association: greenhouse gas emissions lead to an increase in temperature.

Udall's new study examines the relationship between temperature and the impact of precipitation on the river's flow. Udall argues that both factors have to be investigated separately in order to provide useful information. Examining temperature alone can provide a certain prediction—when the effects of precipitation are examined, it is a little more uncertain.

Greenhouse gas emissions alone are predicted to increase temperature from 6.5 degrees Celsius to 9.7 degrees Celsius, average to worst case scenario respectively. Similarly, the Colorado River flow is estimated to decrease by an astonishing 35%. At worst, river flow could decrease by up to 55% in the next century.

Precipitation can counter the effects of temperature on river flow declines, but the uncertainty prevents scientists from agreeing on one prediction. Precipitation is also unable to counter the effects of decade-long droughts.

The author, Chelsey Harvey, aims to help the awareness of climate change—specifically, the troubles water managers face when distributing water. The Colorado River provides water to most of the Western states, and the possibility of water shortage affects millions. Water regulations must be disputed adequately, with regards to climate change.

Harvey, Chelsea. Climate Change Is Already Reducing Flows in the Colorado River, Scientists Report. The Washington Post. WP Company, 27 Feb. 2017.

Iran's Intensifying Struggle with Climate Change
by Tanisha Sheth

Carolyn Kormann, a writer for the New Yorker wrote an article in 2017 about climate change in Iran. She covered the story of Ako Salemi, a photographer who grew up in northern Iran and who was trying to spread awareness through his photographs from his early years and now. In Iran, climate change has led to dessication. Once the sixth largest saline lake in the world, Lake Urmia, is now just ten percent of what it was compared to the nineteen-seventies. The sea level along its coastline is projected to rise more than two feet by the end of this century and by 2070, potentially flood the homes of more than two thousand people annually. Yet Salemi stated that the people around him know about the droughts and lack of clean water, but they don't understand why these things were occurring. In the nineteen nineties, in both northern and central Iran, various factors began depleting the lake – deforestation, an exponentially growing population, water-intensive crops and inefficient irrigation systems. Soon the lake had such a high salt concentration that the brine shrimp could not survive; like this the entire ecosystem began to fall apart.

Today, the lake is a vast expanse of salt flats. Unlike Trump, Iranian President Hassan Rouhani said that he believed fossil-fuel consumption is the main driver of climate change, and his government has committed to reducing Iran's greenhouse-gas emissions by four percent, or up to twelve percent if the United States reverses its sanctions against the country. But efforts to spread a clean energy infrastructure are not yet widespread. Last October, M.I.T. researchers found that by 2070, if worldwide emissions are not significantly reduced, The Persian Gulf would experience heat waves impossible to survive. The oil producing city of Bandar-e Mahshahr already got a preview of this when one day in July, temperature and humidity conspired to make the air feel like a hundred and sixty-three degrees Fahrenheit.

Kormann, Carolyn., 2017. A Witness to Iran's Intensifying Struggle With Climate Change. The New Yorker

Climate Change's Impact on Milk Production
by Tanisha Sheth

India, the world's largest milk producer, may see a loss of milk production by over 3 million tons per year by 2020 due to frequent climate change. This may also lead to a decline in per capita consumption, industry experts have noted. From 2015 to 2016, the country's milk production has steadily been increasing with an output of 16- million tons. However, the impact of rising temperatures, especially on cross-bred cows will make the task of meeting domestic demand difficult. It could eventually lead to a decline in consumption as noted by experts in the 45th Dairy Industry Conference as organized by the Indian Dairy Association.

While stress to animals caused by changes in temperature-humidity index would directly affect the production of milk, indirect effects include feed and water availability due to adverse climate events. Heat stress also impacts animal reproduction by affecting conception rates.

Research states that stress from heat can cause decline in milk yield by 10% to 30% in the first lactation, and 5%—20% in the second and third lactation. The short term heat waves and cold waves can have short and long-term effects on production by cows and buffaloes. Although efforts are being made to reduce greenhouse gas emissions from within the dairy sector, the lack of education and literacy amongst laborers in this field introduces another difficulty to make any effective impact.

Milk continues to be India's single largest agricultural commodity and surpasses the combined value of the two principal cereal crops. It has helped millions of rural households pursue their livelihoods. It accounts for 18% of the world's milk production and the Indian market for milk and milk products, as indicated by economists, is expected to grow 15% annually.

A three-day conference will be held by the National Dairy Development Board which will consist of 23 technical and commercial sessions wherein scientists and industry experts will resent their research papers regarding the topic. Nearly 180 exhibitors from India, Bulgaria, France, Germany, USA and other countries will be showcasing their products, technologies and services and discussing potential solutions.

Mukul, Pranav., 2017. 'Climate change may hit milk production by 3 MT per year by 2020' The Indian Express

California's Droughts and Deluges Traced to Atmospheric Waves

by Charlie Thomson

Researchers have traced the severe winter droughts that struck California from 2013 to 2015 and this year's unusually wet winter that caused widespread flooding in the state to the same phenomenon: wavelike patterns of winds in the upper atmosphere around the globe.

Two scientists at the National Center for Atmospheric Research (NCAR) found that a specific pattern made by the wave prevented incoming Pacific storms from coming on-shore in the winters of 2013 and 2014, keeping the state unusually dry. This winter, the same pattern resurfaced, and scientists named it "wavenumber-5," but it was in a slightly different position that allowed the jet stream to push drenching rainstorms into the state, causing flooding and stressing dams. Haiyan Teng, lead author of the NCAR study, said the wavelike patterns, which consist of five pairs of alternating high- and low-pressure areas, can be grouped with the approach of long-lasting extreme weather events. "As we learn more, this may eventually open a new window into long-term predictability," Teng said. NCAR, which is financed partially by the National Science Foundation, has spent many years looking for ways to extend the predictability of floods, droughts, heat waves and other extreme weather events from weeks to months as a way to give weather-sensitive areas, such as agricultural areas, more time to protect themselves against many costly losses. The idea that atmospheric wave patterns might give scientists a better understanding of approaching seasons was first explored by a Swedish-American meteorologist, Carl-Gustaf Arvid Rossby, in 1939. Using early versions of electronic computers, the patterns he identified are now called Rossby waves. They are caused by the Earth's rotation, but they can have strong impacts on local weather. Some scientists believe that as they wander around the world, their activities can be better weather predictors than variations in sea surface temperatures.

One theory is that heat from tropical rain warms parts of the Earth's upper atmosphere in ways that favor the formation of the classic "wavenumber-5" pattern that has alternately drenched and dried parts of California. What intrigues scientists is that when it does emerge, the pattern comes about 15 to 20 days before major summertime heat waves hit the United States.

Fialka, John, and ClimateWire. "California's Droughts and Deluges Traced to
    Atmospheric Waves." Scientific American. Scientific American, 13 Apr. 2017.
    Web. 17 Apr. 2017.

Flaws in Analyzing the Effect of Climate Change on Food Security
by Kelly Watanabe

How reliable are food prices for determining the effect of climate change on food security? Thomas W. Hertel (2016) addresses this question by arguing that food security—the availability of affordable, nutritious food—does not always diminish when food prices rose. Hertel suggests that the determination of absolute poverty should measure not only minimal food consumption, but also minimal nutritional requirements. He claims that climate change can sometimes benefit household incomes for some socioeconomic groups susceptible to weak food security.

Hertel establishes two groups—urban poor and rural poor—which react differently to climate change. The rural poor include subsistence farmers who are a part of "agriculture-dependent households." Extreme weather events due to climate change destroy the supply of agricultural product, causing agricultural prices to increase. Because agricultural products generally contribute to a large portion of global commodity output, Hertel argues that the rural poor producers benefit from climate change due to increased profits from increasing prices. A study of Bangladesh's rice market showed that in the short run, a climatic catastrophe destroyed the harvest, increased the price, and lowered wages for laborers. In the long run however, sustained high rice prices eventually led to higher wages and overall poverty reduction due to an increased demand for rural labor to regenerate the destroyed rice fields. Derek Headey—a Senior Research Fellow in the Poverty, Health and Nutrition Division at the International Food Policy Research Institute (IFPRI)—conducted a worldwide statistical analysis of 300 poverty occurrences; Headey concluded that higher food prices led to national poverty reduction in developing countries of the rural poor.

From current extrapolation of data, future generations are likely to contribute mostly to urban areas of the developing world. Contrary to the rural poor, the urban poor will suffer from global food price increases due to climate change because the urban poor will not receive income gains from food production. Hertel suggests that the urban poor are the most susceptible to climate change. However, Hertel recognizes that his claims face challenges: the uncertainty of extreme climatic events and the unknown future distribution of the food-insecure population.

Hertel, Thomas W., 2016. Food security under climate change. Nature Climate Change 6, 10-13.

What California's Dam Crisis Says About the Changing Climate
by Jason Yi

Noah Diffenbaugh (2017) discusses the recent flooding at the Oroville Dam. Until recently, California had been in a record setting five year period of drought. The Oroville event occurred during a storm when the precipitation rate was more than twice the average of the previous year. Such conditions may seem odd; however, climate scientists have predicted similar outcomes of long dry seasons followed by short cycles of intense rain since the 1980s.

Moreover, many believe that such an event signifies an end to the drought. However, according to Diffenbaugh, they are incorrect, since California lost as much as three years of precipitation between the years of 2012 and 2016, and it would be impossible to make up the lost water within a couple of days.

Diffenbaugh also reports that the recent event reveals the fact that California's water infrastructure is old. Furthermore, the water system was designed in an "old climate" where hot weather was less frequent and "snowpack was more reliable." As a result, the Oroville Dam was constructed with both the functions of flood control and water storage. Such a system is known to rely on mountain snow. In the winter, precipitation falls as snow and builds up in the mountains rather than immediately flowing into reservoirs. Later, in the summer, the snow slowly melts and flows into the water storage. The problem arises when precipitation falls as more rain than snow, or as rain on snow, melting the accumulated snowpack. In that situation, the dam needs to release water more often for flood control. If it didn't, the dam could reach its maximum storage and could result in a spillover. This is what occurred at the Oroville Dam.

The article concludes on the note that California's water infrastructure needs an upgrade. A few suggested investments were to implement new technologies to increase the water supply during dry seasons, build a new infrastructure that relies less on snowpack, and to prioritize a system that safely supplies water to local cities.

Diffenbaugh. S. Noah. 2017. What California's Dam Crisis Says About the Changing Climate.
New York Times Feb 14

Energy and Climate Change

Gas Company Shifts Stance on Climate Change
by Bryn Edwards

Rex Tillerson, C.E.O. of ExxonMobil was recently nominated by President Donald Trump as Secretary of State. His merging with the Trump administration represents the merging of business and politics, specifically big oil. An analysis of his business, in this case centered around climate change, reveals an interesting history of big oil's involvement with climate change. In 2009, Tillerson shocked the world as he came out in favor of a carbon tax, a tax based on how much carbon dioxide was emitted, as opposed to the "cap and trade" approach that uses a permit system and an overall limit on carbon dioxide emissions. Ironically, prior to this, Exxon Mobil denied climate change, echoing calls from other oil companies that it was a hoax, and paying anti-climate change think tanks to aid their cause. This was a similar approach to that of the tobacco industry in the 1960s, denying that smoking caused cancer. While Tillerson and Exxonmobil's policy decisions in the past ten years acknowledge climate change, they do nothing to help the cause or spread awareness. It would appear that their standpoint on climate change is nothing more than a public relations stunt, with no substantial actions to back up their words. As a nominee to the Trump administration, the leader of which has already claimed climate change is a hoax perpetrated by the Chinese, Tillerson could be instrumental in reversing many of the measures that the Obama administration had put in place to protect against climate change. The political atmosphere of the United States for the next four years will not be a place where talk on climate change is welcome, nof legislation trying to counter it. This could have even more disastrous effects of the environment, with carbon emissions increasing every day. It is sad news for the environment of the planet that climate change will no longer be accepted as a fact of science, and it would seem that already, this new administration, lead by climate-change deniers and big oil

CEO's, will be acting against what needs to be done to slow down the potentially-disastrous effects of climate change.

Schwartz, J., 2016. Tillerson Led Exxon's Shift on Climate Change; Some Say 'It Was All P.R.' The New York Times. https://www.nytimes.com/2016/12/28/business /energy-environment /rex-tillerson-secretary-of-state-exxon.html?_r=0

China's Coal Mining Hypocrisy
by Vikramaditya Jhunjhunwala

In light of President Trump's uncertain stance on climate change, China has assumed the leading role in battling it. In an attempt to mobilize global initiative, China has publically implored its powerhouse compatriots, such as the United States, to acknowledge the science behind the phenomenon, and reduce their dependence on harmful fuels like coal and oil.

However, Keith Bradsher (2016), tells us of a troubling and rather ironic narrative of China mining and burning increased quantities of coal.

Even though there was a dip in production by 3 percent last year in a governmental effort to mitigate pollution and rising sea levels, Chinese coal is still the planet's greatest source of carbon emission from human activities and the reopening of mines spells all kinds of environment-related troubles.

The writer recalls that the future did not always look this bleak: two years ago, China was in a position where it was possible to significantly cut emissions with electricity consumption plateauing enough to have mining operations limits be as low as 276 days a year. However, technical and financial circumstances, such as rising electricity blackouts and unfavorable financial market movements, have forced increased production of coal.

According to Bradsher, it was when mining enterprises started receiving substantial loans from banks that things began to go downhill as, with an increased number of mines, coal prices began to drop. It was at the same time that a dangerous trend in the Chinese financial markets began to take place – Chinese investors began flooding the commodity markets as they believed that coal prices had hit rock bottom. This turned out to be a self fulfilling prophecy as even minute rises in prices made speculators rush in and buy large amounts of coal leading, to massive price hikes. This along with rising power demands because of an abnormally hot summer, rising home mortgages and increasing railway requirements made Chinese coal prices double from those at the start of the 2016 year to those toward the end. As a consequence of rising demand the previous operating limit of 276 days was also extended to 330 days per year.

One can, however, take solace in the fact that China's government is not taking the coal situation lightly and continues to uphold its environmental friendly ideals. Such is the magnitude of the situation that there are already murmurs of President Xi Jinping replacing Xu Shaoshi from his position as China's National Development and Reform Commission's director. Furthermore, China is also heavily investing in ambitious hydroelectric dam projects and wind turbine programs. So, while the situation with powerhouse nations in regards to climate change does not look too rosy, one does hope that China and the rest of the world will soon see better and greener days.

Bradsher K., 2016. Despite Climate Change Vow, China Pushes to Dig More Coal. The New York Times.

Is The End to the Oil Era Nigh?
by Vikramaditya Jhunjhunwala

Since the retirement of the horse-drawn streetcar in 1917, oil has been a cornerstone of the past century. Even though at the time of its introduction, oil was seen as a boon to the environment, its products are now seen in the same light as horse manure in the 19th century: a hazard to society and the environment. Slowly and steadily, the world's reliance on oil is beginning to dwindle.

The downfall of the oil industry is not being caused by a drop in demand of the commodity, but by a shift in investment preference from finding fresh sources of oil to finding alternatives to it.

This shift can be best seen by the signing of the Paris Climate Agreement by 194 countries, which aims to keep global warming to less than 2°C.

According to the International Energy Agency, a global energy forecaster, oil demand would have to peak in 2020 at 93m barrels per day–just above current levels–in order for the agreement's target to be achieved.

While none of the signatories to the Paris agreement have taken the steps needed in order to fulfill this objective, falling costs of renewable energy are making the transition from oil to alternative sources easier.

Recent developments suggest that oil operations around the world are being stifled as concerns about global warming deepen by the day.

In America, the Securities and Exchange Commission has begun investigating ExxonMobil, the world's largest private oil company, over whether it has been disclosing its activity's risks to the environment. Similarly, shareholders in America and Europe alike are putting pressure on oil companies to report on the effect of climate-change regulations on their businesses.

Air pollution in metropolitan cities of China and India are also forcing South Asian countries to look for alternatives to petrol and diesel.

To capitalize on this opportunity, car companies like Tesla, Chevrolet and Nissan have begun pricing their electric vehicles as low as $30,000, and even lower with government rebates.

Such worldwide developments suggest that global oil consumption might begin to wane as early as 2020. In the words of Rabah Arezki, head of commodities at the International Monetary Fund, the world may just be "at the onset of the biggest disruption in oil markets ever". The only question that now remains is the precise time when the hum of a battery eclipses the roar of the engine.

Tricks H., 2016. The future of oil. The Economist. Special report section of the print edition (Nov, 2016).

Coal Mining on the Rise Down Under
by Vikramaditya Jhunjhunwala

According to the Office of the Chief Economist's most recent Resources and Energy Major Projects report, there are 37 major coal mining projects that are currently underway in Australia. If all these projects were to be completed, they would collectively produce almost 300 million tons of coal annually. The completion of such undertakings would make it impossible for Australia to achieve any of its climate change objectives. Troublingly, recent remarks, by the Prime Minister of Australia, advocating subsidies for coal production have made such an occurrence highly likely.

According to the International Energy Agency, countries that are part of the Organization for Economic Cooperation and Development, like Australia, need to shut down almost all of their coal-fired power stations by 2035 to do their part in the Paris Climate Agreement. But by building more coal plants, the country could see its carbon emissions rise until 2030, thus overshooting all its benchmarks.

The decision to subsidize coal production is even more surprising considering that market conditions are ripe for a halt in coal production. According to data from the Office of the Chief Economist, the demand for coal-generated electricity has dropped by more than 15% in the past eight years without any government interference. Additionally, with cleaner sources of energy such as wind and solar becoming more economical by the day, Bloomberg New Energy Finance has also put coal as the most expensive energy source. Furthermore, coal can no longer be seen as reliable source of fuel with today's global energy demands. In a world where wind and solar energy can produce a lot of energy, albeit inconsistently, the need of the hour is not a base-load source of energy but a flexible power source that can serve as a stopgap for any drop in energy supply. In the short term, this need can be fulfilled by gas but the future of this requirement is likely to be in storage from renewable sources, such as batteries, pumped hydro, solar thermal with storage, or geothermal. Irrespective of either time frame, coal does not fit in anywhere.

The potential government handouts to the coal industry can only be seen as Australia's last ditch attempt in salvaging some money out of its unwise investments. Such a decision, however, would be severely short sighted and would constitute an extremely irresponsible decision with significant repercussions.

Slezak M., 2017. Why coal-fired power handouts would be an attack on climate and common sense. The Guardian. Retrieved from https://www.theguardian.com/environment/2017/feb/07/why-coal-fired-power-handouts-would-be-an-attack-on-climate-and-common-sense

Economics of Nuclear Energy
by Vikramaditya Jhunjhunwala

On the face of it, energy produced from nuclear reactors seems like a relatively clean and reliable source of power. However according to Smith (2017), nuclear energy is unlikely to emerge as a predominant source of power in the future.

The main redeeming quality of energy produced through fossil fuels over that produced by wind and solar is that it does not depend on weather conditions, and thus constitutes a regular stream of energy. Nuclear energy provides a similar baseload-like form of power without discharging greenhouse gasses like methane and carbon dioxide that have an unfavorable impact on the environment. Barring accidents, the only time that environmental safety is compromised with nuclear energy is during transportation of the industry's waste. However, rapid progress is being made in the field of nuclear waste transportation and disposal: Finland are France are currently in the process of excavating underground storage facilities that will safely hold radioactive waste for over 100,000 years.

Given the relative safety of nuclear energy, Smith believes that the main deterrent of nuclear power's rise to prominence lies in the astronomical fixed costs of the industry. To put them into perspective, a nuclear plant is 1,000 times as expensive as a fracking well and three times as expensive as the word's biggest and costliest solar plant. The nature of the renewable energy industry is also such that in the next five years, a competitive source of energy can make nuclear energy completely unprofitable. In China, solar panel costs have decreased by nearly 25% in just five months due to evolving technology. However, unlike with wind and solar power, the costs associated with nuclear energy have shown no signs of decreasing. According to a study by the Breakthrough Institute, nuclear plant construction costs have, in fact, increased by 5% and 4% in USA and Canada respectively and have only marginally decreased in countries like Japan, South Korea and India (less than 1%). With plunging prices in competing technologies, people have now become extremely uncertain of making large upfront costs to support a project that has considerable repayment uncertainty.

Smith, N. & Lake, E. (2017). The Dream of Cheap Nuclear Power Is Over. Bloomberg View. Retrieved 6 March 2017, from https://www.bloomberg.com/view/articles/2017-01-31/the-dream-of-cheap-nuclear-power-is-over

The Paris Climate Agreement and Africa
by Vikramaditya Jhunjhunwala

As part of the Paris Climate Agreement in 2016, the world's developed countries agreed to pledge $100 billion annually from 2020 to 2025 in order to play their part in reducing global greenhouse gas emissions. However, these developed countries only include those nations that were signatories of the United Nations Framework Convention on Climate Change that took place in 1992. Therefore, this $100 billion commitment fails to include big greenhouse gas emitters like China and India.

While this has a huge impact on the environmental aspirations of the aforementioned countries, it is likely that countries in Africa will suffer as a result of such an agreement as well. From a global perspective, the environmental impact on Africa can be catastrophic: while the African continent contributes little to global carbon emissions right now, it is estimated that nearly all of the world's population growth in the next 50 years is going to take place in Africa. It should be the onus of African countries and their partners to make sure that this growth is as low-carbon as possible. African countries for their part have taken giant leaps to ensure a clean future for their natives: Morocco is currently building the world's largest solar power station and Ethiopia, Ghana, Kenya, Rwanda, and South Africa have all undertaken huge solar and wind power projects. Despite this, it is expected that only 70% of the expected population in Africa will have access to electricity in 2040. Without climate friendly investment, Africa is being forced to bridge this deficit by allowing countries like China to build coal stations on their soil. Currently, China is in the process of building 17 coal-fired power stations in Ghana, Kenya, Malawi, and Zimbabwe. It is imperative that countries act urgently either to provide alternate finance solutions to such countries or to make all nations responsible for their emissions, otherwise such developments can be damaging in the long run.

Masiyiwa S., (2017). Green investment is the only bet. The Africa Report. Retrieved 27 March 2017, from http://www.theafricareport.com/International/masiyiwa-green-investment-is-the-only-bet.html

Is Bio-energy Clean?
by Vikramaditya Jhunjhunwala

In recent years, burning biomass like wood to produce electricity has emerged as a popular way of generating renewable energy with the quantity of biomass energy doubling from that in 2005 to that in 2015. The EU has particularly embraced this form of energy generation and it is expected that bio-energy will contribute to more than half of EU's renewable energy by 2020.

However, a 2017 study conducted by UK based think tank, Chatham House, claims that the notion that such a form of power generation constitutes a clean source of energy is based on flawed assumptions.

The reason that bio-energy generation is seen as a carbon neutral process is due to the assumption that emissions from the harvesting of wood are balanced by planting new trees. According to the author of the study, this is an especially naïve assumption to make as newly planted trees do not absorb and store the same quantity of carbon that century old trees do.

Furthermore, the EU imports a lot of its wood from US and Canada: during 2015, the UK was the biggest importer of wood pellets with 7.5m tons of wood pellet shipments being imported to the country. Most of these wood pellets are shipped across the Atlantic Ocean and release significant amounts of combustion product in the transport process, which is unaccounted for in most cases.

Indeed, even if the opposing carbon effects were to balance themselves out in the long run, short term emission targets like the ones set by the Paris Climate Agreement would remain unaffected.

There has never been stronger support for bio-energy than there is today, exemplified by recent reports suggesting that the UK is preparing to provide the industry with a £800m subsidy. With clean alternatives like wind and solar power getting more and more inexpensive by the day, authors of the study are calling for an urgent review of such support.

McGrath M., (2017). Most wood energy schemes are a 'disaster' for climate change - BBC News. BBC News. Retrieved 1 April 2017, from http://www.bbc.com/news/science-environment-39053678

Carbon Neutral Air Travel
by Vikramaditya Jhunjhunwala

With demand for air travel growing at an unprecedented rate, more than 30,000 new large aircrafts are expected to take flight in the coming years. As it stands, large commercial airplanes account for 11% of all carbon emissions from the global transportation sector. With the current demand rate, aircraft emissions are expected to rise by nearly 50% in the next 30 years. Curbing these emissions is crucial if the world hopes to keep the global warming phenomenon to less than a 2°C value this century, as per the Paris Climate Agreement.

Fortunately, developments in the 39th Session of the United Nations' International Civil Aviation Organization (ICAO) in October last year seems to have resulted in the formation of the world's first aviation-specific climate agreement.

The objective of the ICAO plan is to attain "carbon-neutral growth" in the aviation sector from 2020. It is intended to provide a guideline according to which countries may require airlines to purchase emission reductions from other economic sectors in order to keep the net carbon emissions of industrial operations to as close to zero as possible. The framework is meant to be in a pilot stage for the first six years and is only to be adopted by countries that choose to partake in it. While this opt-in approach has received some criticism, 64 countries have already agreed to sign the agreement. ICAO hopes that more countries will choose to partake in the program given the environmental benefits of low-carbon growth.

In recent times, environmental sustainability has become a significant marker for investors and customers to associate themselves with a company. The ICAO hopes that a clearly demarcated metric that is uniform among all countries will spur large aircraft manufacturers like Boeing and Airbus to invest in more fuel efficient models.

If such an agreement were to materialize, it could see the prevention of carbon emissions upward of 2.5 billion tons in the first 15 years. Put into context, this is roughly the equivalent of removing 35 million cars from the roads annually from the time the program is enacted. Collective global support for the ICAO plan in conjunction with the Paris Climate Agreement can go a long way in securing a greener future.

Figueres C., (2017). A new age of air travel is dawning. And it's green. World Economic Forum. Retrieved 10 April 2017, from https://www.weforum.org/agenda/2016/10/a-new-age-of-air-travel-is-dawning-and-its-green

How Trump's Administration Can Fight Climate Change
by *Vikramaditya Jhunjhunwala*

While environmentalists around the world are worried that the "green" administration of President Obama is behind us, there is a case to be made for why President Trump's industry-heavy administration might go a long way in decreasing greenhouse emissions. In fact, if Trump's administration succeeds in bringing back the bulk of USA manufacturing to the United States, the world could see unparalleled decreases in emissions.

In recent times, the growing consensus for the most efficient way to reduce emissions in global environment forums seem to be in favor of the carbon tax. However, if such a policy is implemented in the US, the increasing electricity prices might drastically increase the cost of business operations. In such cases, companies might turn to moving manufacturing to China, where 63% of the electricity is coal-based. Historically, whenever the United States or the European Union have instated a carbon tax or increased regulations, their global share of manufacturing has declined and China's share has risen. It can be argued that due to carbon-based restrictions in the West, China's global manufacturing has increased by 357% from 2004 to 2013. This has resulted in a 4.3 billion-ton annual increase in carbon emissions from China, thus making it the highest carbon emitter in the world.

While some may claim that moving the harmful environmental effects to the other side of the world furthers the US's cause, such an opinion is extremely short-sighted. China's coal emits large amounts of sulfur and nitrous oxides that blow over the Pacific Ocean and straight into the coasts of Washington, Oregon and California. Another side-effect of such a policy is that it weakens US's economic position in relation to China. Relocating jobs to China results in national unemployment and stymies the US's economic progress while contributing to China's tax revenues and thereby increasing China's bargaining power. All in all, it is in the United States's best interest to contain manufacturing jobs within its borders as alternative policies are inefficient from both an economic and environmental standpoint.

Cassidy B., (2017). To Reduce Carbon Emissions, We Need More Manufacturing. The Daily Caller. Retrieved 17 April 2017, from http://dailycaller.com/2017/03/29/to-reduce-carbon-emissions-we-need-more-manufacturing/

California targets Dairy Farms in the fight against Climate Change
by Vikramaditya Jhunjhunwala

California has taken an unorthodox route in battling climate change by regulating dairy farm operations involving livestock. Cows and other farm animals are significant sources of methane, a potent greenhouse gas that is released as a by-product by animals during the production of manure. To combat these emissions, Governor Jerry Brown signed a legislation last September that requires farmers to install methane digesters. Methane digesters trap and contain the methane in the atmosphere in storage spaces and slowly convert the gas into electricity. The enactment of such a policy can yield remarkable results given the amount of methane produced by the farm animals in dairy sheds: according to a 2013 United Nations Report, dairy livestock accounted for 14.5% of human-induced greenhouse gas emissions.

As the country's largest milk-producing state, California aims to lead the way in reducing greenhouse gas emissions from the dairy industry and has set aside $50 million dollars for its enactment. While the intention is noble, the new law is also likely to have hugely detrimental effects on dairy farmers. In the face of a five years of drought, declining milk prices and increasing labor wages; such a policy is likely to increase costs for the farmers despite the state subsidy.

Considering that New Hope Dairy, a dairy farm that houses a modest 1,500 cows, spent $4 million dollars in installing a methane digester in 2013; the $50 million subsidy is unlikely to cover the cost of installing methane digesters for the the nearly 1,500 dairies in California today. In an industry with slim margins, the enactment of such a plan could very well drive Californian dairy farmers out of the state and subsequently lead to premium priced dairy goods. Given these economic constraints, one does wonder whether it would be wiser to allocate resources to reduce carbon emissions from other industries such as transport or manufacturing.

Chea T., (2016). California targets dairy cows to combat global warming. The Seattle Times. Retrieved 24 April 2017, from http://www.seattletimes.com/business/california-targets-dairy-cows-to-combat-global-warming/

Long Range Power Transmission
by Matt Johnson

One of the problems that has grappled electrical engineers over the last few decades is the long-distance transmission of power. As the shift towards renewable energy continues, we are finding more and more electricity being generated farther and farther away from consumers. With an unavoidable power loss directly related to transmission distances, engineers have found themselves in a tough situation. The Economist (2017) dives into one technology, ultra-high-voltage direct-current connectors, as a particularly promising solution. Electric power grids were standardized on alternating current (AC) in the late 1880s and 1890s, and have stayed that way ever since. Alternating current travels like a wave: the energy shimmies back and forth through a conducting medium. As the distances of transmission increase, it takes more and more energy to push this wave through. Inherently, the more energy you put in, the more that is lost. Direct current on the other hand is a steady flow of energy, there is no oscillation. Therefore, over transcontinental distances, direct current power lines are much more efficient. The power lines are cheaper to build, because a smaller wire can carry more power: reducing weight and cost. Whereas the transformers for AC are relatively cheap, the comparable thyristors for voltage conversion in DC are pricy; but these prices are justified by increased transmission efficiency, especially over long distances.

The US has found itself a laggard in the adoption of this new technology. China already has a handful built, and more under construction. Their biggest project is a power connector 3,400 Kilometers long. This line carries a behemoth of power equivalent to the average usage of Spain. European utilities also have plans for trans-European connectors: especially useful considering the hydroelectric opportunities present. As the transition towards green energy continues, UHVDC connectors will hopefully lead in the economic transmission of clean, cheap power.

Rise of the supergrid: Electricity now flows across continents, courtesy of direct current. (2017, January). The Economist. Retrieved from: http://www.economist.com

Regional Consequences of Solar Installations
by Matt Johnson

Forecasts about the future of solar energy tend to be rosy and optimistic, but is the solar revolution really a nobody-loses scenario? A study lead by Aixue Hu (2017) titled "Impact of solar panels on global climate" addresses some infrequently mentioned concerns.

It turns out that solar energy systems have consideration-worthy regional consequences. But you may ask: why? Solar panels are not 100% efficient, they are actually fairly far from it. The most efficient solar panels on the market today run at around a 40% efficiency, with some new technologies promising around 60%, however most are much lower. A few issues arise in the conversion of solar energy into electricity. Firstly, a small percent of the solar radiation is reflected, as a result of solar panels' glare. Then, another few percent are lost in the conversion of direct-current into alternating current and along the transmitting wires to centers of population. The authors estimate the mentioned causes to sum to about a 10% loss.

This 10% loss is part of the problem, but not all of it. Mainly, solar panels' reflectivity as well as their solar absorption must be considered in relation to the geography they are planned to occupy. Obviously natural materials like sand and rock will have different reflectivity and absorption qualities than manmade silicon panels. Inherently, the installation of such man-made objects is going to change the characteristics in the region of installation. Interestingly enough, the article states that "In general, the changes in the reflected solar radiation do not directly affect the regional and global climate, but the changes in absorbed solar radiation do". A decrease in overall solar absorption resulting from the addition of solar panels leads to a local cooling effect of around 2°C.

In other regional studies, the results varied. For an Egypt installation, precipitation would be reduced by over 20%, while installations in other regions would increase precipitation. A solar array installed in western North America could increase precipitation by a few inches, for instance. This affects plant life which affects leaf size and therefore transpiration: this in and of itself has effects on the temperature in an area.

The message gathered from this study is that solar arrays have consideration-worthy consequences in most regions of the globe. While solar arrays in some areas may provide consequential benefits, they may have repercussions in others. These consequences, good or bad, must be considered and acknowledged. Luckily, the authors report that overall, "the potential global mean climate changes induced by the use of solar panels are small in comparison to the expected climate change owing to fossil fuel consumption".

http://www.nature.com/nclimate/journal/v6/n3/pdf/nclimate2843.pdf
Hu, A., Levis, S., Meehl, G.A., Han, W., Washington, W.M., Oleson, K.W., van Ruijven, B.J., He, M. and Strand, W.G., 2016. Impact of solar panels on global climate. Nature Climate Change, 6(3), pp.290-294.

Changes in European Wind Power Potentials
by Matt Johnson

Like most sources of renewable energy, wind turbines are dependent on environmental conditions for successful operation. Wind turbines require wind, just as solar panels require sun and hydroelectric plants require water. As our understanding of climate change deepens every day, the consequences of global warming are presenting challenges to these technologies. A study published in IOPscience (2016) uncovers how wind farms in Europe may be affected in the coming decades.

The study forecasted what the European wind infrastructure would look like in 2050, and considered how various atmospheric conditions would change that infrastructure's potential power output over the next century. The study found that wind power potential in Europe as a whole will stay fairly constant through the 21st century: within about 5% of the potential today. However, when the resolution of the study was increased, regional changes in wind potential are much more pronounced. The Iberian Peninsula is predicted to experience the largest reduction in wind potential over the century: as much as 15%. More optimistic projections show a 5–10% reduction. On the other hand, the Baltic is expected to experience an *increase* in wind power potential of about 5–10%: this is believed to be a side effect of melting sea ice.

The predictions made by this article are based on changes in geostrophic conditions. The study predicts that near-surface as well as upper atmospheric wind patterns will change in sync in most regions, but discrepancies arise in northern latitudes, such as the oceanic regions around Iceland. Near-surface wind speeds are predicted to increase in these regions, but the higher altitude wind patterns should stay fairly constant.

The realistic implications of these findings are minimal, as oceanographic regions around Iceland are not practical to build on, and technological improvements in turbine technology are destined to outpace the efficiency reductions due to climate change. However, the scope of the study was only until the late 21st century. While changes in wind power potential may not be drastic for this century, the potential impacts that lie in the future may deserve some more consideration.

http://iopscience.iop.org/article/10.1088/1748-9326/11/3/034013/meta
Tobin, I., Jerez, S., Vautard, R., Thais, F., Van Meijgaard, E., Prein, A., Déqué, M., Kotlarski, S., Maule, C.F., Nikulin, G. and Noël, T., 2016. Climate change impacts on the power generation potential of a European mid-century wind farms scenario. Environmental Research Letters.

Transportation Technologies: EV vs Internal Combustion
by Matt Johnson

A commonly accepted notion is that electric vehicles (EVs) are universally better for the environment than traditional internal combustion vehicles. An environmental research paper by Linda Ellingsen, Bhawna Singh and Anders Strømman (2016) recognizes that a lifecycle perspective is necessary to determine the full carbon footprint of electric vehicles, and describes the many factors that EV benefits are contingent on.

Light duty vehicles (LDVs) consumed about 25% of global primary oil in 2014. As the number of LDVs on the road continues to increase, so will greenhouse gas emissions. The 5th assessment by the Intergovernmental Panel on Climate Change described that the rate of increase in transport emissions could be higher than any other energy use sector. This is where aggressive policies targeting LDVs come into play, but first it is imperative that we know how EV's stack up against internal combustion engine vehicles (ICEVs).

The study considered vehicle models 2010 and newer, and split the vehicles into four segments: mini car, medium car, large car, and luxury car. These segments are all based on gross weight. The study found that there were large variations in total lifecycle emissions from segment to segment. On average, luxury ICEVs produced about 1.8 times as much pollution as mini ICEVs, and luxury EVs produced about 1.7 times as much compared to mini EVs.

A large contributing factor to the lifecycle emissions of an EV is the production and end of life (EOL) treatment of the battery. The study found that the production of electric vehicles is more environmentally intensive than the production of internal combustion engine vehicles. However, the greater efficiency during the usage of electric vehicles more than made up for the higher production emissions. An important implication of this is that from an economic perspective, EVs need to travel considerable distances before their emissions beak even with ICEVs: between 44,000 km and 70,000 km. Since the scalability of electric drivetrains is better than conventional drivetrains for larger vehicles, larger electric vehicles were able to meet the breakeven emissions point sooner, compared to their ICEV counterparts.

While the production emissions from both EVs and ICEVs is considerable, it is relatively small in comparison to operational phase emissions. Operational phase emissions for ICEVs are tailpipe emissions; for EVs, they are indirect emissions from electricity production. Medium size EVs had lifecycle emissions about equal to that of mini ICEVs, and mini EV's produced 5 tons less CO_2 than that. Medium, large and luxury EVs also performed better than their ICEV counterparts by even larger amounts: owing again to the better scalability of electric drivetrains. Overall, EVs had 20%–27% lower lifecycle emissions than ICEVs.

In addition to production emissions, EOL treatment of batteries contributed a considerable amount to the lifecycle emissions of EVs. An EV's battery is about 14%–23% of the end of life treatment emissions. Production and EOL treatment of the batteries combined contributed about 13%–22% to the total lifecycle impact of EVs.

The environmental benefits of electric vehicles over internal combustion vehicles is heavily dependent of the sources of the electrical energy. Coal, on average, produces 1029 grams of CO_2 per kWh produced. Natural gas, 595 grams and wind, 21 grams. Charging EVs with coal-based electricity increased the total lifecycle emissions my 12%–31% *compared to conventional ICEVs*. This brings up some concerns about EVs in the US, considering that about 67% of electricity produced comes from fossil fuels: 33% from Coal, 33% from natural gas, and 1% from petroleum, as of August 2016. When EV's are considered in the context of a European infrastructure, which averages 521 grams of CO_2 per kWh, the benefits of EVs compared to ICEVs increased the longer the vehicles are on the road. When charged with coal-produced electricity, it is the other way around. Natural gas-produced electricity still produces slightly more carbon than the European average. Although, EVs powered by electricity produced from natural gas have a 12% to 21% lower lifecycle impact compared to their ICEV cousins. When powered by wind, all segments of EVs beat even mini ICEVs in terms of lifecycle impacts, with 83–84% lower lifecycle impact than ICEVs.

The takeaway from this article is that EVs have less lifecycle environmental impact than ICEV's, considering the state of the power grid today both in the US and in Europe. The benefits of EVs over ICEVs are only going to increase as the power grid continues to transition to renewable energy sources. Despite the common criticisms of battery EOL treatment and indirect emissions, EVs are the definite vehicle of the future.

Ellingsen, L.A.W., Singh, B. and Strømman, A.H., 2016. The size and range effect: lifecycle greenhouse gas emissions of electric vehicles. Environmental Research Letters, 11(5), p.054010.

Old Meets New: Complications of a Renewable Energy Electric Grid
by Matt Johnson

Photovoltaic solar installations are now growing faster than any other energy source. This is not surprising considering the benefits they offer: almost zero marginal operating cost, flexibility of installation, lifespan, etc. Despite the widespread popularity and support, photovoltaics still only supply about 7% of the world's electricity. That is shockingly little, but one must realize that the fossil fuel infrastructure is massive and stubborn to change. An article by *The Economist* (2017) explains why solar doesn't play nicely with the old.

The transition to a renewable energy grid is going to require a lot of money. The investments in this new electric grid are not all going to be public funds: some, if not most, will be private investments. After all, utilities are businesses, which receive investments from those looking for a return on their capital. Utilities have been popular investments for many because of their stability; utilities provide a low risk return on capital. Due to the inexpensive nature of photovoltaics, and their near-zero marginal operating costs, every new installation of photovoltaics pushes down the average price of power. As *The Economist* states, this decrease in pricing coincides with decreases in profits for the utilities, and in order for investments to continue flowing into these utilities, a profit must exist. If our utilities are left stranded with little investment due to their low margin, the advancement of the grid will slow dramatically. The answer to this dilemma is not less solar, "It is to rethink how the world prices clean energy in order to make better use of it".

Public subsidies for wind and solar have totaled about $800 billion since 2008. The intentions of these subsidies were good, but they have clouded the business reality of wind and solar installations. The infusion of public funds came at a time of decreasing demand for electricity. The subsequent installations led to an electric grid with overbuilt capacity, reducing revenues for the utilities. The utilities have become accustomed to public subsidies, and now rely on such infusions of capital to keep the system functioning. This reliance is mostly due to the maintenance costs of duplicate electric power sources. In order to accommodate the intermittency of sources like wind and solar, conventional fossil-fuel burning generators need to be maintained. Most of the time, utilities are now confronted with power plants sitting idle, generating no revenue.

So what are we to do? This article suggests a redesign of power markets. It asks: why should power rates be so constant? We are transitioning from a dirty yet stable electric grid to a clean one with intermittent power sources. The prices of the produced electricity need to reflect this reality. Prices could fluctuate with the weather, for instance. If the grid is being stressed to its limits, then higher prices should reflect the demand exceeding supply. The increase in prices could prevent a blackout. Rewards should be presented to consumers to incentivize them to shift energy intensive activities to off hours. The article even suggests power bills could be structured based on the reliability of power the consumer desires. The solutions to this dilemma are not complex. All it takes is a few policy changes in electric pricing. But with an established fossil-fuel based infrastructure, will barriers arise? Once again, it all comes down to politics.

February 2017. Wind and solar power are disrupting electricity systems. The Economist.

The Politics Behind Wind Turbines in North Carolina
by Matt Johnson

North Carolina is rethinking its stance on its renewable energy commitment, an article in The Wall Street Journal (2017) reports. With the completion of a 100 turbine wind farm, and a new administration in the white house, a wave of second thoughts is sweeping the state.

North Carolina Republicans are divided over the issue of green energy; specifically, the wind turbines spanning the state. In efforts to curb spending, some Republican politicians oppose the turbines due to their heavy reliance on tax credits. Taking the other side of the discussion, rural Republican residents are rejoicing in the extra income: many land owners get paid about six thousand dollars per turbine per year installed on their property. Seeing that the most attractive regions for wind in the state are also the poorest, the residents directly involved especially appreciate the income. In a state that has seen little development in rural towns, this new wind installation, for example, has become the largest taxpayer in the two counties it overlaps. With rural residents rejoicing, and tax revenues increasing, what's not to like?

With a new administration promising to refocus on fossil fuels, Republican-controlled North Carolina has become uncertain of new green energy installations. Subsidies for green energy and the plans for new green energy installations dependent on such policies have fallen out of favor. Wyoming, another Republican state, has even "proposed barring utilities from using wind or solar power to serve customers". While this proposition was denied in early February, it indicates the increasing hostility some Republicans are showing towards renewables. In all fairness, Wyoming is a coal-producing state, and threats to that industry will obviously not sit well with elected officials. However, with a new administration seemingly in favor of this hostility towards renewables, we may see a real stall in the cutting of carbon emissions.

Valerie, B., Sweet, C., 2017. Winds of Change Hit Renewable Projects. The Wall Street Journal. Vol CCLXIX No. 46. A3

Household Energy Saving
by Matt Johnson

A study lead by an Oregon State University professor in conjunction with two Stanford professors (2016) explores 261 energy-saving behaviors, and clusters such behaviors into four groupings: family style, call an expert, household management and weekend projects. In clustering such behaviors, the authors believe that targeting of selected behaviors towards energy consumers can greatly aid in the sustainability of energy-conserving behaviors.

Collective participation in energy-conserving behaviors is key to successful and meaningful reductions in energy use. However, generalized targeting of energy-saving behaviors has sometimes been ineffective among energy-consumers, and multiple intervention strategies to target consumers have had some negative consequences. Users of energy are consumers just like any other; cost savings are attractive, but, information overload can cause consumers to be overwhelmed, and completely disengage from energy-saving activities. If the intervention strategies become more intrusive, a rebound effect can occur even in consumers who have already adopted energy-saving behaviors. In analyzing the adoption rates of certain behaviors, the authors found five important attributes: relative advantage, compatibility with the lifestyle of the adopter, complexity, trialability or "the degree to which it can be tested at a small-scale before full adoption, and observability to others.

To develop a list of energy-saving behaviors, the authors drew on existing public and commercial lists from within the U.S. and Australia. The authors then narrowed such behaviors down to 261 that they believe to be feasible and practical. Among these behaviors, *install* was the most frequent verb at 32% of the behaviors. The runner-ups were *turn off* at 17%, *set* at 16%, *insulate* at 14%, and *clean* at 12%.

More generally, 38% of the behaviors occurred infrequently —once every three or more years. Thirty-four percent of the behaviors required no skill, 38% involved changes in thermal comfort, and more than half cost less than $20.

The family cluster of behaviors, which makes up 19% of the list are frequent and cost little to nothing. These behaviors generally yield low energy savings. Most of these behaviors relate to thermal comforts and eating. Also in this category are activities like turning off lights and appliances, air drying laundry, and setting the thermostat higher in the summer and lower in the winter. The call an expert cluster, making up 26% of the list, includes infrequent, more expensive behaviors, but yields the highest energy savings. Most of these activities have to do with large appliances and home construction improvements. The largest cluster of behaviors is the household management cluster at 32% of the list, and these behaviors are characterized by cleaning and organization activities, as well as interactions with large appliances, such as changing air filters and light bulbs. The energy savings of behaviors in this cluster are relatively low. Lastly, the weekend project cluster composes 22% of behaviors. These behaviors are infrequent, medium cost, and generally yield high energy savings. Behaviors include painting, and installing awnings, shades, or more efficient appliances. This was the most productive category behind call-an-expert.

By clustering behaviors, studies like this are useful in identifying which behaviors are likely to be adopted by consumers. Instead of pestering consumers with endless lists of 'energy-saving tips', we need to inform consumers of the behaviors that yield high energy savings, and have a low implicit and explicit cost, in hopes of achieving widespread adoption. The clusters that seem to be most productive are the call an expert and the weekend project groupings. The fact that neither of these has to do with day-to-day behaviors tells us that prior intervention strategies may have been misplaced. Instead of informing consumers of the need to take shorter showers, we should be informing consumers of the benefits of a new, energy efficient air conditioner or low-flow shower heads. Other options include installing reflective coatings on windows or installing shades or awnings. When a financial incentive is involved, which there inherently is with energy-consumers, making this sort of information readily available should be sufficient in sparking large changes. And again, high adoption rates are key. The marginal cost of providing such information to consumers is low, and the collective benefits of the implementation of only a few behavioral changes could be quite large.

Boudet, H.S., Flora, J.A. and Armel, K.C., 2016. Clustering household energy-saving behaviours by behavioural attribute. Energy Policy, 92, pp.444-454.

The Diminishing Returns of MPG

by Matt Johnson

Consumers have been indoctrinated over the last few years to always consult one efficiency metric when buying a car: miles per gallon. Miles per gallon, also commonly known as MPG, measures the efficiency of internal combustion engine vehicles. Striving for the most efficient vehicle is obviously a good behavior, but as Jo Craven McGinty (2017) wrote in a Wall Street Journal, the benefits of a high mpg vehicle can be deceiving.

Miles per gallon is not a measurement of consumption, but of efficiency. Why is this important? Let's start with an example. Suppose you are given the opportunity to exchange your SUV that gets 10 mpg for a crossover that gets 20 mpg. Or, you could trade your sedan that gets 40 mpg for a hybrid that gets 50 mpg. Which option do you select? You might say that they would both save the same amount of gas, because it's the same 10 mpg increase. But you would be wrong. Over a 100-mile trip, upgrading from 10 mpg to 20 mpg would save 5 gallons. From 40 to 50 mpg, it would save only half a gallon. Why is this important? What consumers really care about are fuel savings, and therefore consumption is what they are trying to minimize. While efficiency and consumption are direction related, as the author notes "mpg conceals consumption's diminishing returns".

This deception means that people tend to "undervalue improvements to gas guzzlers and overrate improvements to gas sippers". This is one of the reasons that Canada, for instance, mandates liters per kilometer in addition to kilometers per liter to be listed on fuel consumption labels of new vehicles. New fuel economy standards require auto manufacturers to sell a fleet of cars averaging 54.5 mpg by 2025. However, an efficiency gain of 10 mpg for trucks is going to move the mean average the same amount as a 10 mpg gain for hybrids. Therefore, it is important that we focus on increasing the efficiency of gas hogs.

Two Duke University professors argue that we need to address these gas guzzlers before spending more time and resources on already efficient vehicles. Quoting Dr. Richard Larrick: "Right around 30 mpg is the sweet spot. Things get really flat after that". Despite new U.S. fuel economy labels that include gallons per 100 miles, an effort needs to be made both in the consumer sphere and among the manufactures to increase the average mpg of the worst offenders, as that is where the easiest savings lie.

McGinty, J., 2017. Gas Guzzlers' Gains in Fuel Efficiency Go Farther Than Fuel Sippers' Do. The Wall Street Journal.

Britain Takes a Break from Coal
by Alex McKenna

In 2017, Britain celebrated a watershed moment. For the first time since the height of the Industrial Revolution, the country did not burn coal for an entire day. Powering them into the industrial age and the 21st century, coal was the economic backbone of many European countries, especially Britain. It is no wonder that the "pea souper" fogs that many believed to be natural phenomena were in fact caused by coal. However, the industry is beginning to decline. In late 2015, the last deep coal mine was closed. For many living in mining towns along the country, their old way of life is beginning to disappear. While this may be true, steering away from coal as an energy source is saving the environment. Coal-fired power generation contributes to climate change, producing twice as much carbon dioxide as burning natural gases. Increasing the use of renewable energy sources such as solar power may be the only way to mitigate the effects, and taking a break from coal for a day is a step in the right direction.

On path to stop using coal-fired power generation entirely by 2025, Britain continues to close plants and promote cleaner renewables. Sean Kemp, a spokesman for National Grid, stated that this event is a milestone and the end of an era. The first public coal-fired generator opened in London in 1882, and since, the economy has been thriving on it. There have been multiple coal-free periods before, especially during spring when demand is lower, but only lasting for a few hours. Now, officials say that coal-free days will become the norm. Since 2012, nearly two thirds of Britain's coal-fired power generating capacity has been shut down, with many plants being converted to burn biomass such as wood. As a result, the share of coal in total power generation has dropped from 40% in 2012 to just 9% in 2016.

Hannah Martin, head of energy at Greenpeace said that the first day without coal in Britain marks a watershed in the energy transition. Some countries such as Switzerland and Belgium have already left coal completely behind in power generation. And while it still accounts for 30% of power generation in the United States, both in the U.K. and globally countries are moving towards a low-carbon economy.

Bennhold, K., 2017. For the first time since 1800s, Britain goes a day without burning coal for electricity. The New York Times, 1-3. https://tinyurl.com/l5qkyou

NASA Study Confirms Biofuels Reduce Jet Engine Pollution

by Kele Mkpado

Have you ever wondered why airplanes leave those long white clouds behind them? I always thought that they were just clouds, but they are actually called contrails. They are a product of the hot airline exhaust mixing with the cold air to make ice crystals that give it its cloud like appearance. Hidden within these ice crystals are particulate matter that are harmful for our environment. What's worse is that these contrails can stay in the atmosphere for an extended amount of time and reflect CO2 back toward earth, effectively warming it.

Scientists at NASA think that they have found the solution to this growing problem. They have found that creating a fuel compound that is part biofuel using the fatty acids of the camelina plant, they can reduce the amount of soot that jets leave in their wake by 50% to 70%. To gather this data, NASA flew a HU-25C Guardian aircraft as close as 250 meters behind a DC-8 jet to gather particle samples of the biofuel exhaust and analyze their contents. Their research found that the biofuel not only reduced the harmful particulates in the air, but also made the contrails last for a shorter amount of time lessening their long-term effect on the atmosphere. Granted, it is very difficult to determine what effects contrails really have on the environment because there are planes flying all over the world 24/7. Scientists can agree on however, that contrails are harmful and any attempt to reduce their effect is a positive one.

Airplanes allow us to travel, communicate, and venture high up into the air, but we must be more aware of the affects they have on our atmosphere. Evidence shows that contrails are harmful, and biofuel can reduce that harm. Next time you look up and see a contrail, you better hope they are using biofuel.

NASA. "Biofuels Reduce Engine Pollution." Vital Signs of the Planet. NASA, 22 Apr. 2017. Web. 23 Apr. 2017.

Comparison of Carbon Footprints of Electric and Gasoline Vehicles

by Bradley Newton

Authors Yuksel, Tamayao, Hendrickson, Azevedo, and Michalek (2016) have conducted a study concerning the carbon footprints of electric and gasoline vehicles. They cite several past studies looking at a similar topic, but point out that none of those studies accounted for grid emissions (pollution created by generated electricity), people's driving patterns, and how diverse temperatures are in different regions. It is also pointed out that past studies used vehicles of differing battery life spans, which can make comparisons harder. The factors that the authors of the study look at for their comparisons are: availability of electricity for Plug-in electric vehicles, temperatures of studied regions, vehicle miles traveled, and driving conditions (meaning whether it is city or highway driving). The vehicles they used were a mix of conventional, hybrid electric, plug-in electric, and battery-electric vehicles. They were driven to the end of their life-cycle (complete depletion of gas tank or battery) and had their respective CO_2 emissions measured. The authors decided that the driving conditions of an area would be based off its urbanization level, VMT (Vehicle Miles Traveled) would be obtained from the National Household Travel Survey from its respective state, and they assigned marginal grid emission factors (amount of electricity available) for each North American Electric Reliability Corporation (NERC) to the counties that lie within their encompassed area. Other pieces of data, such as energy consumption rate and charging time had to be gathered to be able to effectively measure the CO_2 emissions per life cycle of all the vehicles studied. The energy consumption rates of the vehicles studied were obtained from the combination of the Argonne National Laboratory's Downloadable Dynamometer Database vehicle data, the information gathered on temperature, drive cycles, and VMT patterns from each applicable county. The data for the energy consumption were then used in combination with VMT patterns to calculate what the charging time was for each of the electric vehicles. The results of the study showed that regardless of the vehicle model, none of them had a carbon footprint that was consistently the best across the whole US. Plug-in electric vehicles (such as a Nissan Leaf) showed to produce a smaller footprint in more urban areas, whereas regular gasoline vehicles (such as the Mazda 3). proved to have a smaller footprint in more rural areas Because of this, the authors concluded that it would be difficult for any environmental policy that favors any specific vehicle technology to be successful in lowering emissions across the entirety of the US.

Tugce Yuksel, Mili-Ann M. Tamayao, Chris Hendrickson, Inês M L Azevedo, and Jeremy J. Michalek. "Effect of Regional Grid Mix, Driving Patterns and Climate on the Comparative Carbon Footprint of Gasoline and Plug-in Electric Vehicles in the United States."Environmental Research Letters 11.4 (2016): n. pag. IOP Science. Web. 22 Jan. 2017.
http://iopscience.iop.org/article/10.1088/1748-9326/11/4/044007#top

Reduction in Working Hours to Reduce Carbon Emissions

by Bradley Newton

Policy makers have discussed the idea of reducing the working hours in an economy, since it has been posited that it may hold benefits toward goals of economic, social, and environmental situations. For environmental situations, the perspective behind this is that a reduction in working hours, through reduced incomes, will help to dematerialize our economy which will in turn help to lower energy use due to decreased consumption. The study in the article tested five different work schedule scenarios, with the net amount of working hours cut down by 20% in each. The end game was to see which one resulted in the greatest decrease in greenhouse gas emissions. The different scenarios were: "a three-day weekend, a free Wednesday, reduced daily hours, increased holiday entitlement and a scenario in which the time reduction is efficiently managed by companies to minimize their office space." King *et al.* (2017) analyzed how time was used by individual workers and the business in each scenario and made note of how it might impact the energy consumption of the economy. The study also took into consideration the phenomenon where when people stop using energy in one situation, they will inevitably start consuming it somewhere else due to having filled their free time with a different activity. Because of this it could be argued that reducing work hours would change nothing towards the net energy consumption, however, the article pointed out that "due to differences in energy intensities and efficiencies in distinct areas of the economy and time uses, we do not see a complete compensatory effect," meaning that most other leisurely activities you could be doing in your off time from work probably will not amount to the same magnitude of energy consumption if you were at work. This framework was applied as a case study for the United Kingdom, and the results of the study showed that three of the five scenarios garnered a similar effect, and were preferable to the other two. The common characteristic between the more effective scenarios were that they implemented a four-day work week.

King, Lewis C., and Jeroen C.J.M. Van Den Bergh. "Worktime Reduction as a Solution to Climate Change: Five Scenarios Compared for the UK." 132 (2017): 124-34.ScienceDirect. Web.
http://www.sciencedirect.com/science/article/pii/S0921800916302579

Energy Efficient Hybrids
by Luis Salazar

Warren Brown—columnist with a specialty in automobiles—writes about the progress automakers have made on fuel-efficient and clean cars. This movement is in danger of being derailed by the current administration of the U.S.

He argues that Ford and General Motors, as large automakers, should refrain from changing stands on government fuel economy and emission regulations. Automakers must acknowledge the environmental damage done by refusing to manufacture energy-efficient cars.

Major automakers have begun to make changes in the right direction. For example, Chrysler, Audi, and Toyota have all introduced improvements; Chrysler introduced the Fiat, Audi improved performance, and Toyota introduced hybrid cars. Automakers have always been hesitant to change, from seat-belt regulations to environment regulation. They are more understanding when it is proven that change is both possible and profitable.

The Toyota Prius was introduced in 1997 during an era of safety regulations. It sold more than 6 million gas-electric hybrids and promoted the manufacturing of more hybrid cars.

Brown critiques those who believe that, "we have done enough, that we can go back to our old, gas-burning, zoom-zoom ways." U.S. automakers must continue to compete with other countries in the markets to prevent a loss of jobs and sales. Also, the progress made is incredible—Toyota reduced carbon-dioxide pollution by more than 40 million tons between 1997 and 2013. This reduction in pollution has made air cleaner for those living in populated cities. If carmakers reduce the numbers of energy efficient automobiles they produce, then they will no longer be aiding in the elimination of pollution.

The Toyota Prius has improved drastically and now competes in performance with gas-burning cars. The Prius runs comfortably at around 52 miles per gallon, seating five people. Ideally, the more Prii out on the road, the better.

Brown, Warren. Perspective | A Good Antidote to the Climate Change 'hoax' Rhetoric: Toyota's Prius Three. The Washington Post. WP Company, 31 Mar. 2017. Web.

Greenhouse Gas Emissions Increase Transatlantic Flight Durations
by Kelly Watanabe

Paul D. Williams (2016) conducted one of meteorology's first studies on the effect of climate change on airplane flight planning. The increase in greenhouse gas emissions—which contribute to climate change and global warming—creates a stronger temperature gradient from the equator to the poles. This temperature difference is mostly observed in the troposphere, the atmospheric layer which airplanes travel through. According to Williams, the change in atmospheric chemical composition induces stronger westerly winds, which blow from the west. Hence, westbound transatlantic flight durations increase while eastbound times decrease. Williams's data showed that the net round trip flight times increased because westbound times increased by an increment greater than increment which eastbound times decreased.

Williams designed an algorithm to calculate and predict the optimal routes and flight durations for transatlantic flights between London and New York. The algorithm worked off a hypothetical situation of doubled atmospheric CO_2 levels. By extrapolating data from past wind patterns, Williams calculated wind field direction and magnitude, optimal flight routes, and estimates of round trip flight times. The algorithm processed data on a daily basis for 20 years. Williams's results concluded that there had been an average increase of 66 seconds per round trip flight. While the individual increase in flight duration is insignificant, Williams points out the noteworthy effect on a macro scale. Considering all transatlantic flights in a year, the extra flight time adds up to 2,000 extra flights, 7.2 million gallons of extra fuel, an additional \$22 million cost, and 70 million kg of added CO_2 emissions.

The algorithm's main uncertainty lies in quantifying the many diverse types of wind fields. Williams also acknowledges that in reality, airplanes commonly veer off the calculated optimal path due to daily variability in winds. He encourages further research: the expansion of flight-planning algorithms to other areas of the world, refined quantification of algorithms through analyzing other wind fields from different climate models, and minimization of airplane radiation and greenhouse gas emission.

Williams, P., 2016. Transatlantic flight times and climate change. IOP Science 11, 1-8

Could Cheaper Renewable Energy be Harmful?

by Kelly Watanabe

While the decreasing prices of renewable energy yields a positive environmental impact, The Economist (2017) argues that the push for more renewables has dangerous effects on the energy market. Renewable energy systems rely on subsidies. Over the past decade, governments worldwide have shown a significant increase of investment in wind and solar energy. However, renewables still only account for 7% of global electricity output, and fossil fuels account for 80%. In 2014, the International Energy Agency (IEA) predicted that $20 trillion in investments is needed to decarbonize the global electricity grid over a span of 20 years. The IEA predicts that the availability of these subsidies will decrease over time due to the unreliable revenues of renewables.

Solar and wind energy output suffers from the interruptible inconsistent conditions; we cannot control when the sun shines or when the wind blows. For situations when renewable energy is not available, fossil fuels are a dependable backup. However, the decreasing prices of renewables push fossil fuel companies out of the energy market. Moreover, more customers are generating their own electricity, which increases the price of grid electricity linked to fossil fuels. To keep necessary fossil fuels available in the short run, subsidies are needed even though some fossil fuels are currently uneconomic in comparison to renewables. In the long run, The Economist suggests a need for electricity grids with ample storage capacity to compensate for the variability of wind and solar energy.

Because wind and solar energy have low marginal costs, the price of electricity from renewables decreases, the overall grid price causing a need of more subsidies for renewables, causing an increase the quantity of renewables, which goes back to the vicious cycle of decreasing prices. The Economist fears that eventually, renewable prices will become so low that the subsidies will be more expensive than the revenue yielded from them.

The Economist, 2017. A world turned upside down. Briefing print edition. http://www.economist.com/news/briefing/21717365-wind-and-solar-energy-are-disrupting-century-old-model-providing-electricity-what-will

Proposal to Decrease Motor Vehicle Emissions in London and Beijing

by Kelly Watanabe

Transportation vehicles contribute to the greatest percentage of air pollution. Motor vehicles emit pollutants PM2.5—particulate matter small enough to become permanently embedded in lungs—and nitrogen dioxide (NO_2), which causes asthma and defective lung development in children. Kelly and Zhu (2016) analyze the air pollution policies of two of the world's largest cities: London and Beijing.

In 2002, London initiated the Cleaning London's Air strategy to reduce road traffic pollution. To reduce the number of vehicles on the road, the Congestion-Charging Scheme (CCS) implemented a fine for driving motor vehicles in specific zones. Initially, CCS reduced the number of vehicles by 18%, however, by 2012 the traffic congestion increased back to its high levels in 2002. To reduce the average amount of emissions per vehicle, the government established London-wide low emission zone (LEZ) in 2008. LEZ restricts the entry of outdated vehicles that release too much air pollutantion. On roads, the number of large old diesel engine automobiles decreased while new clean-energy vehicles became more common; thus, carbon pollution deceased. However, NO_2 concentrations remained constant due to the increased use of new diesel cars.

In Beijing, air pollution became a problem when Beijing requested to host Olympics in the 1990s. Dangerously high PM2.5 levels were a threat to public health. Similar to London's LEZ, Beijing's government banned old vehicles that did not pass emission standards; pollution levels did not decrease because emission standards were not strict. From the 2008 Beijing Olympics until present day, cars in Beijing were only allowed on the road 4 out of the 5 weekdays. Driving days were determined by the last digit of the license plate, which was distributed by lottery. As a result, the number of vehicles in Beijing grew from 1.5 million in 2000 to 5.6 million in 2015. Yet, PM2.5 concentrations still decreased. Kelly and Zhu argue that NO_2 levels also decreased because Beijing has the most advanced engine technology and fewer diesel vehicles.

Based on London and Beijing's past actions to reduce automobile emissions, Kelly and Zhu propose solutions for the future. In London, younger people prefer to travel via car-sharing or taxi. Car manufacturers BMW and Ford are starting to launch car-sharing programs that utilize electric cars. Kelly and Zhu emphasize the need to distribute electric plug-in stations in central cities. On a bigger scale, Kelly and Zhu believe that a growing population will only be supported by an expanded mass transit system. Within the next 5 years, China plans to build 87 new metro rail tracks. Kelly and Zhu predict that China will have half of the world's transit rail lines by 2050. With the increase in transit systems, other systems of public transportation are needed to connect people to transit points when transit points are not within walking distance.

Kelly, F., Zhu, T., 2016. Transport solutions for cleaner air. Science 352, 934-936.

The Physical Environment and Climate Change

Nasty Chemicals Abound in What Was Thought an Untouched Environment
by Ellen Broaddus

The Economist (2017) investigates a new study that dispels the notion that Earth's deepest oceans remain unaffected by human activity. The Mariana trench off the coast of Guam is the deepest point on Earth's surface, a staggering 10,994 meters below sea level (which is deeper than Mount Everest is tall). Near the surface of the ocean sunlight and hydrothermal vents provide chemicals and energy to sustain life, but sunlight is unable to penetrate below 5000 meters. In areas deeper than that, organism rely on dead organic material from above. However, once these nutrients flow into the trench, they are unable to escape: meaning any pollutants that reach the bottom remain there indefinitely. Alan Jamieson of Newcastle University in England predicted that these trenches are loaded with pollutants, especially "polychlorinated biphenyls" [PCBs] (which were once used widely in electrical equipment) and polybrominated diphenyl ethers (employed in the past as flame retardants)". To test this, he sent landers to 10 sights at the Mariana trench and the Kermadec trench in New Zealand, depths ranging from 7,227 meters to 10,250 meters. These landers spent 8–12 hours at the bottom, using funnel traps to catch amphipods and other organisms. Once recovered, the samples showed levels of polychlorinated biphenyls that were off the charts. Levels ranged from 495 nanograms per gram amphipod tissue analyzed at 10,250 to 1,900 nanograms per gram amphipod tissue analyzed at 7,841 meters, a staggering amount compared to grossly polluted areas such as the Liao river in China whose levels are only about 100 nanograms per gram amphipod tissue . Dr. Jameison suggested that the high levels of pollutant could be caused by the trench's proximity to the North Pacific Subtropical Gyre, a "whirlpool hundreds of kilometers across that has amassed enormous quantities of plastics over the years, and which has the potential to send the pollutants that bind to those plastics deep into the ocean as the plastics degrade and descend." The effect of these pollutants has not been extensively studied, but polychlorinated biphenyls are known to cause cancer and harm hormone systems of animals near the surface of the ocean, suggesting bleak outcomes for those below. This study serves to show that pollution and human activities cause harm to ecosystems even beyond our immediate reach.

2017. Oceanic pollution: Nasty chemicals abound in what was thought an untouched environment. The Economist. http://www.economist.com/news/science-and-technology/21716891-entrenched-nasty-chemicals-abound-what-was-thought-untouched-environment

Improving Climate Change Education in Vietnam to Improve Adaptation Policies
by Chris Choi

Thi Huong Tra Nguyen *et al.* (2016) studied how climate change adaptation efforts can be improved if climate change education policies were put into action. While climate change has affected every country, poor countries are more heavily affected due to the lack of necessary resources to cope with the sudden changes. Adverse climate change especially affects Vietnam's coastal zones where 70% of the population is in danger of rising sea levels. If sea levels were to rise by one meter, then approximately 10% of the population would be affected and may be forced to relocate to another area. The purpose of this study was to find a solution to increase awareness and education on the effects of climate change in an attempt to mitigate its effects.

Vietnam experiences storm surges, floods, and monsoons which damage the country environmentally and economically and have socio-economic impacts upseting poverty reduction efforts. The current method to deal with climate change is to relocate the people affected by it. In a case study conducted along the Mekong delta, they found that at least 20,000 landless and poor households are expected to be relocated by 2020. This could lead to changes in both the social structure and agricultural culture both for the current residents and the new migrants.

Nguyuen proposes to implement a new climate change education program in Vietnam, especially in the rural coastal sectors. There are three different frameworks. The first is called Climate Change Education for Sustainable Development (CCESD). This is an educational model that primarily focuses on creating a larger understanding and attentiveness towards climate change as well as getting rid of any misconceptions. The second is called ABIA, or Awareness Behavior Intervention Action. The goal this program is to encourage individual and community engagement to help sustainability issues. This is done by conducting interventions using educational materials to inform people of the effects of climate change. The last framework is constructivism. This framework promotes an active learning environment where learners build their own knowledge and understanding of the world and deal with new experiences by reflecting on them. The teachers ensure that the students' previous beliefs are examined and questioned to address them so that they can gain new knowledge from this experience. This method focuses more on thinking and understanding than on memorization. Using these three frameworks, Nguyen hopes to improve residents' awareness of climate change. and find a better way to mitigate the effects of climate change instead of just moving people to different parts of the country.

Nguyen, T. H. T., Boon, H., & King, D. (2016). Education to Enhance Vietnamese Coastal Communities' Adaptive Capacity to Cope With Climate Change. eTropic: electronic journal of studies in the tropics, 14(1).

Climate Change Blamed for Deadly Landslides in Chile
by Bryn Edwards

This article describes a recent landslide just outside of Santiago, Chile. While only three people were killed, millions lost access to clean water, and almost 400 people are stuck because of damaged/flooded roads and bridges. This type of incident is becoming more and more common in areas surrounding mountains in Chile; it is the third disaster in just four years. More frequently occurring landslides can be directly attributed to climate change. Rising temperatures mean rain instead of snow in the Andes, causing unstable alpine areas. Slope material becomes saturated with water, and the solid–liquid mixture can reach densities of up to 2,000 kg/m³ (120 lb/cu ft) and velocities of up to 14 m/s (46 ft/s) More rain and less snow causes these landslides to become more common. Chile is plagued by climate change in other forms as well. Wildfires ravaged the central south region the past few months due to higher than normal temperatures and a drought in the region. Chilean officials are calling for altered infrastructure to adapt to new weather patterns. Ricardo Toro, the director of Chile's National Emergency Office is quoted in the article, calling on the Chilean people to recognize climate change as a "new reality." The government is making plans to build a reservoir in the flood-prone region to provide an area for the water to collect, instead of flooding into towns. The reservoir would also serve to provide secondary water supply as backup for treatment plants during periods of overflow.

Quiroga, Javiera. Climate Change Blamed for Deadly Landslides in Chile. Bloomberg Markets. https://www.bloomberg.com/news/articles/2017-02-27/chile-landslides -kill-three-people-cut-water-supply-to-millions

Innovative Ways to Store Carbon Dioxide
by Bryn Edwards

A new research team in Iceland has developed a new way to store carbon dioxide: by turning it into stone, which has since been dubbed the Carbfix Project. Carbon dioxide is credited with the rising surface temperatures of our planet. We produce it is such massive quantities that the planet cannot sustainably filter it out, thus scientists must come up with innovative solutions like this, also called carbon capture and storage (CCS). Current CCS methods inject gaseous CO_2 into geological formations, often through oil wells, and although its fate is not well-understood, it could escape back into the atmosphere in time. The Icelandic team created a process that mimics how carbonate rock is formed naturally, but shortened the process from hundreds of thousands of years to about two. They pumped the CO_2 into the volcanic rock that makes up most of Iceland, where a chemical reaction between basalts and gas creates the tiny carbonate minerals that make up limestone.The only way this could resurface as CO_2 is through volcanism. Already, the team is transforming 10,000 tonnes of CO_2 every year into limestone, which has practical architectural applications across the globe. Potentially, this new development could capture CO_2 emissions from power plants and re-purpose the harmful emissions into construction materials, slowing down global warming across the planet. However, a lack of support from government and politicians is slowing down the spread of this profoundly powerful technology. There is one test site in the US, located in the Columbia River Basalts, in Washington and Oregon. However, the project requires huge amounts of water per tonne of CO2 buried. Even though saltwater can be used, this could present challenges in desert, land-locked area. If applied properly, however, this could be a huge step in the right direction for CCS, and could lead to other innovative ideas. Testing is already underway by teams of scientists across the country for creating different types of stones, and fuel cells that could trap the carbon dioxide and change it into usable energy instead of wasted emissions.

Carrington, Damian. CO2 turned into stone in Iceland in climate change breakthrough. The Guardian.
https://www.theguardian.com/environment/2016/jun/09/co2- turned-into-stone-in-iceland-in-climate-change-breakthrough

Carbon Sequestration in Coastal Wetlands
by Bryn Edwards

The Climate Agreement reached in Paris two summers ago added to increasing pressure on countries to minimize carbon dioxide emissions and to find innovative new ways to store carbon. Decades of research have shown the staggering capacity of CO_2 that oceans can hold; a new paper published in *Frontiers in Ecology and the Environment* analyzed the sequestration of carbon in coastal wetlands, which span 620,000 kilometers of coastline globally. The study showed that coastal mangroves, seagrasses, and tidal marshes store carbon the longest and most effectively. To be more specific, the study compared carbon sequestration by coastal blue carbon ecosystems to sequestration by algae and marine animals. Coastal areas have very different carbon storage mechanisms than those of plants. Salt or brackish water saturates soil anywhere from twice a day to constantly, inhibiting the decomposition of organic material and traps it in the soil. Carbon storage in soil ranges from 50–90%, a much larger percent that had been previously acknowledged. Full pieces of plants can be found up to 3 meters underground, highlighting the effectiveness of this method of carbon storage; almost nothing is released. Coastal vegetation like seagrass and mangroves stabilize soil with their root systems, and are able to store 2 to 35 times more carbon than the usually credited photosynthetic processes that occur in phytoplankton and kelp. Wetlands, though do more than store carbon; they are the first line of defense for shorelines against storms. Effects of hurricanes up and down the Eastern Seaboard are much more strongly felt in areas with few or small protective wetlands to act as buffers. This causes erosion at an exponential rate, and leaves coastal communities more vulnerable than ever to storms that seem to be getting stronger and more frequent every season. Considering the fact that only 29 out of 150 countries that signed the Paris Agreement have entertained the ideas of coastal protection, the world has a long way to go in recognizing the importance of wetlands.

Derouin, Sarah. Study Finds That Coastal Wetlands Excel at Storing Carbon. https://eos.org/articles/study-finds-that-coastal-wetlands-excel-at-storing-carbon

CO_2 Threshold...
by Ethan Kurz

Recently, the Mauna Loa Observatory observed something startlingly sinister... the CO_2 in the atmosphere reached 410.28 parts per million. Carbon dioxide in the atmosphere hasn't reached that level in millions of years. This new atmosphere is trapping heat and causing climate change.

Carbon dioxide emissions have been breaking records each year. In 1958 when recording of carbon dioxide in the atmosphere began at the Mauna Loa Observatory, it was 280 ppm. In 2013 it passed 400 ppm.

Carbon dioxide emissions have skyrocketed in the past two years due to record amounts of fossil fuels we are burning and the record amounts of trees we are cutting down. If we did reduce our emissions the rate of increase would slow down. We need to reduce our emissions by almost half if we want the carbon dioxide concentration to begin to decrease. Even if we reduce our emissions by half, it is too late. The ramifications of our years of carbon emission will extend far into our future. The planet itself has heated up by 1 degree Celsius, and there are 627 months on record of "above normal heat". Sea levels have risen around a foot already, oceans have become more acidic, and extreme heat is common. These impacts won't end with a simple cut in emissions. What we face now is how intense these adverse effects will be. The sooner we start to do something, the less serious these impacts will be...but they are already serious and beyond fixing.

Kahn, Brian, 2017. Threshold for CO2. Scientific American. <https://www.scientificamerican.com/article/we-just-breached-the-410-ppm-threshold-for-co2/>.

Avalanches and Climate Change
by Ethan Lewis

Amanda Erickson, a writer for the Washington Post, recently published an article addressing the correlation between avalanches and climate change. On January 18th, 2017, an avalanche at an Italian ski resort left 30 people buried under the snow, and countless more dead. The official link to this avalanche was an earthquake, but scientists are coming to the conclusion that climate change also plays a key role in these phenomena.

Avalanches are caused by earthquakes, mountain incline, weather, and snow structure. Because of the warmer weather due to climate change, snow is more difficult to pack together. If you add poor snow quality with an earthquake or gusty wind, an avalanche is destined to occur. Researchers on the Intergovernmental Panel on Climate Change warn that rising temperatures are destabilizing mountains, melting glaciers, and creating more intense snow storms. Tad Pfeffer, a glaciologist at the University of Colorado at Boulder says, "People will get in trouble if they rely on what they knew in the past, They have to have their eyes open and not go somewhere simply because it worked out five years earlier."

The Alps have been hit especially hard by climate change due to the fact that they are warming at a quicker rate than the global average. Also, snow storms are more erratic, making the base of the snow weak and poorly packed. A statement by Vice says "As more snow piled on top of the weak layer, temperatures remained warm, the upper, moisture-laden layers become vulnerable to sliding."

Similar trends have been found on mountains all across the world. From 1977 to 2010, Nepal's average temperature change was two to eight times above the global average which led to a increase in the total number of avalanches. In May 2012, 60 people were killed due to a avalanche on Mount Annapurna. In 2014 on Mount Everest, 16 Sherpas were killed in another avalanche, deeming it the worst disaster in Everest history.

Erickson, Amanda. "Avalanches are becoming more common due to climate change, researchers say." Washington Post, January 19th, 2017.

Climate Change and Earth's Ocean
by Ethan Lewis

Chris Mooney, a writer from the Washington Post, summarizes a paper published in Nature about oxygen content in our oceans. Scientists have detected a decrease in the amount of dissolved oxygen in the worlds oceans. This decrease is due to climate change and could have severe consequences for not only marine life but also humans. Worldwide, a decline of two percent occurred in ocean oxygen content between 1960 and 2010. The Arctic Ocean had the steepest decrease while the Pacific had the largest total oxygen decrease. This is the first time that this decline in oxygen has been recorded on the global scale, and in the deep ocean.

Ocean oxygen is essential to marine life, but only one percent of the Earths oxygen can be found in its oceans. Climate change models predict that oceans will lose oxygen primarily because warmer water holds less dissolved gas. As the upper layer of the ocean which contains majority of the oxygen warms, it is more difficult for the water to cycle to the deep ocean. This means that the oxygen supply of deeper ecosystems is also significantly reduced.

Mooney concludes that although it is not conclusive that these changes are human-driven, the data strongly suggest it. Some of the consequences of this oxygen decrease are that more "dead zones" will be created. In these dead zones, microorganisms tend to produce nitrous oxide, which is a greenhouse gas that is stronger than CO_2. Also, coral reefs and kelp forests are beginning to die off. Warmer oceans have also begun to destabilize glaciers in Greenland and Antartica, which in turn freshens oceans and changes the nature of their circulation. Studies suggest that the ocean will loose up to 7% of its oxygen by 2100, which could be catastrophic.

Mooney, Chris: "Scientists have just found a major change to Earth's oceans linked to climate change." Washington Post, February 17th 2017.

Early Spring's Ties to Climate Change
by Ethan Lewis

Chelsea Harvey, a writer for the Washington Post, analyses one of the warmest Februarys America has seen in decades. USGS recently shared an analysis released by the USA Nation Phenology Network that an early spring is sweeping over the United States, starting in the Southeast. The analysis reaffirms the fact that climate change is advancing the onset of spring. The analysis uses a "spring index," which defines the start of spring as temperatures falling in certain ranges and the emergence of flowers and leaves on plants. The index was created by volunteer citizens collecting data across the country. Mark Schwartz, a climatologist working at the University of Wisconsin, used these data to create an algorithm that detects where "spring" has arrived across the country.

Scientists using Schwartz's algorithm are comparing this year's spring to those of previous years. Washington D.C. saw its spring 22 days earlier than its average. Spring season is also spreading from the south eastern states into states like Colorado, New Mexico, Arizona, and California. The same "spring index" was used to study spring in national parks. From data spanning the past 112 years, springs are earlier than 95 percent of the historical record.

A downside of early springs is the warmer weather helping parasites and insects reemerge more quickly. Also, agriculturally, early springs followed by sudden frosts, or by droughts in the summer, devastate a crop that is in mid growth. This has happened frequently in the past. In 2012, a grape harvest in Southwestern Michigan was devastated by a sudden switch of temperatures, and in 2007, an identical incident hit a tree nut harvest in the Southeast. As far as other news, there are other indicators of long term climatic changes, but spring is a more dramatic red flag.

Harvey, Chelsea. "The U.S. Geological Survey hails an early spring — and ties it to climate change." Washington Post, February 24, 2017.

Effect of Climate Change on our Oceans
by Ethan Lewis

Chelsea Harvey, a writer for the Washington Post addresses the issue of the effect that climate change can have on our worlds oceans. Climate change can cause rising temperatures, acidification, lower oxygen levels, and decrease food supplies. Scientists predict that by 2050, almost 80% of the ocean will be affected by one of those situations. Harvey comments on a paper published in the journal Nature, which used computer models to examine how oceans would fare over the next century. Almost the entire ocean is acidifying because of greenhouse gasses being absorbed by the water. Researchers do say that reducing emissions can significantly delay the negative effects allowing marine life to adapt or migrate.

Harvey quotes Stephanie Henson, a scientist at the National Oceanography Center who said, "Things that live in the ocean are used to regular variability in their environments." But Henson noted that a warming climate will cause changes that have never happened before. Hotter temperatures, lower pH, or less oxygen may exceed the organisms ability to tolerate the changing conditions. These organisms will either be forced to migrate, evolve as a species, or face extinction.

There is lot of uncertainty of how individual organisms will react but evidence does show that major challenges lie ahead. Large sections of coral bleaching in the past few years can be directly attributed to unusually warm temperatures. Henson and her team now want to know when climate change will actually push the system outside its range of natural variability. Some parts of the ocean are already beyond their limits. 99% of the ocean is experiencing ocean acidification. Henson's team also believes that multiple different factors are occurring at the same time, Henson said, "for example, the combination of warming and ocean acidification may be even more detrimental than just one of those factors alone."

Mitigation will not stop the emergence of stressors in the ocean, but it does slow it down. This delay could buy time for organisms to move or adapt. Fast-moving fish may be able to travel to more stable areas while organisms with quick generation times like plankton, may be able to evolve to the changing environments. Scientists are still trying to figure out what certain organisms will do, but one thing is for certain, there will be winners and losers.

Harvey, Chelsea. (2017, March 7). By 2030, half the world's oceans could be reeling from climate change, scientists say. https://www.washingtonpost.com/news/energy-environment/wp/2017/03/07/by-2030-half-the-worlds-oceans-could-be-reeling-from-climate-change-scientists-say/?utm_term=.aa64713ff5a9

Oman's Mountains may Hold Key to Climate Change
by Ethan Lewis

Sam McNeil, a writer for the Washington Post, wrote an article regarding how mountains in Oman could hold the secret to reversing climate change. Scientists are coring samples from deep canyons in the mountains to uncover how carbon dioxide gets transformed into limestone and marble. These canyons are some of the world's only exposed sections of the mantle. They deepest part of these mountains reaches roughly 12 miles into the earth's crust.

McNeil says that as the world mobilizes to confront climate change, the main focus is clean energy and reducing emissions in fuel efficient cars. But some researches are also testing ways to remove or recycle carbon already in the seas and sky. Currently, a geothermal plant in Iceland injects carbon into volcanic rock and a fertilizer plant in China, carbon is used as fuel. In total, 16 industrial projects capture and store 27 million tons of carbon a year.

Peter Kelemen, a geochemist at Columbia University has been excavating Oman's mountains for nearly three decades. Kelemen says, "Every single magnesium atom in these rocks has made friends with carbon dioxide to form solid limestone, and we are attempting to fully understand that process." Kelemen and a team of 40 scientists have formed the Oman Drilling Project to see if that process could be used to scrub the earth's carbon-laden atmosphere. The $3.5 million project has support from across the globe, including NASA.

Around 13 tons of core samples from four different sites will be sent to the Chikyu, a state-of-the-art research vessel off the coast of Japan, where Keleman and other geologists will analyze them in round-the-clock shifts. They hope to answer the question of how rocks managed to capture so much carbon over the course of 90 million years and see if there's a way to speed up the timetable.

McNeil☐ | ☐AP, Sam. "Oman's mountains may hold clues for reversing climate change." The Washington Post. WP Company, 13 Apr. 2017. Web. 14 Apr. 2017.

Could the Antarctic Ice Shelf Collapse?
by Alex McKenna

In 2016, scientists made a disturbing discovery. In less than a century, the Antarctic ice shelf could completely collapse. How do they know? Using satellite images, researchers were able to find evidence of a rift in Pine Island, one of West Antarctica's largest glaciers, just days before a 225 square mile iceberg broke off. Even more troubling, the break occurred from the inside out, a sign that Ian Howat, glaciologist at The Ohio State University, thinks could mean that the ice sheet is still melting. In fact, he no longer doubts that the West Antarctic Ice Sheet will melt. For him, it is only a question of "when". He believes that a collapse is imminent, as rifting adds to the probability of a rapid retreat of these glaciers.

The base of the rift they detected on satellite images was located nearly 20 miles inland and spread upward for nearly two years before breaking. Researchers have observed similar subsurface rifts in the Greenland Ice Sheet, where warm ocean water had seeped inland, melting ice from underneath. Thus, because the Pine Island break had a rift originating from the center, implying that the ice was weakened by warm water at the bedrock, scientists think that the West Antarctic Ice Sheet could collapse within the next 100 years, leading to a 10-foot rise in sea level and massively increased coastal flooding around the world. They determined that with rising temperatures due to global warming, warmer ocean temperatures may cause so much ice in the Antarctic shelves to melt, that many parts simply break off and crumble into the ocean.

After studying this rift in the Pine Island Glacier, the scientists predict that other glaciers, including the nearby Thwaites Glacier, will rapidly retreat and melt as well. According to them, over 10 percent of the West Antarctic Ice Sheet could drain into the sea in the next few years. This poses many threats to wildlife, even to terrain inhabited by humans. Thus, scientists are prepared to launch more air and field campaigns so that they can gather the information they need to study ice-shelf stability and look into any methods they can use to slow down the melting process.

Deamer, K., 2016. Antarctic ice shelf could collapse within 100 years, study finds. Live Science, 1-4. http://www.livescience.com/57016-west-antarctic-ice-shelf-melting-inside.html

Using Architecture to Adapt to Climate Change
by Alex McKenna

Recently, the JDS Development Group built two new copper-clad apartment towers along the East River of New York City. However, unlike most posh NYC apartment buildings, these towers were designed with a purpose in mind: to withstand the changing climate. Hogged by five emergency generators and equipped with advanced electrical switchgear, the building is designed to withstand floods, surges, and high winds, all allowing residents to live in their apartments for weeks when floodwaters are high. Simon Koster, principal at JDS Development Group, explained that the reason behind his project is to provide a safe place for people to live when the effects of climate change intensify.

JDS and the American Copper Building aren't alone. Since Hurricane Katrina in 2005 and Hurricane Sandy in 2012, tenants, planners, regulators, and private developers across the country have been fortifying infrastructure against storms and rising sea levels. In New York City, an area particularly susceptible to flooding, the senior director for climate change policy under Mayor Bill de Blasio stated that while these changes present a challenge for his city, they also provide it with an opportunity to become more resilient and sustainable.

The idea for this project came between 2012 and 2013 when the site of the American Copper Buildings was inundated by Hurricane Sandy, turning an excavated pit into a small lake. This incident led Mr. Koster to believe that the $650 million project would be designed to resist severe flooding. If residents may be forced to live for weeks without electricity, then emergency generators must be installed to power elevators, water pumps, refrigerators, and outlets. To produce this power, five 400 kilowatt generators were installed in the west half of the north tower. More importantly, they are all powered by natural gas that is piped in and do not depend on the bulk delivery of fuel.

Although this equipment takes up square footage, including the entire penthouse, Mr. Koster believes that ample emergency power is an asset and selling point to buyers scarred by Hurricane Sandy. In fact, as of 2014, New York requires that mechanical systems be installed above the design flood elevation, especially at buildings like American Copper that stand in floodplains. In addition, many buildings are beginning to use stone rather than wood in their lobby walls, and are installing advanced pipes in their basements to drain water.

One thousand prospective tenants have already inquired about the American Copper apartments, though they will not officially open until next month. There is clearly a significant amount of interest in the project, proving that people are still comfortable moving to the waterfront so long as they feel their homes can weather the changing climate.

Dunlap, D., 2017. Building to the sky, with a plan for rising waters. The New York Times, 1-5. https://nyti.ms/2k6Ladf

Climate Change and Flooding in Latin America
by Alex McKenna

In 2017, a catastrophic mudslide devastated the village of Barba Blanca in Peru. Although all 150 residents managed to escape unscathed, their homes, churches, and stores were all destroyed. Even worse, this event was not an anomaly. The number of floods and destructive mudslides in South America has drastically increased in the last few years. In April, the city of Mocoa in Colombia was leveled by a flood that left 293 people dead. In Peru, mudslides have killed more than 100 people and left 150,000 homeless in the last decade. These catastrophes, while serious on their own, point to an even larger problem: climate change. There is little doubt that rising temperatures and increased rainfall, all consequences of climate change, are responsible for the mudslides and floods. Juan Manuel Santos, the president of Colombia, stated that the recent flooding was caused by the changing climate and that they must prepare for even more intense rains to come. Moreover, economic expansion in Latin America over the past three decades has spurred migration into coastal desert towns, areas that have not been buttressed by preparation for natural disasters. Leopoldo Monzon, a civil engineer in Peru, stated that many of these areas have long been unsettled because they are susceptible to flash flooding and that politicians have developed them in exchange for votes. Now, in Lima alone, more than 100,000 people live in flash flooding zones.

Making matters worse, the arrival of El Niño, a rise in ocean temperatures in the Pacific, has made normally scorched desert towns susceptible to devastating mudslides. In response to El Niño, a Peruvian weather expert said that the desert is turning tropical. For example, in the village of Barba Blanca, the land sat on a dry approach to the Andes for centuries before flooding occurred. But now they must face a difficult decision: should they rebuild Barba Blanca or resettle in a safer location? The roar of the mud and devastation has left many scarred, but this village is the only home many of these natives know. In Latin America, especially Peru, climate change is becoming a reality that people must finally face.

Casey, N., 2017. Mud erased a village in Peru, a sign of larger perils in South America. The New York Times, 1-5.
https://www.nytimes.com/2017/04/06/world/americas/peru-floods-mudslides-south-america.html

NASA Studies a Rarity: Growing Louisiana Deltas
by Kele Mkpado

NASA is known for many things, like getting us to the moon and back, but one thing that makes them particularly useful to our society today is their satellites. It is one way that we can view the world like never before, and provide new perspectives on what might be changing year to year along with warnings for future disasters. Carol Rasmussen, a NASA scientist decided to study the differences in sea level, from a greater than birds-eye view. If she could accurately plot where sea levels might be rising disproportionately to other parts of the country, it might give us a head start as to how to protect our most vulnerable coastlines.

Observing the Louisiana coastline from one of NASA's satellites, she noticed that it was sinking into the Gulf of Mexico at a faster pace than other areas of coastline around the country and the world. Louisiana is losing land at an alarming rate of one football field per hour (approx 18 sq. miles per year). She did notice however that this is mostly caused by the fact that Louisiana has so many deltas feeding inland that the rising water levels are magnified because of the surface area the water shares with the land. She notes that growing deltas are very hard to measure because doing research in a swamp is difficult, especially those filled with alligators and snakes. There is also such an extensive network of rivers in the state that they are impossible to cover in a reasonable amount of time and some just aren't even accessible. The researchers were also able to match the data they received from the satellites to data they began to collect using unmanned aerial vehicles (UAV drones). This allowed them to cross-analyze the data to see which was more accurate, and use that method in the future.

With these new data, the researchers plan to model the advancement of water throughout the swamps of the southern part of the country and decide how to cope with the imminent rise of sea levels.

Rasmussen, Carol. "NASA Studies a Rarity: Growing Louisiana Deltas." NASA. NASA, 08 Feb. 2017. Web. 20 Feb. 2017.

Changes to the Jet Stream will Cause Planes to Spend Longer in the Air and Suffer more Turbulence
by Kele Mkpado

For many of those who think that climate change will have little effect on the developed world, think again. An article by DailyMail suggests that climate change is affecting those of us who travel through the air. A british scientist named Paul Williams made the prediction a while ago, and we are beginning to see it come true.

First off, climate change has a direct effect on the air, changing its composition constantly. You could see how this could have a large effect on those very things that rely on air to work. Research has found that the rising is global temperatures speed up the jet stream, which is an area of the atmosphere where planes fly. The jet stream propels air west to east, making eastbound flights faster and westbound flights slower. This speed increase to the jet stream will cause westbound flights to significantly decrease in air time, and only slightly increase the speed of eastbound flights, but the total time of all flights will increase. You may think this has little effect on airliners as a whole, but for every 2 extra minutes a plane is in the air, it burns approximately 100 gallons of fuel. Thats over 75 million dollars a year for airliners.

Second factor that comes into play is turbulence. Aviators have noticed a slight increase in turbulence over the past years but scientists are unsure as to what the actual cause is. Many wish to attribute the anomaly to climate change but they are not sure if it is the only factor or one of many. It is safe to say that climate change is not helping the situation. Turbulence seldom results in an aircraft crashing, but an increase in would make many more wary of flying and possibly hurt the industry's credibility.

It is not just longer flights that people may have to worry about. Longer flights result in longer wait times at airports and higher ticket costs. Extreme turbulence may frighten some so much that they would rather drive now that self driving cars are coming along, or take the hyperloop if that ever materializes. The contribution airplanes have made to climate change is finally coming back to haunt them.

MailOnline, Sarah Griffiths for. "The Latest Impact of Climate Change? Flight Delays: Changes to the Jet Stream Will Cause Planes to Spend Longer in the Air and Suffer More Turbulence." Daily Mail Online. Associated Newspapers, 09 Feb. 2016. Web. 21 Mar. 2017.

Sea Ice Extent Sinks to Record Lows at Both Poles
by Kele Mkpado

NASA satellites have been used to monitor changes to our Earth in locations all over the planet, in particular the poles, where ice has been melting at an alarming rate. This is concerning on many levels, mainly the fact that once ocean temperatures are raised, it will take a long time to restore them to their previous temperatures.

On march 7th 2017, NASA satellites viewing the North and South Poles recorded the least amount of sea ice in those areas since the satellites began collecting data in 1979. They recorded that total polar sea ice covered 6.26 million square miles, which is 790,000 square miles less than the average global minimum. In more visual terms, the loss of sea ice could have covered the country of Mexico. Now this is not to be taken too seriously as sea ice freezes and melts as the seasons change, but it was a larger decrease in ice than ever before. It was also noted that at the season's peak (coldest weather), frozen ice was 37,000 square miles less than the previous record low, so obviously the amount in the hotter months would build upon that. The Arctic's maximum amount of ice has dropped by 2.8% per decade since 1979, and the summertime minimum amount of ice has dropped 13.5% per decade.

The freezing and melting of the 90% of sea ice that is under water has little effect on sea level rise, but it must foreshadow what is to come. By recording how the ice is reduced in the seas over a period of time, there might be a way to configure a timetable as to how quickly land ice in the form of ice caps and glaciers will melt and flow to the ocean, causing rapid sea level rise. At any rate, the loss of sea ice affects the whole ecosystems of the Arctic and Antarctic, and we must not neglect that just because it does not affect us directly.

Maria-José Viñas. "Sea Ice Extent Sinks to Record Lows at Both Poles." NASA. NASA, 24 Mar. 2017. Web. 29 Mar. 2017.

Human-Caused Climate Change has Rerouted an Entire River
by Kele Mkpado

Many see climate change as a threat that is to be dealt with later because it is tough to determine which disasters today are directly a product of climate change. Though this may be some people's opinion, a team of scientists in Canada recently discovered the first documented river reorganization due to c

The Kaskawulsh glacier in northern Canada has been retreating for more than a century, but a warm spring in 2016 caused unusually high levels of melting. Dan Shugar at the University of Washington Tacoma and his colleagues combined satellite and drone imagery with data from lake and river gauges to reconstruct the path of water flowing from the glacier. The melting in 2016 formed an ice-walled canyon, which redirected water south into the Alsek River instead of into the Slims River to the north. This cut the flow to Yukon's largest lake and instead channeled water to the Pacific Alaskan coast instead of the Bering Sea. This change in the direction of the river has heavy implications for the species that depend on it for survival. Kluane Lake is a habitat for animals, but also human river communities who depend on it for their livelihood. Due to this river problem, the water level might sink below its outlet point, causing the lake to be classified as a "dead basin" which would change its' chemistry.. The scientists working on the project deemed that this phenomenon would be impossible during a "constant climate", and the increases in our Earth's temperatures are believed to be the culprit. Researchers do not expect the glacier and the river system that depends on it to flip back—rather, it has entered a new state.

Changes to an ecosystem can be drastic for the flora and fauna living in it, and rivers and lakes are vital to many species survival. Granted, a new river system on the other side of the glacier will probably introduce a new habitat for animals, but it is not an excuse for the effects we are having on our planet.

Mooney, Chris. "Human-caused Climate Change Has Rerouted an Entire River." The Washington Post. WP Company, 17 Apr. 2017. Web. 19 Apr. 2017.

New Tactics for Combating Flooding
by Bradley Newton

Water is an important part of sustaining any sort of human settlement, but too much of it can be a detriment to infrastructure and people's lives. The article Flooding: Water potential by James M. Gaines outlines a couple of types of flooding situations, and the solutions that urban designers and researchers have proposed to combat these situations.

In areas along the west coast of the United State, such as San Francisco, flooding is not so much a problem from rainwater as it is from groundwater. An urban designer from the University of California, Berkeley, Kristina Hill has studied and participated in the prevention of urban flooding, specifically in New Orleans post Hurricane Katrina. More recently she has been applying what she knows to the San Francisco Bay Area. California has been experiencing an intensified drought the last few years, however, rising sea levels are the concern in this area. The coast acts as a sponge to seawater, with the saltwater being absorbed inland. The saltwater is denser than the freshwater found underground in aquifers, and the increase in saltwater intrusion will inevitably start pushing the freshwater aboveground, causing flooding. Another effect will be that when the rains come, the ground will saturate more quickly due to already being full of water, worsening the flood. Hill's current solution to this problem is to effectively waterproof underground infrastructure, especially in areas with gas pipes, electrical lines, and communication cables. She admits, however, that there will be some low-lying areas that will need to be abandoned eventually, such as parts of New York, due to just not being ready.

At Stanford University, there is a research group headed by Richard Luthy that focuses on urban water management, specifically with water situations caused by storms. Luthy states that generally cities try to deal with storm water by trying to get rid of it as quickly as possible. Sometimes though, the storm drains that channel away the water are overwhelmed by too much water and it causes destruction. Luthy's goal is to find a way to slow down the water flow in these channels, and maybe even find a way to store the excess water away for later use. He is working on storm water reservoirs in Sonoma and Los Angeles that are meant to be places for the water to pool and collect. Vegetation can be planted around and in these reservoirs to help purify the water, and then can be purified by way of other methods before being allowed to drain into underground aquifers for use during droughts. There is also the idea of the tree trench, basically an extra absorbent area for water to pass through before being accepted by the storm drains. It is meant to slow down the flow of water and purify it to help protect the city. These are especially helpful because they are smaller and can be placed alongside streets since a full-sized reservoir would never fit. The concrete and asphalt in urban areas are impervious to water, making it more difficult for the ground to help control flooding. Because of this, Philadelphia is working on another method of controlling water by experimenting with pervious paving.

Gaines, James M. "Flooding: Water Potential." Nature International Weekly Journal of Science. N.p., 17 Mar. 2016. Web. http://www.nature.com/nature/journal/v531/n7594_supp/full/531S54a.html

Usage of Enhanced Weathering
by Bradley Newton

Negative emission strategies are ways of permanently removing carbon dioxide from the atmosphere, on human timescales. Edwards *et al.* (2017) talk about a specific type of negative emission strategy called enhanced rock weathering. The article talks about an example of the practice where crushed reactive silicate rocks are introduced to land areas of vegetation to help increase atmospheric removal rates of carbon dioxide. The minerals, after having been distributed among the vegetation, will begin to chemically break down, leaving behind base cations and bicarbonate. Introducing these minerals also creates the potential of increasing the vegetation's ability to capture and store atmospheric carbon dioxide. Subsequently, the minerals will make their way to rivers where they will be flushed out sea. In the ocean, they will be stored as either dissolved inorganic carbon or as carbonate. The resulting lower atmospheric carbon dioxide and the increase of alkalinity in the ocean due to the enhanced weathering could help to counteract against ocean acidification. Potential positives from this practice include improved productivity and reduced carbon dioxide emissions, land sparing (if the introduction of silicate rocks improves crop yield, then the need for deforestation decreases), and a reduced risk phytoplankton blooms in rivers and reefs (the excessive application of fertilizers at incorrect times of year lead to rivers picking up runoff from crops, causing eutrophication). However, the practice is accompanied by potential pitfalls as well. The drawbacks consist of greenhouse gas emissions from the grinding and transport of the minerals (however, the amount by which this affects things should decrease due to global transitioning toward methods and activities that output less carbon emissions), yield quality ("Potentially toxic elements contained in some silicate minerals could become bioavailable under enhanced weathering"), unknown biodiversity impacts, reduced nearby water quality, and the possible expansion of mining operations.

Edwards, David P., Felix Lim, Rachael H. James, Christopher R. Pearce, Julie Scholes, Robert P. Freckleton, and David J. Beerling. "Climate Change Mitigation: Potential Benefits and Pitfalls of Enhanced Rock Weathering in Tropical Agriculture." Biology Letters 13.4 (2017): 20160715. Web.
http://rsbl.royalsocietypublishing.org/content/13/4/20160715#sec-2

Disappearing Permafrost
by Luis Salazar

New studies attempt to describe the relationship between temperature and disappearance of permafrost—for every degree Celsius (1.8°F), nearly 1.5 million square miles of permafrost disappear. This updated study shows an increase of 20%.

The Paris climate agreement aims to have less that 2°C warming. These 2° could make nearly 2.5 million square miles of permafrost disappear. Throughout the next century, it possible for all of permafrost to disappear.

The increase in greenhouse gas emissions directly affects the disappearance of permafrost. Losing permafrost results in the release of methane, a greenhouse gas. Increased gas emissions leads to more warming, which in turn leads to more permafrost disappearing. It is an ongoing cycle.

Permafrost affects land too. When permafrost thaws, it causes water damage to architecture. Researchers of the earlier study describe the need to have strict climate change regulations. These regulations will be the difference the thawing of permafrost and the damage of buildings.

The Paris agreement aims to keeping temperature increase from 1.5 to 2°C. The more we allow temperatures to increase, the more permafrost we lose. Clearly, the more ambitious goal is to remain at or below the 1.5°C increase.

If things get out of hand and the earth's temperatures increase by 6°C, we would be facing the release of more gas emissions, which become a concern for the climate. This is one of the first studies aimed at linking the thawing of permafrost and the increase in temperatures. A critique of this study is that recorded observations would have been more accurate in predicting permafrost.

Assistant professor and permafrost expert, Donatella Zona suggests that this model, while uncertain, illustrates the connection between permafrost and climate change. Researchers are working hard to provide more reliable cost estimates of climate change in the Arctic. Similarly, researchers applaud the usage of air temperature and the design of the research between permafrost and temperature.

It is important to carefully analyze all factors that affect permafrost and how climate change will affect future behavior. In addition, it takes a while for permafrost to disappear after temperature increases, which results in uncertainty. This uncertainty calls to question the speed of change. Still, we are able to see the following: increase in temperature leads to the thawing of permafrost.

Harvey, Chelsea. Climate Change Could Destroy Far More Arctic Permafrost than We Thought — Which Would Worsen Climate Change. The Washington Post. WP Company, 10 Apr. 2017. Web.

What is the Future of Carbon Capture Technology?
by Tanisha Sheth

John Schwartz, a science writer for the New York Times recently wrote an article regarding carbon capture technology. Carbon capture involves pulling carbon dioxide out of smokestacks and industrial processes before the gas can escape into the atmosphere. However, Donald Trump's denial of climate change might potentially hamper this environmental initiative.

The new Petra Nova plant which is 30 miles southwest of Houston is currently being completed within its budget and on time. The plant is attached to one of NRG's coal-burning units and is capable of drawing in 90% of the CO_2 from the emissions produced by 240 megawatts of generated power. This is equivalent to the greenhouse gas produced by driving 3.5 billion miles, or the CO_2 from generating electricity for 214,338 homes.

Petra Nova uses the most common technology for carbon capture. The exhaust stream is exposed to a solution of chemicals known as amines, which bond with carbon dioxide. This solution is then pumped to a regenerator which heats the amines and releases the CO_2. The gas is then drawn off and compressed for further use and the amine solution is cycled back into the system for the absorption of CO_2. The compressed CO_2 will then be pushed through a new pipeline 81 miles to an oil field. This gas will then be used in enhanced oil recovery where it will be injected into walls to increase the quantity of oil produce from 300 to 15,000 barrels a day.

Nonetheless, the good news is that one of the pillars of Mr. Trump's campaign was his intention to revive the fortunes produced by the coal industry by supporting clean coal. While the exact meaning of the phrase is open to interpretation, it generally includes not just technologies that remove soot and smog-causing pollutants, but also carbon dioxide

The success of the Petra Nova translates into a boost for carbon capture. Despite the problems associated with carbon capture, its supporters include the IPCC (Intergovernmental Panel on Climate Change) and the IEA (International Energy

Agency) call the project crucial for meeting the emission standards that can potentially prevent some of the worst effects of climate change.

Schwartz, John., 2017. Can Carbon Capture Technology Prosper Under Trump? The New York Times

Research on Geoengineering to Combat Global Warming?
by Tanisha Sheth

The White House for the first time has recommended research into geoengineering which is the concept of intervening in nature to slow down or reverse global warming. The document lays out a plan for climate-related research at 13 federal agencies until 2021 and calls for studies into two approaches to geoengineering: distributing chemicals in the atmosphere to reflect more heat producing sunlight away from the earth, and removing carbon dioxide from the air so the atmosphere traps less heat. This report was submitted to Congress by the U. S. Global Change Research Program. However, it is unclear how the Trump administration will employ technologies to counter climate change. Opponents of geoengineering argue that the risks are too great: Geoengineering might have unintended damaging effects on weather patterns, or might be used unilaterally as a weapon by governments or even extremely wealthy individuals. Environmentalists oppose the concept of geoengineering research on the ground that it would be a distraction from the task of reducing the impact of climate change by cutting carbon dioxide emissions. Others say that scientists should at least be getting a head start and well-versing themselves with the concept of geoengineering in case it is needed someday. The report suggests modest recommendations such as research to improve how computer models represent the interaction of clouds and aerosol particles of the type that may be used to reflect sunlight. Still the recommendations illustrate the importance geoengineering has gained in official circles. For years the Obama administration avoided even mentioning the term but a government-sponsored panel of the National Academy of Sciences recommended that some research into the field must be made, with proper oversight.

Fountain, Henry., 2017. White House Urges Research on Geoengineering to Combat Global Warming. The New York Times

Geoengineering Earth's Atmosphere: How It Could Affect Astronomy

by Charlie Thomson

In an article written by Nola Taylor Redd, a contributor for Live Science, the issue of geoengineering was discussed. While considered by many in the scientific community to be a potential large-scale solution to the issue of climate change, geoengineering could directly affect astronomers. At one of the United States' largest astronomical conferences on January 4th, scientists discussed what effects geoengineering could have on the sky such as how well astronomers would be able to see it. Some studies have shown that adding clouds to the atmosphere via geoengineering can increase the brightening of the night sky by 25 percent. Panel members at the conference unanimously agreed that geoengineering is only a short-term solution to help dial back the planet's temperature before reaching catastrophic levels, and as one panel member said "solar radiation management is not a substitution for mitigation". Despite the panel's partial view in favor of their profession, the panel admitted that "fixing global warming is more important than astronomy". If we as a planet are truly going to do everything possible to reverse the change in climate, at some point geoengineering will be an unavoidable practice. To alleviate the most serious consequences of global warming, climate scientists have agreed that the rise in earth's temperature must be capped at no more than 3.6 degrees fahrenheit. Long term strategies for climate change reduction require burning less fossil-fuels, but climate scientists say that this is not enough on its own in order to meet the climate change goals set by the IPCC.

At the end of the day, astronomers will just have to accept the fact that the cost of lowering our world's climate and the impact that these changes have on our environment might involve lowering the sky's visibility at night which would have a minor effect on astronomers and the astronomy community as a whole. Personally I believe this is a cost that is far outweighed by the benefit of climate change reduction.

Redd, Nola Taylor. "Geoengineering Earth's Atmosphere: How It Could Affect Astronomy." LiveScience. Purch, 20 Jan. 2017. Web. 11 Feb. 2017. <http://www.livescience.com/57567-geoengineering-earth-atmosphere-could-affect-astronomy.html>.

Arctic Sea Ice Sets Record-Low Peak for Third Year

by Charlie Thomson

Consistent warm temperatures alongside this winter's heat wave slowed sea ice growth in the Arctic this winter — leaving the winter sea ice cover with a missing chunk the size of California and Texas combined. This set a record-low ice cover maximum for the third year in a row. Even in comparison to the decades of greenhouse gas-driven global warming and ice loss in the Arctic, this winter made a serious impression on scientists. "I have been looking at Arctic weather patterns for 35 years and have never seen anything close to what we've experienced these past two winters," Mark Serreze, director of the National Snow and Ice Data Center, which keeps track of sea ice levels, said in a statement. The sea ice that surrounds Antarctica also set a record low for its annual summer ice cover minimum—which alarmingly was very far from record highs recorded in recent years. Researchers are still investigating which variables, including global warming, are behind this new trend in sea ice. The portion of the Arctic Ocean that is covered in sea ice usually hits its winter peak in early to mid-March when the freeze season ends with the re-appearance of the sun above the horizon. It is estimated that this year's maximum ice coverage reached on March 7, the NSIDC (National Snow and Ice Data Center) said Wednesday, when sea ice covered 5.57 million square miles, a 38 year low according to satellite records. This measurement came in just below 2015's maximum ice coverage of 5.605 million square miles—471,000 square miles below the 1981-2010 average. Arctic sea ice was not only less is terms of square miles, but also thinner as well. The Arctic sea ice this year is thinner than it has been in the last four years, according to data from the European Space Agency's CryoSat-2 satellite. The reason for this thinness and smaller ice area was how temperatures stayed warm consistently throughout the fall and winter. All across the Arctic Ocean, temperatures during this time were about 4.5°F above average, and in parts of the Chukchi and Barents seas coming in at 9°F above average. The Antarctic summer sea ice coverage minimum was 813,000 square miles — 900,000 square miles below the 1981-2010 average and 71,000 square miles below the previous record low that was set in 1997. As shown by these statistics, Antarctic sea ice is far more volatile than the Arctic — scientists are still looking into how climate change and various natural climate cycles might be interacting to affect sea ice levels there.

Thompson, Andrea, and Climate Central. "Arctic Sea Ice Sets Record-Low Peak for Third Year." Scientific American. Scientific American, 22 Mar. 2017. Web. 23 Mar. 2017. <https://www.scientificamerican.com/article/arctic-sea-ice-sets-record-low-peak-for-third-year/>.

Acidity in the Arctic Ocean Increases Rapidly
by Jason Yi

Chelsea Harvey (2017) discusses the current climate change situation in the Arctic.

She further points out that the effects of climate change are greater in the Arctic than any other region in the world. As a result, many native species are suffering from their diminishing habitat.

To make the situation worse, a recent study revealed that the Arctic Ocean is becoming more acidic due to greenhouse emissions. Researchers have suggested that similar situations are occurring in different parts of the world. However, the acidity levels in the Arctic have risen to the point where they can no longer be ignored.

More specifically, the acidification occurs when "carbon dioxide dissolves out of the air" and flows into the ocean waters, causing the pH levels to decline. Furthermore, with the icecaps melting at a rapid rate, the cold water allows the carbon dioxide to dissolve more easily. Consequently, as the pH levels drop, the formation of aragonite, which many marine species use to create their outer shells is inhibited.

As a result, many scientists have been using the aragonite saturation levels to estimate the amount of carbon dioxide diffusing into the sea. After comparing the data between 1994 and 2010, it was discovered that the "unsaturated area[s]" of aragonite rose from 5 to 31 percent. Scientists also revealed that at the current rate, aragonite saturation levels in the Arctic Ocean will be too low to allow marine organisms to construct shells in twenty years. While many treat climate change as a trivial matter, it seems that the once negligible problem of climate change is quickly becoming a pressing issue.

Harvey. Chelsea. 2017. Scientists just measured a rapid growth in acidity in the Arctic ocean, linked to climate change. Washington Post Feb. 27

About the Authors

The authors of this book are first-year students at Claremont McKenna College. The book is a work product of a Freshman Humanities Seminar—*The Human Response to Climate Change*—taught by Dr. Emil Morhardt, the George R. Roberts Professor of Environmental Biology, in the W.M. Keck Science Department of Claremont McKenna, Pitzer, and Scripps Colleges.

The students' task was to write journalistic summaries of interesting academic technical papers having something to do with climate change, but not written by natural scientists (*i.e.* not written by anybody who might be housed in the W. M. Keck Science Center). A way into the project, the criteria were relaxed to include pieces written by journalists and fiction writers, as well as writing about art and theater projects—all obviously important aspects of the humanities. The summaries were due weekly and were returned with editorial comments shortly thereafter.

The editor remembers how difficult it was for him to learn to write as a freshman at Pomona College (another member of the Claremont Colleges), and suspects he was not nearly as good at it as the students who wrote this book. They have done a terrific job.

www.ingramcontent.com/pod-product-compliance
Lightning Source LLC
Chambersburg PA
CBHW031424270326
41930CB00007B/562